Researching Widening Access to Lifelong Learning

This authoritative volume is a truly international contribution to the worldwide debate on how best to widen access to lifelong learning.

The first section of the book comprises research studies from around the world, reflecting the diversity of contexts in which widening access is researched, and considers issues central to the access debate, including different understandings of the concept of access, organizational and structural change, curriculum development, entry policies, performance and retention, and labour market outcomes.

The second illustrates a range of diverse and innovative methodological approaches that have been employed by researchers in the field and considers the range of approaches available to researchers.

Given the growing concern around the world on the need to combat social exclusion and to improve economic circumstances through access to lifelong learning, this book acts as a unique reference point informing the ongoing debate, exploring the interrelationship between research, policy and practice. It will be essential reading for students, academics and policymakers researching the global phenomenon of widening access to education.

Michael Osborne is Professor of Lifelong Education, Co-Director of the Centre for Research in Lifelong Learning, University of Stirling and editor of the *Journal of Adult and Continuing Education*. **Jim Gallacher** is Professor of Lifelong Learning and Co-Director of the Centre for Research in Lifelong Learning, Glasgow Caledonian University. **Beth Crossan** is Research Fellow at the Centre for Research in Lifelong Leaning, Glasgow Caledonian University.

Researching Widening Access to Lifelong Learning

Issues and approaches in international research

Edited by Michael Osborne, Jim Gallacher and Beth Crossan

RoutledgeFalmer
Taylor & Francis Group

LONDON AND NEW YORK

First published 2004
by RoutledgeFalmer
2 Park Square, Milton Park, Abingdon, Oxfordshire OX14 4RN

Simultaneously published in the USA and Canada
by RoutledgeFalmer
270 Madison Avenue, New York, NY 10016

Transferred to Digital Printing 2005

RoutledgeFalmer is an imprint of the Taylor & Francis Group

© 2004 Michael Osborne, Jim Gallacher, Beth Crossan and
individual contributors

Typeset in Goudy by
HWA Text and Data Management, Tunbridge Wells
Printed and bound in Great Britain by
Antony Rowe Ltd, Chippenham, Wiltshire

British Library Cataloguing in Publication Data
A catalogue record for this book is available from the British
Library

Library of Congress Cataloging in Publication Data
Osborne, Michael, 1954–
    Researching widening access to lifelong learning : issues and
approaches in international research / Michael Osborne,
Jim Gallacher, and Beth Crossan
        p. cm
    Includes bibliographical references.
    1. Education, Higher–Aims and objectives. 2. Educational
equalization. 3. Inclusive education. I. Gallacher, Jim, 1946– II.
Crossan, Beth, 1964– III. Title.
        LB2322.2.083 2004
        379.2´6–dc22   2003027156

ISBN 0–415–32236–7

Contents

Figures

Tables

Contributors

Peter Alheit is Chair in General Education at the Georg-August University of Göttingen. He is a philosopher and sociologist working mostly in the fields of adult and higher education. His research interests include biographical research, access and experiences of adults in higher education, comparative higher education, exclusion, education, work and lifelong learning. He is a member of ESREA Steering Committee and a co-founder of the Inter-university Network for Biographical and Lifeworld Research.

Jo Barraket is a lecturer in the Department of Political Science at the University of Melbourne. She has research interests in social policy and the socially transformative effects of emerging technologies and has conducted government-commissioned and independent research in these areas.

Hunter R. Boylan is a Professor of Higher Education and the Director of the National Centre for Developmental Education at Appalachian State University in Boone, North Carolina, USA. He is the author of numerous books and articles on adult and developmental education, a frequent speaker at conferences, and is quoted widely in the media for his views on higher education.

David Boud is Professor of Adult Education and Associate Dean (Research) in the Faculty of Education at the University of Technology, Sydney. He has written extensively on teaching, learning and assessment in higher and professional education. Currently he is involved in research on informal learning in workplaces and sustainable assessment practices for lifelong learning.

Ronald M. Cervero is Professor and Head of the Department of Adult Education at The University of Georgia. He has written extensively in the area of the politics of education, including *Planning Responsibly for Adult Education: A Guide to Negotiating Power and Interests* and an edited book, *Power in Practice: Adult Education and the Struggle for Knowledge and Power in Society*.

Beth Crossan is Research Fellow at the Centre for Research in Lifelong Learning, based at Glasgow Caledonian University. She has worked on numerous research projects which have explored aspects of access and widening participation.

Chris Duke is Director of Higher Education at the National Institute of Adult Continuing Education (NIACE) and Director and Professor of the Community and Regional partnership at RMIT University, Melbourne. He is also Honorary Professor of Lifelong Learning, University of Leicester.

Sara Ferlander is a lecturer at the University College of South Stockholm working in the research project 'Stockholm Centre on Health of Societies in Transition'. She is also a Research Fellow in the Centre for Research and Development in Learning Technology at the University of Stirling. Her research interest concerns the impacts of ICT on social capital and community, but she is also interested in the role of social capital in Eastern Europe.

Ramón Flecha is Professor of Sociology at the University of Barcelona and director of CREA, the Centre for Social and Educational Research at the Science Park of Barcelona. His extensive research is dedicated to the analysis of social inequalities and how to overcome them. Among his latest publications are *Contemporary Sociological Theory* and *Sharing Words, Theory and Practice of Dialogic Learning*.

Alasdair Forsyth is Research Fellow at the Centre for Research in Lifelong Learning, Glasgow Caledonian University, and has been involved in researching a variety of youth issues since 1985, but during the past five years he has concentrated his work in the education field. Currently his main interests lie in the relationships between socio-economic advantage/disadvantage and participation in higher education.

Andy Furlong is Professor of Sociology in the Department of Sociology, Anthropology and Applied Social Sciences at the University of Glasgow. His research interests focus on youth transitions, labour markets and education.

Jim Gallacher is Professor of Lifelong Learning and Co-director, Centre for Research in Lifelong Learning, Glasgow Caledonian University. He has undertaken numerous research projects on issues associated with widening access to further and higher education and links between further education colleges and universities. He is also involved in research into work-related learning and the accreditation of prior experiential learning (APEL). He has also worked with the Scottish Parliament's Enterprise and Lifelong Learning Committee and is a Vice Chair of the Universities Association for Continuing Education (UACE) in the UK.

Jesús Gómez is Associate Professor in Educational Research Methods at the University of Barcelona. His professional interests include communicative methodology, and the discourse on interpersonal relations and emotions in education. He is co-author of *Why Romà Do Not Like Mainstream Schools: Voices of a People Without Territory* for the Harvard Educational Review.

Juanita Johnson-Bailey is an Associate Professor at the University of Georgia in the Department of Adult Education and the Women's Studies Program. She specialises in researching race and gender in educational and workplace settings. Her book, *Sistahs in College: Making a Way Out of No Way*, received the Phillip E. Frandson Award for Literature in Continuing Higher Education.

Ewart Keep has worked in the University of Warwick since 1985, firstly in the Industrial Relations Research Unit (IRRU), and, since 1998, as deputy-director of the ESRC centre on Skills, Knowledge and Organisational Performance (SKOPE). He has acted an advisor to the National Skills Task Force, the Cabinet Office, the Department for Trade and Industry, the Department for Education and Skills, and the Scottish Parliament, and has published extensively on UK vocational education and training policy, work-based learning for the young, the links between skills and competitive strategy, and the learning society and learning organisation.

Joseph Lo Bianco holds the Chair of Language and Literacy Education at the University of Melbourne. He is the author of Australia's first language policy, the 1987 National Policy on Languages and founder of the National Languages and Literacy Institute of Australia (Language Australia). His research interests include language policy and planning and bilingualism in the context of globalisation. Recent books include: *Australian Literacies: Informing National Policy on Literacy Education* (2001); *Australian Policy Activism in Language and Literacy* (2001); *Voices from Phnom Penh: Development and Language* (2002) and *Teaching Invisible Culture: Classroom Practice and Theory* (2003).

Rob Mark has worked as a teacher, staff developer, and researcher in the field of adult literacy. He first became interested in adult literacy while working as a volunteer tutor in the mid 1970s. Since then he has worked as a literacy tutor and manager in a range of different contexts including further education, the voluntary sector and in community education. He is currently responsible for tutor training in adult literacy and numeracy at the Institute of Lifelong Learning, Queen's University Belfast.

Barbara Merrill is Senior Lecturer in the Centre for Lifelong Learning, University of Warwick. Her research interests are access and experiences of adult students in further and higher education, gender, class and adult education, citizenship, community-based learning and biographical methods. She is also involved in comparative European research and is Chair of SCUTREA.

Brenda Morgan-Klein is Senior Lecturer in Education at the Institute of Education, University of Stirling. The focus of her research interest is on educational inequality. She has recently researched widening access to Scottish higher education and temporal and spatial aspects of participation in higher education.

Mark Murphy is Lecturer in Education at the University of Stirling. His main areas of interest include university adult education, educational sociology, critical theory and education, political economy of post-compulsory education and international adult education. He has numerous publications in the fields of adult and higher education, and his work has involved him in educational debates in Ireland, Scotland and the United States.

Michael Osborne is Professor of Lifelong Education and Co-director, Centre for Research in Lifelong Learning, University of Stirling. He has worked in the field of access to higher education since 1980, first as a lecturer in some of the earliest adult access courses in the UK at the then City and East London College and later at the then South London College. His work in access research started at South Bank Polytechnic in the mid 1980s, and this has been a major theme of his work since. He is author of numerous papers and monographs in the area of access to higher education, university continuing education and lifelong learning. He is editor of *The Journal of Adult and Continuing Education*.

Peter Scott is Vice-Chancellor of Kingston University in London and was formerly Professor of Education at the University of Leeds and Editor of *The Times Higher Education Supplement*. He is Chairman of the Universities Association for Continuing Education and a member of the board of the Higher Education Funding Council for England.

Shirley Walters is Professor of Adult and Continuing Education at the University of Western Cape, South Africa. She is founding director of the Division for Lifelong Learning which is concerned with widening access for adult learners into higher education. She is involved in a number of cultural, educational and women's organisations and is presently Chair of the Learning Cape Festival Steering Committee. This is a pioneering initiative of government, civil society, business, and labour to promote the Western Cape Province as a learning region.

Part I

Key issues

Chapter 1

An international perspective on researching widening access

Michael Osborne and Jim Gallacher

Introduction

Whilst there is a substantial interest internationally with issues pertaining to increasing and widening access to Higher Education at both policy and practice levels (e.g. Davies 1995; Council of Europe 1996; Eggins 1999; EURYDICE 2000; Woodrow 2002), there have been few overviews of the field as an area of research concern. Given the emphasis internationally on the need to combat social exclusion and improve economic circumstances through access to education (UNESCO 1998; Council of Europe 2001; European Commission 1995, 2001; OECD 2003), and the increasing concern with evidence-informed policy, this collection as a whole aims to provide a reference point for these debates.

This initial chapter explores international perspectives on widening access research. After setting the scene by considering what is encompassed by the territory, it seeks to map out the dominant themes of research.

The territory

The thrust to increase and, to a lesser or greater degree, to *widen* access to Higher Education in most societies is associated with a number of themes within the larger banner of lifelong learning. They include 'the economic imperatives created by global competition, technological change and the challenge of the knowledge economy, individual responsibility and self-improvement, employability, flexibility of institutions and individuals, social inclusion and citizenship' (Osborne 2003a, pp. 45–58).

In recent articles (Osborne 2003a, 2003b), we have detailed some of the main international trends in the field of access to Higher Education, and drawing upon that work we initially provide an overview of the domain covered within that broad-reaching field.

In many parts of the world where once there was a small elite sector with as few as 5 per cent of school-leavers participating, most immediately after leaving the compulsory sector, there now exists a greatly expanded *mass* and in some cases a *universal* system.[1] According to recent OECD (2003)[2] statistics for 30 of its member countries, on average 47 per cent of school leavers are likely to participate in higher tertiary A education[3] in the course of their lives. This phenomenon to a certain extent is a reflection of changing demography, but only in a few countries does increasing population size account for significant change. Even then, as in all nations, actual increases in participation rates account for significantly more of the overall change.

The issue of access to Higher Education is not of course the preserve of the rich economies of the world, though they have the privilege to give the issue precedence given that in the main access to compulsory education is universal and literacy levels are comparatively high. However, the scale of the task to even provide school education is so great in many countries (see Oduaran 2001) that access to HE is a secondary issue. Largely we have not sought to deal with this aspect of the access agenda in this text, though in chapters concerned with South Africa (Walters) and literacy (Lo Bianco and Mark), we begin to explore that wider domain of work.

Structural differentiation and access

Gellert (1993, p. 17) has suggested there are a number of 'essential areas of change' in HE systems. A number of these features are closely linked to the expansions that have occurred from the 1960s onwards and which, particularly in Central and Eastern Europe, continue today. Amongst the trends that Gellert identified were institutional differentiation, which includes the establishment of new forms of higher education institution and new forms of programme, functional modification, new modes of teaching and learning, increased concern with access and educational opportunity, the greater prevalence of government intervention and accountability, and the greater influence of the European Union. These trends combine both the developing features of systems and some of the factors that have influenced these developments, and form one of a number of useful frameworks for the analysis of recent trends in participation.

Thus in an international context, an analysis of the forms that initiatives to widen participation take is best contextualised within an understanding of the degree to which HE systems around the world are structurally differentiated.

At one pole, at a system level it is possible to identify countries where there is a well-integrated unified Higher Education system and highly equitable procedures for ensuring access irrespective of individual background. For instance, in Sweden since reforms in 1977, when a number of new Higher Education colleges (HECs) were set up in all regions of the country, there has been a unified sense of mission and purpose across the whole HE sector. Furthermore since national university aptitude tests were introduced to increase the prospects for entry of adults over the age of 25 and with four years work experience, there has been widespread access to HE. Whilst the system is not completely open in the sense that it does operate certain forms of selection through limitations at programme and subject level (*numerus clausus*) and there is differentiation between universities and HECs in particular in relation to research, the system is one in which 'the idea of lifelong learning has become a reality not only to politicians, but, most of all, to Swedes themselves' (Bron and Agélii 2000, p. 98). Most other countries, by contrast, present much less integrated provision, although some systems such as that of the UK, in its post-binary phase (of universities and polytechnics), might be seen as being unified, but with continuing stratification.

In many countries, there exist two more distinct parallel sectors of higher level provision within a dual or binary system, and a set of tertiary establishments outside the university sector that are largely unconnected to these. Most well known is the German system of both universities and *Fachhochschulen*. The latter were introduced in 1970/1 and are characterised by shorter three or four-year programmes, a practice-oriented bias, an integrated semester or two of work experience, and lecturers who have, in addition to their academic qualifications, gained professional experience outside the field of Higher Education. It is the establishment of the *Fachhochschulen*, which can provide access for those without the traditional school-leaving qualification, the *Abitur*, together with the expansion of academic-track upper school education leading to the *Abitur* that has led to the massification of the German HE system (Wolter 2000). A binary line exists in a number of other countries. In some nations, this has involved the creation of new HE forms in very recent times, such as the polytechnics (*ammatikorkeakoulu*) established in 1992 in Finland. In Finland as elsewhere, the creation of a new form of HE has involved rebranding and upgrading vocational provision in the coming together of a number of diverse institutions under one banner, and this has also been the case in the establishment of the Institutes of Technology in Ireland. The *ammattikorkeakoulu* and the Institutes of Technology, as is the case with *Fachhochschulen*, have been developed with specific labour market objectives in mind.

The HE systems of North America with its two year Community College (CC) programmes that are designed to articulate to universities provide the most well-known forms of stratification, with Canadian CCs very explicitly playing the role of 'commuter colleges' for universities (Bonham 2002; Burtch 2002). As the Higher Education systems of Central and Eastern Europe are seeking to transform, they too are looking to increase participation through the creation of new forms of stratified HE structure with links between sectors. For instance, Marga (2002, p. 133) reports the creation since 1998 of a national network of university colleges in Romania offering short-cycle Higher Education. Cerych (2002, p. 112) reports that the 'German *Fachhochschule*, the Dutch HBO (*Hoger Bereops Onderwijs*) or the OECD concept of "short-cycle" or "non-university" sector higher education … have certainly inspired reforms in Czech education'. Hence Higher Professional Schools (*Vyssi odborna skola*) based on the HBO have been set up in the Czech Republic. This tendency is of course accelerated by the desire of the majority of countries in this region in Europe to harmonise with those of the Western countries within the framework of the Bologna agreement[4] and subsequent Communiqué of the Conference of Ministers responsible for Higher Education (2003) in Berlin.

These delineations are of course approximations and many systems such as that of the UK demonstrate further complexity. As we have said, whilst there is in principle a unified HE system, there is also stratification. The siting of increasing proportions of higher tertiary B provision in Further Education Colleges (FECs), has been based on its accessibility to students in terms of geographical locality, cost and educational ethos, and the relatively lower cost to government. The use of these institutions both as providers of qualifications with national recognition and as feeders to the second or third year of universities has effectively established a new, but fuzzy, binary line, and an HE structure that increasingly is assuming the characteristic of a stratified system[5] (Gallacher 2003; Morgan-Klein and Murphy in this volume). In certain UK institutions the links between HEIs and FECs have in recent years led to complete amalgamations, and the creation of dual sector post-16 institutions similar to those established in some Australian states (Wheelahan 2002).

In summary, we can identity three structural forms of Higher Education (unified; binary/dual; stratified, with links between universities and colleges), although each will be complex with variations. Some systems may have elements of more than one form such as the case of the UK. These forms in themselves afford elements of structural flexibility to varying degrees. Though it is difficult to associate particular forms categorically with specific types of initiative, the degree of differentiation in systems is a basis for understanding the degree to which particular types of activity are emphasised in particular nations.

Forms of access initiatives

It is difficult to make broad generalisations that cross international boundaries when considering the forms that particular initiatives to widen access have taken. However, it is clear that across societies around the world, a plethora of measures have been taken at national level. As we have reported in the study that stimulated this book (Murphy et al. 2002), these actions are best conceptualised in terms of supply and demand. Drawing upon a categorisation originally proposed by Toyne (1990, pp. 63–5), we first identified two broad types of access initiative – initiatives that focus on people 'getting in' to HE, and access initiatives that emphasise the staff of universities 'getting out' of the campus into the community to reach people under-represented in HE. We refer to these as *in-reach* and *out-reach* respectively (Murphy et al. 2002). A number of initiatives, however, can neither be categorised primarily as in- or out-reach, and have more to do with transformations and adjustments to the structure, administration and delivery of HE programmes and are referred to in our study broadly as *flexible* access initiatives.

The category of forms described as in-reach refer to those actions of Higher Education associated with improving supply, by creating new ways for students to access existing provision. These include alternative entry tests for adults, customised courses and other procedures that allow a second opportunity to demonstrate potential often accompanied by relaxation of entry requirements. Such actions have a long history, and include such practices as the UK's mature access courses (see Parry 1996) and in-house summer schools and the affirmative action efforts within the US dating from the 1960s, now under considerable challenge (Orfield and Miller 2001). Widening participation in the out-reach mode is concerned with collaboration and partnership. Emerging university partnerships with schools, communities and employers refer to those schemes whereby HEIs actively engage with under-represented groups and the socially excluded outside their own boundaries. The primary objective of such out-reach initiatives is to target individuals who believe HE is 'not for them'. A strong element therefore in out-reach is the attempt to counter dispositional barriers by creating greater awareness of what might be possible, and thereby stimulating new demand. Flexible arrangements are not completely distinguishable from out-reach activity as is evident in links between the Vocational Education and Training (VET) sector and universities. Flexibility implies significant structural modification in systems, which may or may not be accompanied by collaboration, although in many cases it is a facilitating mechanism. Flexibility in the context of widening participation refers to both spatial and temporal matters, namely changes that allow students access to education in locations and modes (e.g. in the workplace and via the use of information and communications technology [see Boud and Barraket later in this volume]), and at times that to at least a certain degree are of individuals' rather than institutions' choosing. It also refers to those mechanisms that challenge constructions of what constitutes knowledge at Higher Education level and the means by which knowledge can be acquired and demonstrated.

The dominant research questions

The research questions within the field of widening participation can broadly be categorised within three broad areas, each of which will be covered in greater depth within this book by individual authors. The first set of questions pertains to the extent to which structural modifications to the HE system, and particular policies and practices at national, local and institutional level have succeeded in changing the constitution of the HE population. Linked to this question is the related matter of what particular forms of intervention provision have been most successful. However, simply providing wider access in itself might be considered to be only the first step. A third set of questions centres on the student experience of HE, the performance of a more heterogeneous population and their retention within the system. The subsequent and final set of questions relates to the ultimate outcome of access, particularly in relation to labour market opportunities for individuals and the economic benefit that they, enterprises and society more widely accrue from participation.

The impact of structural change, and particular policies and practices

With regard to the first set of questions, at a macro-level, it is the quantitative indicators that provide a starting point to answer questions about the changing nature of HE systems. However, despite the range of system level changes, the move to greater institutional differentiation and the introduction of numerous explicit interventions to widen participation that have occurred in many countries around the world, there is limited evidence on a global level as to their effect on traditionally excluded groups in Higher Education. For instance, using the statistical indicators of organisations such as the OECD, it is difficult to gather data across a range of socio-demographic indicators that would indicate the extent to which participation has been *widened* as against merely been increased. A number of commentators (e.g. Schuetze and Slowey 2000; Murphy *et al.* 2002) have reported that the quantitative expansion of Higher Education has not necessarily been accompanied by a system-wide improvement in access for those groups in society who have historically not participated. Such evidence is most readily available from those countries where routine and detailed data collection is made. For instance in the UK, data available on applicants and entrants gathered by the Universities and Colleges Admissions System (UCAS) and the Higher Education Statistical Agency (HESA) has allowed increasingly sophisticated profiles of participation to be created.

The assertion that there has been rather limited success in widening participation is therefore best made in countries such as the UK, the USA and Australia, where sophisticated quantitative data exists. In the UK where the aim of widening access as an aim of government is heavily embedded in policy and practice, there is still considerable skewing of participation by social class and clear evidence that it is those more recently established universities and the non-university HE that accommodate most readily the 'non-traditional' student (see Morgan-Klein and Murphy in this volume). Thus an ostensibly unified HE system reflects in its widening participation practices its historic binary origins. The Australian government of the early 1990s was one of the first to routinely monitor quantitative indicators of equity performance, following the target setting of *A Fair Chance for All* (DEET 1990) with the setting of equity targets for six under-represented groups in HEIs. Postle *et al.* (1996) have shown that students from isolated areas, from low socio-economic backgrounds, and from rural areas were all under-represented in higher education and this situation showed little change during the period 1991–5.[6] Evidence is also found beyond the Anglo-Saxon world. In Spain, reforms in the university curricula in 1989 were introduced to both update their content and provide greater flexibility within the system, and brought about the expansion of three-year short cycle programmes, creating greater possibilities of access for young people from lower socio-economic groups (San Segundo and Valiente 2002). Even so recent analyses would suggest that inequality of opportunity by socio-economic status still remains a major problem (Albert 2000; Petrongolo and San Segundo 2002). A number of references to policies and practices at national level in other countries are found in Murphy *et al.* (2002).

The nature and effectiveness of provision

This analysis at a system level of course is by no means the dominant thrust of research that pertains to the nature and effectiveness of access provision itself. Most of the work carried out within this broad area has been relatively small-scale in nature and mainly, though not exclusively, qualitative. A number of general sub-themes can be identified as strands of research, although they are far from mutually exclusive.

First there has been considerable work on the profile of participants with emphases on both socio-demographic and psychological characteristics, and their interaction. This field of work includes studies of the factors that motivate students to participate, their attitudes to constraints such as those associated with finance, and how these interact with personal and individual factors. A recent study in the UK of the decision-making processes of potential mature student applicants summarises much of this literature (Davies *et al.* 2002).

Second there is much work on the experiences of participants in their preparation for HE. For instance, Haggis and Pouget (2002), in a study of young students taking a special entry to university programme, highlight three themes. First their sample carried a sense of injustice and alienation deriving from their learning experiences, second they lacked effective learning strategies for coping with formal learning and third their performance depended greatly on the strength of relationships and support mechanisms. As in other studies of this type, there are a complex set of interactions between these themes.

Third there is considerable research on the form and effectiveness of particular forms of intervention. We have already alluded to the tripartite fashion in which access mechanisms can be differentiated as in-reach, out-reach and flexible, and the particular types of activity within each of these strands of the typology has been shown to result in differential outcomes as measured by indicators of widening participation to under-represented groups. Other work has considered the particular efficacy of specific types of initiative,[7] particular forms of targeting[8] and the specific content of the curriculum.[9]

A fourth strand relates to the policy and practices of institutions, and includes such areas as the relationship between mission and action (Davies *et al.* 1994), collaboration with other bodies (Thomas 2002) and case study work of practice in the area of diversity such as that commissioned by the Higher Education Funding Council for England (HEFCE 2001, 2002).

The experience of Higher Education, performance and retention

A recent report from the National Center for Postsecondary Improvement (NCPI) in the US reports that despite 'notable progress on the frontiers of reform since the 1960s and 1970s, higher education's core practices remain largely unchanged', and 'achievement gaps in higher education persist between students of lower and higher socio-economic status, and across ethnic and racial groups' (NCPI 2002, p. 3). Referring to Australia, Postle and Sturman (2003) report a study of the Australian Vice Chancellors Committee (AVCC) (1998). In that study, it was found that Aboriginal and Torres Strait Islander students are significantly out-performed by other students; those with disabilities are significantly out-performed by other students; non-English-speaking students are significantly out-performed by English-speaking students but this was not the case in all States; low socio-economic status (SES) students are significantly out-performed by middle/high SES students although this was a result of significant differences in one State only – Victoria; female students in non-traditional areas are significantly out-performed by other female students. These are but two studies that make reference to performance; both sets of authors, rather than suggesting that the phenomena they describe are functions solely of the characteristics of the new and diverse student population, raise questions as to the suitability of HEIs themselves.

So in seeking explanations of the performance of students admitted through schemes to widen access, a range of issues must be considered. In a universal system, it is not simply a question of the preparedness of students for the HE experience, though clearly many are not prepared for the demands of a still largely inflexible system, but it is also the degree to which institutions respond to the challenges of diversity. In the US for instance, there is considerable evidence that the success of minority students is related to the extent to which they feel marginalised in institutions (Cuyjet 1998; Gloria and Rodriguez 2000; Schwartz and Washington 1999; Stanley et al. 1999). More generally, there is therefore a considerable research agenda that relates to the support of 'non-traditional' students within Higher Education, including around the role of counselling and support from academic staff (Bolam and Dodgson 2003), peers, family and others, approaches to teaching and learning (Sutherland 1997), academic literacy and developmental education (see Boylan later in this volume), and the content of the HE curriculum (McGivney 1996). This work in turn relates to a more general Higher Education literature concerned with the links between the student experience of Higher Education and wider social processes of elite reproduction (e.g. Bourdieu and Passeron 1990; Haselgrove 1994; Pascarella and Terenzini 1991), and the more recent focus on learning trajectory and learner identity (Gorard et al. 1998). It also relates to the well-known literatures that are concerned with student approaches to and their conceptions of learning in the Swedish phenomenological tradition such as Marton and Saljo (see Tickle 2001). Despite the plethora of general literature in this domain, Merril (2001) usefully points out the relative paucity of material that pertains to how mature adult learners experience the processes and interactions of learning.

Considerable research effort in particular is beginning to be focussed on issues pertaining to retention in those countries where the expansion of HE has been accompanied by increased attrition rates (e.g. the UK [National Audit Office

2002]). In certain other countries with a longer-standing universal system such as the UK, there is already a substantial research base pertaining to approaches that tend to improve student persistence in HE (Kerka 1995).

The outcomes of participation

There is increasing interest in the outcomes of participation in HE, as measures of satisfaction expressed by individuals in general terms, in terms of wider societal good and as demonstrated in terms of labour market opportunity and financial benefits to individuals, enterprises and society. In this context, whilst many studies demonstrate the financial benefits of achieving graduate status, for those accessing HE through schemes designed to widen participation, the outcome is not so clear. Conlon (2002) has demonstrated that whilst there is a private financial benefit to participation, it is not one that is easy to calculate (see Keep later in this volume). Egerton (2000) points out that there are many intervening variables that determine the market value of a degree achieved by a mature candidate, including their own socio-economic status and the nature of the HEI attended. Wolter and Weber (1999) in a Swiss study demonstrate that delaying the investment in education reduces the relative benefit, an issue also addressed in a recent OECD (2001b) publication.

Concluding remarks

The succeeding chapters therefore focus largely on the themes of 'getting in, getting through, and getting on', namely the stages prior to HE entry, the period within HE and the subsequent outcomes. Part 1 is concerned with key issues and Part 2 is concerned with approaches to research. And whilst the thrust of the collection concerns itself with the particular issue of widening participation to Higher Education, we also are keenly aware of the wider issues that provide barriers in many nations. We have therefore developed sections that begin to tackle broader issues such as that of literacy.

The research agenda in the field of widening participation is both broad, and potentially deep. The scope of this initial overview cannot possibly give full justice to the considerable work that has taken place in this field and which continues. The succeeding chapters will provide some of that detail.

Notes

1   The terms elite, mass and universal here refer to the delineations made by Trow (1973).
2   See Table C2.1 (OECD 2003). Entry rates to tertiary education and age distribution of new entrants (2001).
3   According to OECD (2001a) definitions, higher tertiary level A education requires a minimum cumulative theoretical duration of three years full-time equivalent study and normally are four years equivalent in duration. They are not exclusively

delivered at universities, and conversely it is not only type A programmes that universities offer. Type B programmes focus on practical, technical and occupational skills leading to direct entry to the labour market, though may contain some theoretical components, and are of a minimum of two years equivalent in duration.

4   See for instance the recent UNESCO-CEPES report on Bulgaria (Georgieva et al. 2002).

5   Scott (1995, p. 35) suggests that HE systems can be classified as dual, binary, unified and stratified. Both dual and binary systems contain alternative forms of HEI; in the case of the latter alternative institutions have been set up to complement and rival existing traditional structures. In unified systems, there is no formal differentiation of institutions and in stratified systems institutions are allocated a role within a total system.

6   Data at institutional level was readily available until 1997, thus allowing comparisons of HEIs in meeting performance targets. The DEST publications website (http://www.dest.gov.au/highered/repts.htm) provides full online documents for DEETYA/DETYA/DEST publications. *Equity in Higher Education* provides a detailed statistical analysis by institution, but has not been updated since 1997. *Higher Education Equity Plans* provides the mandatory equity plans for all individual universities.

7   E.g. Adult Access courses (Capizzi 1996), Inter-institutional links (Woodrow 2002), E-learning (Gorard and Selwyn 1999), Accreditation of Prior Experiential Learning (Davies 1999), Workplace Learning (Reeve et al. 1995), Summer Semester provision (Harris and Fallows 2002).

8   E.g. Women Returners (Pascall and Cox 1993), Men (Marks 2003), Minority Ethnic Groups (Imel 2001 (Native Americans)), Postle et al. 1996 (Aboriginals and Torres Strait Islanders)), Disabled Students (Riddell et al. 2002).

9   At a European Union level a current Socrates Grundtwig project, Chagal, focuses on Curriculum Guidelines for access programmes into higher education for under-represented adult learners (see the URL http://www.vwu.at/chagal/index.php).

References

Albert, C. (2000) 'Higher education demand in Spain. The influence of labour market signals and family background', *Higher Education*, 40(2), 147–62.

Australian Vice Chancellors Committee (AVCC) (1998) *Designated Equity Groups in Australian Universities: Performance of Commencing Students 1996 – Undergraduate Award Courses*, Canberra: AVCC.

Bolam, H. and Dodgson, R. (2003) 'Retaining and supporting mature students in higher education', *Journal of Adult and Continuing Education*, 8(2), 179–94.

Bonham, B.S. (2002) 'Educational mobility in the U.S. through the community college transfer function', in M.J. Osborne, J. Gallacher and M. Murphy (eds) *A Research Review of FE/HE Links – A Report to the Scottish Executive Enterprise and Lifelong Learning Department*, Stirling/Glasgow: Centre for Research in Lifelong Learning.

Bourdieu, P. and Passeron, J.C. (1990) *Reproduction in Education, Society and Culture*, London: Sage.

Bron, A. and Agélii, K. (2000) 'Non-traditional students in higher education in Sweden: from recurrent education to lifelong learning', in H. Schuetze and M. Slowey (eds) *Higher Education and Lifelong Learners – International Perspectives on Change*, London: RoutledgeFalmer.

Burtch, B. (2002) 'Review of further education/higher education links in Canada', in M.J. Osborne, J. Gallacher and M. Murphy (eds) *A Research Review of FE/HE Links –*

A Report to the Scottish Executive Enterprise and Lifelong Learning Department, Stirling/ Glasgow: Centre for Research in Lifelong Learning.

Capizzi, E. (1996) 'Measuring the effectiveness of access; methods and minefields', *Journal of Access Studies*, 11(1), 34–58.

Cerych, L. (2002) 'Higher education reform in the Czech Republic: a personal testimony regarding the impact of foreign advisers', *Higher Education In Europe*, XXVII(1–2), 111–21.

Communiqué of the Conference of Ministers responsible for Higher Education (2003) *Realising the European Higher Education Area*, Berlin, 19 September 2003. Online at: http://www.bologna-berlin2003.de/pdf/Communique1.pdf, accessed on 12 October 2003.

Conlon, G. (2002) 'One in three? The incidence and outcomes associated with the late attainment of qualifications in the United Kingdom', *Journal of Adult and Continuing Education*, 8(1), 14–45.

Council of Europe (1996) *Project on Access to Higher Education in Europe: Working Report. Part 1 Synthesis and Recommendations*, Strasbourg: Council of Europe.

Council of Europe (2001) *Lifelong Learning for Equity and Social Cohesion: A New Challenge to Higher Education*. Final Conference, Paris, 15–17 November 2001, Strasbourg: Council of Europe.

Cuyjet, M.C. (1998) 'Recognising and addressing marginalisation among African American college students', *College Student Affairs Journal*, 18(1), 64–71.

Davies, P., Osborne, M. and Williams, J. (2002) *For Me or Not for Me, That is the Question. A Study of Mature Students' Decision-making and Higher Education*. DfES Research Briefing No. 297.

Davies, P., Williams, J., Webb, S., Green, P. and Thompson, A. (1994) 'Mission possible? Institutional factors in patterns of alternative entry to higher education', *Scottish Journal of Adult and Continuing Education*, 1(2), 18–28

Davies, P. (1995) *Adults in Higher Education: International Perspectives on Access and Participation*, London: Jessica Kingsley.

Davies, P. (1999) 'Rights and rites of passage: crossing boundaries in France', *International Journal of Lifelong Education*, 19(3), 215–24.

Department of Employment, Education and Training (Australia) (1990) *A Fair Chance for All: Higher Education that's Within Everyone's Reach*, Canberra: DEET.

Egerton, M. (2000) 'Pay differentials between early and mature graduate men: the role of state employment', *Journal of Education and Work*, 13(3), 289–306.

Eggins, H. (1999) 'European approaches to widening participation in higher education: A commentary in light of the role of the Society for Research into Higher Education', *Higher Education in Europe*, 44(4), 561–6.

European Commission (1995) *White Paper – Teaching and Learning: Towards the Learning Society*, Brussels: EC.

European Commission (2001) *The Memorandum on Lifelong Learning*, Brussels: EC.

EURYDICE (2001) *Thematic Bibliography: Lifelong Learning*. Online at: (http://www.eurydice.org/Documents/Bibliographie/Lll/en/FrameSet.htm).

Gallacher, J. (2003) *Higher Education in Further Education: The Scottish Experience*, London: Council for Industry and Higher Education.

Gellert, C. (ed.) (1993) *Higher Education in Europe*, London: Jessica Kingsley.

Georgieva, P. with Todorova, L. and Pilev, D. (2002) *Higher Education in Bulgaria*, UNESCO-CEPES Monograph Series, Bucharest: UNESCO-CEPES.

Gloria, A.M. and Rodriguez, E.R. (2000) 'Counselling Latino university students: psychosociocultural issues for consideration', *Journal of Counselling and Development*, 78(2), 145–54.

Gorard, S., Rees, G., Fevre, R. and Furlong, J. (1998) 'Learning trajectories: travelling towards a learning society?', *International Journal of Lifelong Education*, 17, 400–10.

Gorard, S. and Selwyn, N. (1999) 'Switching on the learning society? Questioning the role of technology in widening participation in lifelong learning', *Journal of Education Policy*, 14(5), 523–4.

Haggis, T. and Pouget, M. (2002) 'Trying to be motivated: perspectives on learning from younger students accessing higher education', *Teaching in Higher Education*, 7(3), 323–36.

Harris, R.W. and Fallows, S.J. (2002) 'Enlarging educational opportunity: summer-semester provision in UK higher education', *Quality in Higher Education*, 8(3), 225–37.

Haselgrove, S. (ed.) (1994) *The Student Experience*, Buckingham: SRHE/Open University.

HEFCE (2001) *Strategies for Widening Participation in Higher Education – A Guide to Good Practice*, Guide 01/36, Bristol: HEFCE.

HEFCE (2002) *Successful Student Diversity – Case Studies of Practice in Learning and Teaching and Widening Participation*, HEFCE 02/48, Bristol: HEFCE.

Imel, S. (2001) *Adult Education for Native Americans*, Trends and Issues Alert No. 28, Educational Resources Information Center. Online at: http://ericacve.org/tia.asp, accessed on 12 October 2003.

Kerka, S. (1995) *Adult Learner Retention Revisited*, Educational Resources Information Center Digest No. 166. Online at: http://ericacve.org/digests.asp, accessed on 12 October 2003.

Marga, A. (2002) 'Reform of education in Romania in the 1990s: a retrospective', *Higher Education In Europe*, XXVII(1–2), 123–35.

Marks, A. (2003) 'Welcome to the new ambivalence: reflections on the historical and current cultural antagonism between the working class male and higher education', *British Journal of Sociology of Education*, 24(1), 83–93.

McGivney, V. (1996) *Staying or Leaving the Course: Non-Completion and Retention of Mature Students in Further and Higher Education*, Leicester: NIACE.

Merril, B. (2001) 'Learning and teaching in universities; perspectives from adult learners and teachers', *Teaching in Higher Education*, 6, 5–17.

Murphy, M., Morgan-Klein, B., Osborne, M. and Gallacher, J. (2002) *Widening Participation in Higher Education: Report to Scottish Executive*, Stirling: Centre for Research in Lifelong Learning/Scottish Executive.

National Audit Office (2002) *Improving Student Achievement in English Higher Education*, HC 486 Session 2001–2, 18 January.

Oduaran, A. (2001) 'Access initiatives in Botswana and Nigeria', *Journal of Adult and Continuing Education*, 7(1), 51–62.

OECD (2001a) *Education at a Glance*, Paris: OECD.

OECD (2001b) *Economics and Finance of Lifelong Learning*, Paris: OECD.

OECD (2003) *Education at a Glance*, Paris: OECD.

Orfield, G. and Miller, E. (2001) *Chilling Admissions: The Affirmative Action Crisis and the Search for Alternatives*, Cambridge: Harvard Education Publishing Group.

Osborne, M. (2003a) 'Policy and practice in widening participation – a six country comparative study of access as flexibility', *International Journal of Lifelong Education*, 22(1), 43–58.

Osborne, M. (2003b) 'A European comparative analysis of policy and practice in widening participation to lifelong learning', *European Journal of Education*, 38(1), 5–24.

Parry, G. (1996) 'Access education in England and Wales, 1973–94: from second chance to third wave', *Journal of Access Studies*, 11(1), 10–33.

Pascall, G. and Cox, R. (1993) *Women Returning to Higher Education*, Buckingham: SHRE and Open University.

Pascarella, E.T. and Terenzini, P.T. (1991) *How College Affects Students. Findings and Insights from Twenty Years of Research*, San Francisco: Jossey-Bass.

Petrongolo, B. and San Segundo, M. (2002) 'Staying-on at school at sixteen. The impact of labour market conditions in Spain', *Economics of Education Review*, 21(4), 353–65.

Postle, G.D., Clarke, J.R., Skuja, E., Bull, D.D., Batorowicz, K. and McCann, H.A. (eds) (1996). *Towards Excellence in Diversity: Educational Equity in the Australian Higher Education Sector in 1995: Status, Trends and Future Directions*, Toowoomba: USQ.

Postle, G. and Sturman, A. (2003) 'Widening access to higher education – an Australian case study', *Journal of Adult and Continuing Education*, 8(2), 195–212.

Reeve, F., Gallacher, J., Sharp, N., Osborne, M., Land, R., Whittaker, R., Dockrell, R. and Neal, P. (1995) *Developing Employment-based Access to Learning (DEAL) – Final Report*, Glasgow: Glasgow Caledonian University/University of Stirling/Napier University.

Riddell, S., Wilson, A. and Tinklin, T. (2002) *Disability and the Wider Access Agenda: Supporting Disabled Students in Different Institutional Contexts*. Paper presented to the Eleventh European Access Network Annual Conference, Italy: Under-Privileged but not Under-Achieving: Promoting Completion Rates among Disadvantaged Students. Online at: http://www.ed.ac.uk/ces/Disability/publications.htm, accessed on 11 August 2003.

San Segundo, M. and Valiente, A. (2002) 'Widening access in Spain: the unexpected effects of two policy changes', *Journal of Adult and Continuing Education*, 8(1), 46–59.

Schuetze, H. and Slowey, M. (eds) (2000) *Higher Education and Lifelong Learners – International Perspectives on Change*, London: RoutledgeFalmer.

Schwartz, R.A. and Washington, C.M. (1999) 'African-American freshmen in a historically Black college', *Journal of the Freshman Year Experience*, 11(1), 39–62.

Scott, P. (1995) *The Meanings of Mass Higher Education*, Buckingham: SRHE/Open University.

Stanley, C., Rohdiek, S. and Tang, L. (1999) 'An exploratory study of the teaching concerns of Asian American students', *Journal on Excellence in College Teaching*, 10(1), 107–27.

Sutherland, P. (1997) *Adult Learning – A Reader*, London: Jessica Kingsley.

Thomas, L. (2002) 'Collaboration with and between HEIs in England: a review of policy and practice', in L. Thomas, M. Cooper and J. Quinn (eds) *Collaboration to Widen Participation in Higher Education*, Stoke-on-Trent: Trentham Books.

Tickle, S. (2001) 'What have we learnt about student learning? A review of the research on study approach and style', *Kybernetes: The International Journal of Systems and Cybernetics*, 30(7–8), 955–69.

Toyne, P. (1990) 'Achieving wider access', in G. Parry and B. Wake (eds) *Access and Alternative Futures for Higher Education*, London: Hodder and Stoughton.

Trow, M. (1973) *Problems in the Transition from Elite to Mass Higher Education*, Berkeley: Carnegie Commission for Education.

UNESCO (1998) *Mumbai Statement on Lifelong Learning, Citizenship and the Reform of Higher Education*, Online at: http://www.unesco.org/education/uie/online/olpub.html, accessed on 5 July 2003.

Wheelahan, L. (2002) 'Links between vocational education and training and higher education in Australia', in M.J. Osborne, J. Gallacher and M. Murphy (eds) *A Research Review of FE/HE Links – A Report to the Scottish Executive Enterprise and Lifelong Learning Department*, Stirling/Glasgow: Centre for Research in Lifelong Learning.

Wolter, A. (2000) 'Germany: non-traditional students in German higher education: situation, profiles, policies and perspectives', in H. Schuetze and M. Slowey (eds) *Higher Education and Lifelong Learners – International Perspectives on Change*, London: RoutledgeFalmer.

Wolter, S.C. and Weber, B.A. (1999) 'Skilling the unskilled – a question of incentives?', *International Journal of Manpower*, 20(3–4), 254–69.

Woodrow, M. (2002) *Pyramids or Spiders? Cross-sector Collaboration to Widen Participation: Learning from International Experience*, Edinburgh: Scottish Funding Councils.

Chapter 2

Researching widening access
An overview

Peter Scott

Introduction

The aim of this chapter is to provide an overview of research into widening access. But the topic itself – research into widening access – contains within it a tension, if not a contradiction. On the one hand, widening access has become a dominant policy preoccupation. Higher education in England is embarking on a third wave of expansion, on a scale that is equivalent to and potentially outstrips the first wave associated with the Robbins report in the mid-1960s and the second wave unleashed by the abandonment of the binary system between 1988 and 1992. The target is 50 per cent participation for 30-year-olds and younger by 2010, even if the target has been downplayed in recent ministerial statements. Widening participation is the key motif of this third wave. If Scottish higher education has not been set a specific expansion target, this is because an 'access' perspective has already been wholeheartedly accepted. On the other hand, research into widening access is still an emerging rather than a mature research field. It remains a sub-set of a wider research field, post-compulsory education, which is itself something of a poor relation of educational research which, in turn, has had to fight hard to gain and maintain academic respectability.

There can be no doubt about the growing importance of 'access' as a policy domain – and, in particular, of widening participation. It has moved from the margins of policy to the mainstream, challenging (if not yet superseding) the dominance of research, and is increasingly embroiled with debates about the future funding of higher education. The 50 per cent target is derived from a commitment in the Labour Party's Manifesto for the 2001 General Election – the only substantial reference to higher education in that document. It is one of the key performance indicators for the Department of Education and Skills. Widening participation has been identified by the Higher Education Funding Council for England (HEFCE) as one of four core areas (the others are teaching and learning, research and out-reach to business and the community) in which all higher education institutions are expected to engage. Indeed HEFCE approval of institutional strategies, and action plans, for widening participation has now been made a condition of grant – following a decision by the Scottish Higher Education Funding Council (SHEFC) to impose a similar condition a year earlier.

A 'Partnerships for Progression' initiative has been launched by HEFCE to extend the work of existing access partnerships between universities, further education colleges and schools (HEFCE 2001; HEFCE 2002). As part of this initiative regional targets have been set for increasing participation, designed to achieve the overall 50 per cent target.

A lively debate about the Government's plans for widening participation has ensued. Some have criticised the 50 per cent target as unrealistic and/or undesirable. They have argued that it is impossible to provide higher education for such a high proportion of the population without sacrificing standards – or even undermining what is meant by higher education (even in an extended post-binary form). Even if such an expansion were possible, they further argue, it would be undesirable because the most urgent national need is for the expansion and improvement of technician education and training of skilled workers. (Such critics typically ignore – or are ignorant of – the involvement of higher education institutions in the first of these categories.) The Institute of Directors, an organisation which represents the business community in the UK, has been a vocal exponent of this point of view, arguing that Britain needs plumbers not media studies graduates. Similar concerns about the dangers of 'dumbing down' are also well represented in influential sections of the press. Other, more generous, critics of the 50 per cent target in England have argued that its concentration on young adults tends to downgrade the importance of lifelong learning, the real challenge both in terms of enhancing employment skills and offering individuals greater opportunities to participate in higher education. This danger to a large extent has been avoided in Scotland, partly because of higher levels of participation and partly because of the emphasis on lifelong learning in the determination of ministerial portfolios within the Scottish Executive. A further concern in England has been that the target was calculated by using projections of future demand for graduates in the workforce rather than by reference to any idea of democratic rights. However, whatever opinions are expressed, these lively debates demonstrate just how central access and widening participation have become in higher education policy.

Yet this has not been accompanied by a similar enlargement, or elaboration, of the research base in access and widening participation. It is far from easy to define the scale and scope of research in this field. However, of the 172 journals scanned by the Society of Research into Higher Education's publication *Research into Higher Education Abstracts* only six are specifically concerned with these subjects. This may be an overestimate because journals concerned with adult education and lifelong learning have been included. However, this journal count does not tell the whole story. First, the journals that were scanned for *Abstracts* – inevitably – are biased towards mainstream higher education. Several reputable journals are not included, such as Staffordshire University's *Widening Participation and Lifelong Learning*. Second, many of the articles published in other journals are concerned with widening participation. Anecdotal sampling suggests that the proportion of these articles is increasing. Nevertheless, it is revealing that *Abstracts* groups articles into seven areas – such as 'national systems and comparative studies', 'institutional management' and 'curriculum' – which do not include access or participation.

A further indicator of the limited research based in the field is that there is only a small number of university research centres which focus on access and participation. However, universities do generate a large amount of informal research in this area in the course of developing policies on widening participation, which may be only loosely linked (if at all) to the more academic research being undertaken in these centres. Much of the institutional research in this area is practitioner-led and practitioner-focused and it is often published as 'grey' literature – official reports, institutional policy-papers and so on. Consultants in various guises also make a significant contribution to access research. As a result the access research community is poorly defined (administrators and consultants are members as well as academic researchers); widely distributed (not only across different academic departments, but also between academic and administrative departments and outside higher education institutions); and highly eclectic in epistemological and methodological terms. These are important – and not necessarily negative – characteristics which will be discussed in greater detail later in this chapter.

Several reasons can be suggested for this apparent asymmetry between access as a policy preoccupation, more important as each year passes, and access as a research field, immature and weakly institutionalised. One, which has already been hinted at, is that this is an immature research field. If this essentially optimistic view is taken, the asymmetry is one of timing; it would be reasonable to expect research on access and widening participation to develop and to mature, to match the much higher policy profile now enjoyed by these subjects. Another, less optimistic, reason is that access research is poorly institutionalised, both in a concrete and cognitive sense. No matter how mainstream the issue of access may have become in terms of policy, in the context of research it remains a marginal activity within Departments of Education where the natural centre of gravity continues to be research in schools. (The position of access research within Departments of Adult or Continuing Education is more favourable – but these Departments still sometimes occupy peripheral positions within the wider university.)

A third, still more gloomy reason is that, despite the rhetorical emphasis on evidence-based policy-making, in practice policy is no longer so clearly grounded in research. Several factors may account for this change: the frenetic volatility of post-modern sound-bite politics; the shift from planned welfare-state regimes to chaotic quasi-market environments; even the under-development (and intellectual poverty) of much access research. An example may be the contrast between the research commissioned by the Robbins committee, much of which was fundamental groundbreaking social science research, and the research commissioned by the Dearing committee, which more typically took the form of reviews of existing literature supplemented by a limited amount of qualitative research. A fourth reason

– and the one that will receive the greatest emphasis in this chapter – is that the nature of the research enterprise is being transformed in ways that fundamentally change the balance between theory and practice and the articulations between researchers, practitioners and policy-makers. If this view is accepted, the asymmetry between policy and research appears in a new light. Notions of intellectual immaturity or insecure institutionalisation cease to be so relevant.

This chapter is divided into three main sections. The first section considers these wider changes in the production, or generation, of knowledge within which formal research is now only a sub-domain. As a result our definitions of research and researching are changing all the time – and becoming wider and wider. These changes are particularly relevant to a research domain such as widening access, which is engaged, highly distributed, and close to policy formation. The second section, instead of offering an inevitably selective review of the research literature on widening participation, attempts to develop a broad typology of research in this area and distinguishes between three main levels. The first is macro-level studies of the evolving aims and purposes of higher education, which inevitably embrace notions of entitlement, access and widening participation. The second is intermediate-level studies of specific policy initiatives aimed to widen access and increase participation (although the two need to be carefully distinguished because they are not necessarily the same; logically access can be widened without increasing participation). The third is micro-level studies of the experience of access students and of the intellectual, pedagogical and organisational challenges they pose to institutions. Many of these studies are – literally – enthused with strong value commitments to the political project represented by widening access. The third section of this chapter consider two main modes of research into widening access, namely policy studies (typically with a strong emphasis on evaluation) and academic studies (generally with a stronger theoretical bias).

New patterns of research

New patterns of research – or, more broadly, knowledge generation – have been emerging in recent years. Although the novelty of these changes has been questioned, their visibility and intensity are not in doubt. A radical shift can be observed not only in research practices but also in definitions, and conceptions, of what constitutes valid research. The first element, the shift in research practices, is incontestable. The evidence is everywhere – the growth of commissioned and sponsored research, the increasing popularity of near-market or policy research, the emphasis now placed on user-perspectives. Researchers have embraced these new practices largely in order to secure adequate funding, but their epistemological (and, to a lesser extent, their methodological) purity has been preserved. Their life-world remains unsullied. However, the second shift, in definitions of valid research, continues to be sharply contested. Some argue that, at the best, it is a crude justification of the priority now attached to applied research and, at the worst, a treacherous rationalisation of irrationality, a deplorable dumbing-down of standards and a dangerous lurch into relativism, post-modernism (or worse!). The reason for the greater controversy aroused by shifting definitions of research is that, potentially at any rate, they penetrate deeply into the life-world of research. Everything is up for grabs – epistemology as well as methodologies, research outcomes as well as research questions.

These changes in research practices and definitions of valid research have been theorised in a number of different ways. Some authors have tried to accommodate (and domesticate) these changes within intellectual frameworks that preserve the essence of an 'objective' science unsullied by social constructivism while acknowledging the growing impact of risk and uncertainty (Ziman 2000; Pollack 2003). Others have attempted to describe and explain the more intense engagement of science with society and the economy without totally abandoning science's claim to represent a separate, and relatively autonomous, domain. The best example is the notion of a 'Triple Helix' of science, the state and business (Etzkowitz and Leydesdorff 1997). A third group has analysed these changes in terms of a transition from 'Mode 1' science, research that is denominated in disciplinary domains and policed by scientific communities, to 'Mode 2' knowledge production that is problem- or action-oriented; is highly distributed with proliferating research sites and research actors (who are no longer easily categorised as 'producers' or 'users'); and produces knowledge that is not only reliable (whether through verification or falsification) but socially robust, in the sense that it can stand up to the rough-and-tumble of the politics arena or the marketplace (Gibbons et al. 1994; Nowotny et al. 2001). Inherent in this third theoretical perspective are the ideas of de-differentiation and co-evolution. The first of these ideas is fiercely resisted by more traditional scientists as potentially denying the autonomy of science and acquiescing in its effective incorporation into the political and/or market domains. The 'Triple Helix' and 'Mode 2' accounts have come to be regarded as alternatives, or even rivals, although they have much in common (Shinn 2002).

There is no space in this chapter to enter further into these debates, or to attempt to assess the validity of these rival accounts. However, these debates and rival accounts are themselves evidence of the important changes that have taken place in the empirical landscape of research. They are a – theoretical – acknowledgement of the observable enlargement of the scope of research (or knowledge generation). Arguably this enlargement is especially significant for apparently immature research fields that are weakly institutionalised and cognitively heterogeneous, even eclectic. Because their stake in a more traditional research paradigm is comparatively weak, they have less to lose (and potentially much to gain) from a shift to a more open paradigm of knowledge generation. One effect of this shift has been to break down the former dichotomy between established scientific research and alternative forms of enquiry, of which 'action' research was and is a good example. The norms of established scientific research obliged researchers (especially in less mature, and less confident, research fields) to adopt a conservative approach both to theory, which typically was imported from more prestigious fields, and to methodology, which had to demonstrate its rigour by being *plus royaliste que le roi*. In contrast, the norms of alternative modes of enquiry, whether highly applied or action-oriented, encouraged researchers in these fields to challenge this innate conservatism by embracing innovative, but often vulnerable, methods and by celebrating passionate engagement and disparaging disinterested detachment.

The breaking-down of this sharp demarcation between established and alternative modes of research has been especially significant for research in post-compulsory education – and, in particular, access research. Although there was – and is – a significant amount of 'standard' research in these fields, there has always been an important strand of 'alternative' research as well. One reason is structural. Many access research projects have been comparatively small-scale. As a result access researchers have not always had access to the elaborate resources and infrastructure required for 'standard' research. Furthermore they have found it difficult to compete with other research fields in the increasing competition for external research funding from the Economic and Social Research Council (ESRC)[1] and major foundations. But another reason is quasi-ideological. Much of access research has been conducted by practitioners who were committed to advocacy on behalf of those who were likely to benefit from the implementation of access policies or whose administrative responsibility it was to develop and implement such policies. However, a result of the far-reaching changes in the way that knowledge is generated and research undertaken is that instead of two rival – and, maybe, incommensurable – research traditions there is now a broad spectrum of epistemologies and methodologies, all of which are now recognised as more or less valid. Of course, there are still fierce controversies about the relative weight that should be attached to different research traditions. But the bias against 'alternative' research styles has tended to diminish.

This is likely to have important effects. One is that access researchers may now be in a better position to attract funding from the ESRC and the other mainstream research funders. This has already begun to happen during the past decade. The emphasis on programmatic research, which can be seen as one aspect of the emergence of a much more heterogeneous research paradigm, has presented research into post-compulsory education (and widening participation) with new opportunities. A few years ago the ESRC's Learning Society Programme and, more recently, the Teaching and Learning Research Programme (TLRP) are good examples. Another effect has been to raise the self-confidence of researchers in these fields and to encourage the growth of more, stronger research communities. Also significant has been the growth of policy-oriented research programmes developed by HEFCE and similar agencies which, for all their faults such as their abbreviated time-scales and rather less than open agendas, have provided valuable additional resources for access researchers. The parallel growth of practitioner-focused research programmes, again despite faults such as a bias towards over-simplification and 'practical' outcomes, has had a similar effect. The work of the Learning and Skills Development Agency (LSDA),[2] and its off-shoot the Learning and Skills Research Centre (LSRC),[3] is a good example of this development. Finally institutions themselves have become significant generators of informal research, as they develop, implement and evaluate access policies. As a result of these changes a more eclectic repertoire of research styles and methods, and a more diverse range of funding sources, are available to access researchers.

Widening participation research

It is possible to develop a comparatively simple taxonomy of access research. As has already been indicated three broad types can be identified: (i) macro-level studies of the evolution of modern higher education systems; (ii) intermediate-level studies of specific policy initiatives aimed at widening participation; and (iii) micro-level studies of 'access' in terms of student experiences, progression, outcomes and so on. In this section each will be discussed. But it is important to emphasise that this taxonomy of access research should not be taken to imply any kind of hierarchy. There is no warrant for assuming that macro-level studies are more likely to be conceptual (and, therefore, the most rigorous in conventional academic terms), or that micro-studies are necessarily the most practical. The development of new research paradigms and new forms of knowledge production mean that these conventional characterisations of research have become an anachronism.

The evolution of modern higher education systems

Nevertheless it is in some sense true that macro-studies tend to be more academic in two senses. First, they are more concerned with the development of new concepts and a new language, to describe the evolution of modern higher education systems; the development of these new concepts and that new language are key transformative elements in the mainstreaming of access policies. Second, these macro-studies are more likely to be undertaken within the context of 'standard' social science research because they draw from and contribute to established disciplines. This is both an advantage and a disadvantage: an advantage because these macro-level studies are less inhibited by the constraints inherent in commissioned research or evaluation studies; and a disadvantage because such studies may be over-influenced by internal disciplinary agendas and hierarchies.

The transformative potential of these studies is crucial because the language of access is a key driver of changing conceptualisations of modern higher education systems, conceptualisations that are not merely of academic interest but have real political bite. Nearly all theories of mass higher education are derived from a single dominant phenomenon, the remorseless expansion of student numbers – and that expansion, in turn, both leads to (and also is dependent upon) widening participation (Scott 1995). This may be particularly true at times when more conventional forms of student demand appear to be growing only slowly, which makes the search for new student constituencies more urgent and the need to transform higher education to accommodate these new kinds of student more essential. Arguably, the emphasis on access policies is even more intense in these circumstances. In England ministers draw a clear distinction between increasing participation (more of the same, leading to levels of near-universal participation by middle-class students) and widening participation (reaching out to new, predominantly working-class and ethnic-minority students).

Almost every theory, every conceptual framework, every research topic about the growth of mass higher education flows from this single dominant phenomenon. The most familiar categorisation is still that developed in the 1970s by Martin Trow, admittedly in the rather different context of the development of Californian higher education. He emphasised a succession of shifts – first from élite to mass higher education; and subsequently from mass to universal higher education, with transition zones at 15 and 40 per cent participation levels (Trow 1973). Trow's taxonomy raises key issues of categorisation. Is 'higher education', which took over from 'university' around the time of the Robbins Report (1963), any longer a defensible, or a distinguishable, category? If it is not, what happens to the intellectual and cultural norms – and, of course, the social practices – embodied in the now redundant idea of 'higher education'? Can 'lifelong learning', the most probable successor category, be as effective a creator, and transmitter, of intellectual culture and scientific knowledge? Then, at a more practical level, nearly all the issues raised about higher education funding, institutional management or student learning also can be regarded as being derived from the same dominant phenomenon, widening participation, which has led to massively increased expenditure on higher education, produced larger and more complex institutions, encouraged the recruitment of new kinds of student and led to a revolution in learning and teaching, courses and curricula, admissions and assessment.

Policy development and evaluation

The second type of access research is intermediate-level studies which can be divided into two main categories. The first is pre-initiative studies where a broad policy objective has been identified but there is a need for research either to 'scope' the context and options or, in a more limited way, to provide a review of earlier research findings that seem to be relevant. The second is post-initiative evaluation studies which review the effectiveness of particular policies against their original objectives. Because the policy world is always moving on, these post-initiative studies inevitably suggest some pointers towards the development of future policies and so connect back to, and have a lot in common with, pre-initiative studies. A major source of the funding for such research comes from Government Departments, Funding Councils and other national agencies; the Scottish Executive and National Assembly for Wales; Regional Development Agencies and other regional bodies in England; local authorities; and voluntary organisations. One of the benefits of devolution, in Scotland and Wales, and of regionalism in England, has been to produce a wider range of players. Not only has this increased the potential number of funding sources, it has also increased the emphasis on widening participation. Although it is a very broad generalisation, it is nevertheless probably true that in an exclusively Westminster-Whitehall perspective widening participation was probably a less prominent policy preoccupation than it is in the more fragmented multi-layered perspective provided by European institutions, national Government, devolved Administrations, and regional and local agencies.

It can be argued that there is still not a sufficiently strong commitment to evidence-based policy development in higher education – compared, for example, with the National Health Service. However, many higher education initiatives – and access initiatives, because of their prominence, are not an exception – are still developed with inadequate research underpinning. Many also are never seriously evaluated (in the sense that such evaluation leads on to policy improvements rather than simply closing the books on a particular initiative). Once, the prime cause was the unwillingness of Government Departments and Funding Councils to take research seriously. In other words it was a demand problem. That unwillingness has not disappeared. But the main problem may now be the lack of adequate (and adaptable) research capacity within universities. In other words a supply problem. This lack of research capacity has many causes – including, of course, the rather weak institutionalisation of higher education research in the research system. But there is an opportunity to build research capacity which would produce not only the obvious advantage of critical mass and continuity in research groups but also the less obvious advantage of developing a wider range of more independent research perspectives.

Practitioner-based studies of the 'access' experience

The third type of access research is micro-studies of student experiences and outcomes. The bulk of access research probably falls in this third category, although it is difficult to draw a firm line between the second and third types. Nearly all higher education institutions have now developed detailed and sophisticated strategies on widening participation either because these strategies are central to overall institutional strategies or because these strategies now have to be approved by the Funding Councils. These strategies need to be 'scoped', and then evaluated, in the same way as national policy initiatives. So institutional research is no longer an add-on predominantly driven by practitioner curiosity and enthusiasm; it has become much more of a key element within institutional management. This is an important shift. Once, the pattern of publication in this third type of access research was dominated, first, by bottom-up research undertaken by practitioners who wanted to improve their understanding of the needs – but also the potential – of students from less traditional backgrounds (often with a view to developing good practice); and second, by 'advocacy' research undertaken by participants in access networks – or, in the case of 'old' universities, staff in adult and continuing education departments, the old extra-mural departments – whose mission was – and is – to promote widening participation.

Neither practitioner nor activist research was necessarily intended to be scholarly in a traditional sense. Nor was it necessarily closely aligned with corporate objectives; indeed, in some cases it was consciously going against the institutional grain. Such research still exists – and much of it is of very high quality. But it has now been supplemented by more mainstream research more closely aligned with corporate objectives. (One example might be research into ways to improve retention rates among less traditional students.) This has its advantages and disadvantages. The advantages include better funding than that typically available to practitioner-focused and activist-driven access research. Also its findings are more likely to be followed up by action. The main disadvantage is that this institutionally-driven style of access research may have lost that quality of radical insurgency that was one of the most important, and appealing, characteristics of earlier styles of grass-roots access research.

Policy studies and academic research

The third section of this chapter is concerned with the contrast between policy studies and more academic forms of research. This contrast has already been discussed in terms of the taxonomy of widening participation research outlined in the preceding section. However, it would be misleading to equate academic research in the field of access studies with the first and third types (macro-studies of the evolution of higher education systems and micro-studies rooted in practitioner and activist perspectives), and policy studies with the second type (intermediate-studies of policy initiatives, often with a strong element of evaluation). The real pattern of research production is much more complicated. Researchers, policy-makers and practitioners form a complex, and overlapping, array of actors – even research actors to different degrees (Scott 2000). Much of the apparently theoretical research in this field is ultimately driven by policy developments, even if it is not sponsored by policy-making agencies. Equally, many of the policy studies, or evaluations, usually commissioned by such agencies, can – and do – make an important contribution to the development of theory (and so increase our basic understanding of higher education).

There is a second qualification which must also be emphasised. It is inherent in the new research paradigm, the new forms of knowledge generation discussed earlier in this chapter, that the distinctions between academic research and policy research are anachronistic and misleading. It is no longer true, if it ever was, that there is a hierarchical relationship between them with policy studies being dependent on academic research for its concepts and methodologies. Policy research is now far more than simply looking at the research evidence and then using that evidence to explore policy options. Even the phrase 'evidence-based' policy/practice is potentially misleading, because it implies that the 'evidence' (i.e. the research findings) can be regarded as unproblematic; it also implies an essentially linear model of knowledge production starting with disinterested academic research and then moving through a process of application and/or knowledge transfer to produce better goods, services or policies. If this (naïve) model is rejected and if instead it is accepted that knowledge is generated within a context of application (or even implication), that it is increasingly trans-disciplinary and that it is produced within a much larger and more eclectic 'knowledge space', it must follow that policy formation is itself a primary site of knowledge production not an arena in which pre-existing research findings are merely applied.

However, while it is difficult to establish a clear conceptual distinction between academic research and policy studies, it is possible to differentiate in a more practical sense. The key difference is not that academic research and policy studies tend to have different intellectual norms, which may or may not be true, but that their social practices are differentiated. The key differences are between the character of the actual researchers, the institutions which are their bases and the conditions under which they are employed. Also important are differences in funding regimes and dissemination protocols. If this essentially pragmatic distinction between academic research and policy studies is accepted, it is probably true that most of the large-scale access research falls into the policy studies category, while the bulk of the academic research in this field is still comparatively small-scale. This has two main consequences. The first, which has already been discussed, is the rather weak institutionalisation of access research. Because there are still too few sufficiently large and stable research groups, there continues to be a critical-mass issue and it is also difficult to build and sustain research careers. The second, and less obvious, consequence is that there are very few, if any, 'canonical texts', or highly influential books that have shaped the field. As research fields still tend to be defined in terms of their key ideas, as expressed in key texts, this remains a disturbing weakness.

Conclusion

It would be unfair and misleading, however, to end an overview chapter on a negative note. Access research is important – in two senses. First, it is an excellent example of an emerging research paradigm, whether described as a 'Triple Helix' or 'Mode 2', that differs in material respects from traditional styles of scholarly and scientific inquiry. The asymmetry between the ever-increasing significance of access within the policy domain and the under-development or immaturity of access studies as a research domain becomes much easier to explain. The apparent weaknesses of access research – its insecure institutionalisation within higher education (but its spread into other institutions), the range of research actors, the eclecticism of its concepts and methodologies, the diversity of its funding sources, its varied and heterogeneous patterns of publication and dissemination – may be, in fact, strengths (or, at any rate, characteristics of this emerging research paradigm).

Second, the impact of access research is far from being negligible. This impact has been felt at two levels. The first level is the inexorable accumulation of grass-roots research that has spread good practice and informed policy development across (nearly) all our institutions. None of this research, by itself, may be paradigm-busting, but the cumulative effect may have been. The second is that access research is helping to develop a new language – of access and participation, mass higher education, lifelong learning and so on. It is a language now used by almost everyone in higher education, even by those who are not especially committed to the causes this language represents. This language is now so familiar it is difficult to recall how strange, even alien, it was until very recently. In both respects, access research is transforming higher education – through the remorseless accumulation of good practice, and by helping to create a new language (or discourse).

Notes

1   The ESRC is the main UK government funding body for research in the social sciences, including education.
2   The LSDA is a strategic unit for the development of policy and practice in post-16 education and training for England.
3   The LSRC is a government sponsored research centre which focuses on post-16 education and training for England.

References

Etzkowitz, H. and Leydesdorff, L. (eds) (1997) *Universities and the Global Knowledge Economy: a Triple Helix of University-Industry-Government Relations*, London: Pinter.

Gibbons, M., Limoges, C., Nowotny, H., Schwartzman, S., Scott, P. and Trow, M. (1994) *The New Production of Knowledge: The Dynamics of Science and Research in Contemporary Societies*, London: Sage.

Higher Education Funding Council for England (2001) *Partnerships for Progression: Proposals by the HEFCE and the Learning and Skills Council*, Bristol: HEFCE (01/73).

Higher Education Funding Council for England (2002) *Funding for Widening Participation in Higher Education*, Bristol: HEFCE (02/22).

Nowotny, H., Scott, P. and Gibbons, M. (2001) *Re-Thinking Science: Knowledge and the Public in an Age of Uncertainty*, Cambridge: Polity Press.

Pollack, H.N. (2003) *Uncertain Science... Uncertain World*, Cambridge: Cambridge University Press.

Robbins Report (1963) Higher Education. Report of the Committee appointed by the Prime Minister under the Chairmanship of Lord Robbins, 1961–3, London: HMSO.

Scott, P. (1995) *The Meanings of Mass Higher Education*, Buckingham: Open University Press.

Scott, P. (2000) 'Higher education research in the light of a dialogue between policy-makers and practitioners', in Ulrich Teichler and Jan Sadlak (eds) *Higher Education Research: Its Relationship to Policy and Practice*, Oxford: Pergamon Press (for the International Association of Universities).

Shinn, T. (2002) 'The triple helix and new production of knowledge: prepackaged thinking in science and technology', *Social Studies of Science*, 32/4(August), 599–614.

Trow, M. (1973) *Problems in the Transition from Élite to Mass Higher Education*, Berkeley CA: Carnegie Commission on Higher Education.

Ziman, J. (2000) *Real Science: What It Is, and What It Means*, Cambridge: Cambridge University Press.

Chapter 3

Researching access in a rapidly changing context

Experiences from higher education in South Africa[1]

Shirley Walters

Introduction

It has been ten years since South Africa attained its hard won democratic status. Since then there have been changes to policies and practices in virtually every aspect of the nation's life. Within the context of the legacy of racial oppression, poverty and low educational levels, access to education and training at all levels has been a major concern.

It is taken for granted at policy level that broadened access has to occur in terms of changing the demographic profiles of students and staff within higher education institutions (HEIs). Implicit within this is the push for greater social justice for those historically disadvantaged by the system of apartheid. For purposes here, the particular groups that are of interest are the adult learners and workers.

The chapter begins with a brief overview of the material conditions in South Africa. It then moves to a discussion of the rapidly changing higher education scene and the issues of access and equity particularly for adult learners and workers within it.

Political and socio-economic snapshot of South Africa

Since the first democratic elections in South Africa in 1994, the society has been undergoing dramatic changes in virtually all areas, within a changing global context. South Africa is a middle income country with one of the most unequal distributions of wealth in the world. The Gross Domestic Product (GDP) per capita for South Africa is $2,560, which compares unfavourably with the world average of $4,797. For the period 1985–94, life expectancy at birth was estimated at about 54.12 years for males and 64.38 for females. For 1996 the estimates were 52.11 years for males and 61.6 for females. The first set of figures provides a pre-AIDS baseline, whilst the second set falls within the period when HIV/AIDS has emerged as a serious health problem.

At the time of the 2001 South African Census[2] there were just over 44,819,778 people living in South Africa of whom 52.2 per cent were women and 43.2 per cent were under the age of 19 years.[3] Five per cent were seriously disabled preventing full participation in life activities. It is a culturally diverse society with 11 official languages. The racial breakdown[4] is: 'Black African' – 79 per cent, 'Coloured' – 8.9 per cent, 'Asian' – 2.5 per cent and 'White' 9.6 per cent. Languages spoken in the home: 23.8 per cent isiZulu; 17.6 per cent isiXhosa; 13.3 per cent Afrikaans; 9.4 per cent Sepedi; 8.2 per cent English; 8.2 per cent Setwana; 7.9 per cent seSotho; 4.4 per cent Xitsonga; 2.7 per cent Siswati; 2.3 per cent Tshivenda; 1.6 per cent IsiNdebele; 0.5 per cent other. The unemployment rate is 41.6 per cent which includes the not economically active.

The level of education amongst those aged 20 and older is reported in Table 3.1.

This means that 40.4 per cent of those over 20 have no more than primary education. In the 1996 census 19.3 per cent had no education compared to 18 per cent in 2001, 16.4 per cent had Grade 12 compared to 20.4 per cent and 6.2 per cent had higher education compared to 8.4 per cent; this indicates some levels of improvement.

Higher education and access in South Africa

South Africa's National Plan for Higher Education was released in 2001. It set out to address key challenges facing South African higher education, which are 'to redress past inequalities and to transform the higher education system to serve a new social order, to meet pressing national needs, and to respond to new realities and opportunities'.[5]

The National Plan addresses five key policy goals and strategic objectives, which in the Ministry's view are central to achieving the overall goal of the transformation of the higher education system. The goals and strategic objectives are:

- To provide *increased access* to higher education to all irrespective of race, gender, age, creed, class or disability and to produce graduates with the skills and competencies necessary to meet the human resource needs of the country.
- To promote *equity of access* and to *redress past inequalities* through ensuring that the staff and student profiles in higher education progressively reflect the demographic realities of South African society.
- To ensure diversity in the organisational form and institutional landscape of the higher education system through mission and programme differentiation, thus enabling the addressing of regional and national needs in social and economic development.
- To build high-level research capacity to address the research and knowledge needs of South Africa.
- To build new institutional and organisational forms and new institutional identities through regional collaboration between institutions.

Table 3.1 Levels of education amongst those age 20 and older

Level of education	No. of people	Percentage
No schooling	4,587,497	18.0
Some primary	4,083,742	16.0
Completed primary	1,623,487	6.4
Some secondary	7,846,125	30.8
Grade 12/standard 10	5,200,602	20.4
Higher	2,151,336	8.4
Total	25,492,789	100.0

Source: South African Census 2001

In other words, higher education must help erode the inherited social and structural inequities and provide opportunities for social advancement through equity of access and opportunity. It must produce, through research, teaching and learning and community service programmes, knowledge and person power for national reconstruction and economic and social development to enable South Africa to engage proactively with and participate in a highly competitive global economy. Given the apartheid legacy and the social and developmental challenges, the higher education transformation agenda has to be radical and comprehensive.

In terms of the National Plan, access is concerned with participation rates regarding race, gender, class, creed, physical ability, and age. It is concerned both with access and success of different students in a range of different fields of study. It is also concerned with redress of past inequalities through ensuring that staff and student profiles in higher education progressively reflect the demographic realities of the society. In addition, it refers to economic access through discussion of the financial aid schemes and epistemological access through discussion of the needs for certain competencies and curricula orientations.

Access of workers and adult learners

The National Plan for Higher Education prioritises, amongst others, the need to broaden the social base of higher education by increasing access to higher education of workers and professionals in pursuit of multi-skilling and re-skilling, and of adult learners who were denied access in the past. They propose to promote Recognition of Prior Learning (RPL) initiatives to increase the intake of adult learners. In the short-term, it is proposed to establish a 5 per cent target for such enrolments.

The major structural shifts in the economy over the last twenty-five years, the endemic shortage of high-level professional and managerial skills, and the impact of HIV/AIDS on the labour force, has ensured that there is recognition of the significant need for continuing education of workers. In addition, the inadequate numbers of school-leavers with the necessary entry requirements means that the demands for higher education graduates in the economy have to be met by ensuring adult learners gain access.

Generations of black women and men were excluded from higher education for either political or economic reasons. In a small study done amongst candidates for recognition of prior learning at university (Hendricks 2001), the overwhelming majority of respondents (70 per cent) identified poverty or the 'need to assist their families financially' as the main reason for leaving school before Grade 12. A much smaller number (12 per cent) cited political repression. Another reason was that many trades and professions, like teaching or nursing, allowed 'coloured' and 'black African' people to have only a Grade 9 or 10 to begin training. It is therefore projected that of the approximately 50 per cent over 20 years old who have achieved some level of secondary schooling, there are many people who have the potential to enter and succeed in higher education. It is for these reasons that organised labour, government and individuals have asserted the need for redress for those workers and adult learners who were excluded from access to higher education.

This thrust also complements the National Skills Development Strategy of the Department of Labour to increase the education and training levels of the workforce.

However, while the rhetorical commitments are there in the policy statements, as a researcher it is very difficult to ascertain what this may mean in practice. A key question is why is there seemingly so little interest in 'non-traditional students'? This will now be explored as an illustration of attempting to research access in South Africa's rapidly changing context.

Rapidly changing higher education context

Higher education, like most other sectors in South Africa, is undergoing major changes. In a useful forthcoming chapter, Saleem Badat, who is Chief Executive Officer of the Council on Higher Education, elaborates the changes that have occurred. He states that the establishment of a comprehensive agenda of higher education transformation has included: the generation of values and principles; the adoption of frameworks in the form of legislation, regulations, policy texts; formulation and adoption of policies of different kinds – symbolic, substantive, procedural, material; establishment of governmental and non-governmental infrastructure; planning and the implementation of policies; and evaluation and review of policy.

Since 1999 the ambitious reconstruction of a national system of higher education has been undertaken. Until very recently, there were 21 public universities and 15 public technikons, which are more vocationally and technically orientated, whose student enrolments during 2000 were 386,000 and 199,000 respectively. Previously there was a binary system and the new plan shifts this to a unitary higher education system. Many of these institutions had their genesis in the apartheid era and were used to further the apartheid ideology. Today there is an active restructuring process to try to move away from the historically defined 'white advantaged' or 'black disadvantaged' institutions. The 36 institutions are going through mergers in order to reduce them to 21; this includes the merging of some universities and technikons which have had different missions and cultures. There are few higher education institutions unaffected.

In addition to the 36 HEIs, the *White Paper* of 1997 stated that colleges would be incorporated into the higher education sector in phases, beginning with the colleges of education. The universities and technikons are a national competence while the colleges have been a provincial competence.

During the pre-1994 apartheid period there were 120 colleges of education. Their numbers have been gradually reduced and during 2001 all the colleges of education were incorporated into universities and technikons. There are also 24 nursing colleges (6,647 students in 2000) and 11 agricultural colleges (2,033 students in 1999), which presently exist under provincial rather than national jurisdiction. Higher education is a national competence while all other educational levels falls to the nine provinces, therefore these shifts have major implications for their administration.

The scale of the institutional restructuring is vast. It is too early to know what the outcomes of these moves may be but there are sure to be contradictory results. For example, there is speculation that with the amalgamation of colleges, which in many instances were based in rural areas, into universities and technikons, which are often in urban areas, there will be a limiting of access for rurally based students to higher education.

The South African HEIs produce a total of 75,000 graduates annually. Twenty-five thousand leave with qualifications in the broad humanities, 10,000 with teaching qualifications (most of which are upgrading of qualifications of teachers already in service) and 20,000 with qualifications in business (including office administration), accountancy, and management. Only 20,000 graduate in fields related to science, engineering and technology. Black people and women mainly graduate in the humanities. In order to shift this, the new HE Plan focuses on increasing participation in specific disciplines. Over the next 5–10 years the goal is to shift the proportion of learners studying in the humanities from 49 per cent to 40 per cent, Business from 26 per cent to 30 per cent and Sciences from 25 per cent to 30 per cent.

A new funding formula is to be introduced in 2004 which will be based on 'planned enrolments in different programmes and levels of study in line with national, social and economic goals'.[6] It is not anticipated that increased levels of funding will be allocated by the Treasury to higher education. An Act, approving the National Student Financial Aid Scheme, was passed in 1999. In 2002, according to Hall (2002), R687 million was allocated to the National Student Financial Aid Scheme to support some 100,000 students. The available amounts barely begin to meet the financial needs of students who are required to pay for their own tuition and the majority of whom come from impoverished homes.

While the higher education sector itself restructures, it does so within the context of many other changes, for example the implementation of the ambitious

National Skills Development Strategy and the Equity Legislation, which impact HEIs directly. Also the schools and colleges in the Further Education and Training sector are undergoing similar change. At a recent meeting of university leadership, it was stated that HEIs were having to cope with 36 major new policy initiatives simultaneously, and there was now 'policy fatigue'.

Some key challenges

The pressures on HE to contribute to equity, redress and economic development, are daunting. Some key challenges in relation to access are participation rates, equity, institutional change and HIV/AIDS. These will be touched on briefly.

Participation rates

In 1996 massification of higher education was predicted in South Africa with the participation rate increasing from 20 per cent in 1996 to some 30 per cent in 2005. The enrolments in private and public higher education were predicted to double. This has not happened. On the contrary the participation rate in public higher education has decreased from 17 per cent to 15 per cent in 2000. The decrease in headcount enrolments is mainly the result of two factors. First there has been a sharp decline in the number of school-leavers with matriculation exemption, which is a precondition for entry into universities and to a lesser extent technikons. The second factor is there has been a significant fall in the retention rate in higher education, that is, the proportion of students in a given year who re-register. Reasons for this need to be researched but a major reason would be the high drop-out rates due to financial stress and the increased cost of higher education.

The government is concerned with the overall participation rates in higher education and they note the evidence which suggests that there is a correlation between economic development and the participation in higher education. The average higher education gross participation rate is just over 40 per cent in high income countries, just over 20 per cent in middle income countries and 5 per cent for low income countries. The 15 per cent in South Africa is well below that of comparable middle income countries. They are therefore planning to increase the overall rate of the 20–24 age group in the next ten to fifteen years to 20 per cent. They, however, used the international convention for participation rates which are skewed to younger students and did not set targets for other age groups.

In terms of increasing the number of participants in higher education, as discussed above, the system can draw on new matriculants, older adults and people from outside South Africa. In terms of new matriculants, currently the number of candidates obtaining school-leaving certificates,[7] which enable them to enter higher education, is dropping rather than increasing. The school sector has established a variety of strategies to reverse the situation, but to date these initiatives have yet to bear fruit. Thus the role of alternative admission strategies becomes increasingly important in allowing a wider range of learners into the HE system. At present a number of institutions are experimenting with alternative admission policies, such as the recognition of prior learning.

Another issue, which impacts on the ability of HEIs to shift the ratio of learners from humanities to science, is the number of learners eligible to enter science programmes. According to Cloete and Bunting (2000) the current school system produced in 1998 just over 20,000 matriculants with passes in higher grade mathematics and 22,000 higher grade science passes. This is barely sufficient to meet an annual flow of 30,000 students into programmes which place a strong emphasis on mathematics and on mathematics plus science. This presents a challenge to the school system, but also to HE to adapt their admission (and support) policies. Hall (2002) states that this is being addressed through a comprehensive programme on improving mathematics and science education in the schools, including the in-service training of 10,000 teachers.

Access and equity

In terms of 'race' equity there has been significant movement. The change in racial composition has been striking. The enrolments of black students increased by 61 per cent between 1993 and 1999, from 53 per cent to 71 per cent of the total headcount enrolments. 'Black African' student enrolments increased from 191,000 to 343,000 in the same time – in 1999 they constituted 59 per cent of the total headcount.

While the change in the number and proportion of black students indicates that higher education is becoming more representative, there is concern that, first, the overall changes do not necessarily translate into representivity in individual institutions, second, the overall participation rate continues to be characterised by gross inequalities. Although the participation rate of 'black African' students has increased from 9 per cent to 12 per cent it still remains well below that of 'white' students at 47 per cent, and 'Asian' students at 39 per cent. Third, the spread of black students across different programme areas is uneven. The 'black African' students remain clustered in humanities, with low enrolments in science, engineering and technology, business and commerce and in postgraduate programmes. Fourth, there are wide disparities in the graduation rates of black and 'white' students. Average graduation rates of 'white' students are double those of black students.

Gender equity has been achieved in terms of headcount enrolments. Female enrolments increased by 44 per cent from 1993 to 1999. Females now make up 52 per cent of the enrolments. However, gender equity, as with 'race' equity continues to remain a problem in terms of types of institutions, programmes, and levels. Female enrolments are clustered around humanities and at undergraduate level. The National Plan notes that institutions place greater emphasis on race equity than gender with few strategies in place to address issues of gender equity.

Social class equity is not as easy to assess. Because of the racial capitalist system that has existed there is some correlation between racial categories and social class. This is particularly the case with 'black African' students. The question of financial assistance for studying is critical to possibilities for access by poorer students. The present financing arrangements are inadequate and 'financial exclusions' are putting pay to the equity ideals for many people. The National Plan recognises the problem and proposes to investigate the matter further.

Age equity has not been achieved. At present it is very difficult to obtain age related statistics at either national or institutional levels. It is not common practice for HEIs to record the age of students. It is also difficult to gain statistics on part-time studies, where students are usually older. Part-time students are also excluded from accessing the National Student Fund.[8] The lack of statistics and access to resources reflects the marginalised position of part-time students in South Africa, which seems to occur elsewhere as well (Davies 1999).

Changes in the demographic profile of the student body have generally not been accompanied by a similar change in staff profile so that black people and women remain under-represented in academic and professional positions, especially at senior levels.

There is very little data on access of disabled students and the employment of disabled staff. Present indications are that the numbers are unacceptably low. The increase in the representation of women and black people has not necessarily changed the curricula, the pedagogical processes, the structural arrangements or the culture.

Institutional change

In the National Plan there is rhetorical recognition that numbers are not what it is about and that it does need deep transformation. In a recent document the Council on Higher Education stated:

> Equity should mean more than access into higher education. It must incorporate equity of opportunity – environments in which learners, through academic support, excellent teaching and mentoring and other initiatives, genuinely have every chance of succeeding. Equity, to be meaningful, is also ensuring that learners have access to quality education, and graduate with the relevant knowledge, competencies, skills and attributes that are required for any occupation and profession.
>
> (Council on Higher Education 2001, p. 10)

However, it is doubtful whether the radical curricular, pedagogical and organisational transformation will be supported with resources. There is barely any mention of staff, and organisational development needs and support for them.

Importantly, students' academic support and development is recognised and may be funded by the government for the first time, but this is yet to be elaborated.

While the policies commit the HE system to lifelong learning and the increase in numbers of adult learners and workers, the realities are that the picture that holds many HEIs captive is still that of institutions for young, mainly men, studying full-time. The challenges of changing this dominant picture can be seen, for example, in the debates and practices of widening access to HEIs for 'non-traditional students' and 'non-traditional ways of learning' (Schuetze and Slowey 2000). This is of course not a South African issue alone. In many countries women have become the majority in HEIs but the organisational cultures, including curricula, do not necessarily reflect this. This would be true of several South African HEIs.

HIV/AIDS

South Africa is known to have one of the fastest growing AIDS epidemics. Approximately 1,700 people are estimated to be infected each day. The SAUVCA Report (Chetty 2000) highlights a growing concern about HIV/AIDS within HEIs, particularly as the 20–30 year age group represents the largest population group in both the HE and HIV/AIDS populations. SAUVCA estimates that currently the HE population is 22 per cent HIV/AIDS positive and will be 33 per cent positive by 2005. The 18–30-year-olds in HE are amongst the most capable and promising members of societies as they represent the future highly skilled base of any economy.

The SAUVCA report believes that it is not enough to regard HIV/AIDS as a health issue as it should also be seen as a developmental issue that affects organisations as well as individuals. In their planning HEIs need to consider both the direct and indirect impact of AIDS. These include loss of skilled labour, loss of work time due to illness, and loss of motivation to study and teach. As a teaching and learning institution they should also teach about managing AIDS.

HIV/AIDS is compounding, in dramatic ways, the complexity of human development planning in every part of the society, including that relating to access into higher education.

Researching access for adult learners and workers?

In a context where there are so many changes happening simultaneously, it is very difficult to stand still long enough to be able to describe, analyse and understand what is going on. The funding for research is also very limited and this goes some way to explain the lack of research on 'access'.

Researching access of adult learners and workers into higher education is difficult as there is no South African literature on 'non-traditional' students in higher education. There is the beginning of a literature on aspects like recognition of prior learning (Castle 2002), but little else. As mentioned earlier, age statistics are not recorded as a matter of course, there is little information on the work lives of students, and limited information on part-time students. There has been and still is a privileging of young students who are full-time. In the most recent National Plans this is reinforced by the fact that no participation targets are set for adult learners and workers and there is no clarity on what it will mean to implement the 5 per cent target for adult learners gaining access via RPL.

This raises questions of what would need to be done to widen access to adult learners and workers and how serious the intent is to improve access and equity in relation to age. Is the policy merely symbolic, one that was accepted politically at a given time, but with no intention of implementing?

The educational policy of broadening and deepening access to higher education is a fundamentally political process. As Scouffe states:

> The assumption that education policy could be the result of simply identifying and choosing the alternative that is 'best', ignores the obvious political fact that 'best' has to be determined in the political crucible of competing interests.
> (Scouffe 1985, p. 116)

For widened access to be successful it demands the political will of the government and institutions over extended periods and, no doubt, long-term, sustained political action by the groups who are presently marginal. In a context where racial and gender equity are most pressing and are mainstreamed into equity legislation for the society as a whole, it is not surprising that equity in relation to age is not a priority. Also, in a context of high unemployment, organised labour would not necessarily see campaigning to have increased access for workers into HE as a priority. The reality of the age profile of the population as being skewed towards youth, with 43.2 per cent under 19 years, may also make the argument for prioritisation of adult learners less pressing.

Competing priorities

Badat (forthcoming) puts forward the reality of South African higher education having to work simultaneously on many fronts. He recognises the considerable strengths that the sector has but notwithstanding these, he states that 'there are a number of conditions internal and external to South African higher education that are major obstacles to the achievement of key national goals'.

He recognises that the transformation agenda is 'riveted with paradoxes'. He takes the tensions and paradoxes, for example, between equity/redress on the one hand and quality on the other. As he says, the

> exclusive concentration on equity/redress can lead to the unadulterated privileging of equity/redress at the expense of quality, which could result in the goal of producing high quality graduates with the requisite knowledge,

competencies and skills being compromised. Conversely, an exclusive focus on quality and 'standards' can result in equity being retarded or delayed and therefore no or limited erosion of the racial and gender character of the high level occupational structure. The concentration on either equity/redress alone or quality alone leads to the formulation of policies that are abstracted from the conditions in which the policies must be applied and constrains the formulation of policies appropriate to the contemporary situation in South Africa.

(Badat forthcoming)

He argues that 'government and progressive social forces are impelled to pursue *simultaneously*, a number of goals and strategies that stand in severe tension with one another. This in turn establishes difficult political and social dilemmas and choices and decisions'. He states that this is the nature of transformation and that trade-offs become inevitable and that these should not be hidden. In summary, he states:

policy making and efforts to build a new society are conditioned by not just visions and goals but equally also by the paradoxes, ambiguities, contradictions, possibilities and constraints of structural and conjunctural conditions. What can be achieved and can be won is not simply a matter of will – it is also shaped by what is possible, even as progressive actors may seek to maintain an adherence to particular values and principles and push the bounds of possibility to the limits.

(Badat forthcoming)

In summary, the challenges confronting research on access into higher education include the fact that many interrelated parts of the society and the higher education sector are changing simultaneously. It is therefore impossible to understand fully what is happening while it is happening. There are tensions and paradoxes in the range of goals and policies that are being pursued. It is therefore essential to recognise the political nature of the transformation processes. In relation to the adult learners and workers, research is more difficult because there is no database that can be taken for granted as a starting point. It seems that there has first to be a political struggle to convince institutions and the system as a whole to move from symbolic to substantive policy and to collect the necessary data in order to be able to build a platform from which to study and analyse developments. Without this political commitment it is difficult to imagine being able to make headway beyond small-scale research studies.

While this may be so, it is important to suggest the kinds of studies that are needed to further access for adult learners and workers. These include base studies: to establish the age profiles and study patterns of students in a range of HEIs; to understand the relationships between work and study and the barriers or incentives to enabling workers to study successfully; to understand the adult learner or prospective learner, identifying social characteristics of participants and non–participants, investigating the factors associated with the decision to participate or not, and analysing the experiences, expectations and perceptions of the learners; in terms of equity and redress, to clarify what it is that propels people across ages successfully through higher education and what inhibits this progress; to analyse the meaning of being a 'part-time' student and to question the value of the definition of 'part-time' for funding and other purposes; to understand how AIDS is impacting women, men, at different ages, in different regions and to project the implications of this for access to HE for adult learners and workers; to research and develop teaching/learning innovations which both are preventative and supportive of staff and students with AIDS; to research and develop supportive institutional cultures for adult learners and workers; and to understand more deeply why there is seemingly so little interest in 'non-traditional students' when the policy states otherwise.

Notes

1   I wish to acknowledge the research assistance from my colleague, Kathy Watters.
2   Figures obtained from www.statssa.gov.za.
3   This compares to approximately 72 per cent over 25 years in Japan and 70 per cent in the UK as quoted in the ICAE Report 2003: 22.
4   Racial classification continues to be used in South Africa for purposes of affirmative action in terms of the Equity Legislation. Inverted commas are used to signify the classifications. When the term black is used it describes all people who are described as 'coloured', 'Asian', 'black African'.
5   Ministry of Education 2001; 1:1.
6   EduSource Data News, November 2000; 31: 6.
7   Known as matriculation exemption certificates.
8   In December 2003 this was changed to allow part-time students access to the NSFAS.

References

Badat, Saleem (Forthcoming) *Transforming South African Higher Education, 1990–2003: Goals, Policies, Policy Initiatives and Critical Challenges and Issues.*

Castle, J. (2002) 'The prior learning paths of mature students entering a postgraduate qualification in adult education', *Journal of Education*, 29 (2003), 29–55. University of Natal, Pietermaritzburg, South Africa.

Chetty, D. (2000) *Institutionalising the Response to HIV/AIDS in the South African University Sector: A SAUVCA Analysis.* Pretoria: South African Universities Vice Chancellors Association (SAUVCA), Occasional Publications and Reports (2).

Cloete, N. and Bunting, I. (2000) *Is Higher Education in South Africa Moving Towards National Transformation Goals?* Pretoria: Centre for Higher Education and Training.

Council on Higher Education (2001) *Towards a New Higher Education Landscape: Meeting the Equity, Quality and Social Development Imperatives of South Africa in the 21st Century.* Shape and Size of Higher Education Task Team, Pretoria: Council on Higher Education.

Davies, P. (1999) 'Half full, not half empty: a positive look at part-time higher education, *Higher Education Quarterly*, 53(2), 141–55.

Department of Education (1997) *Education White Paper 3: A Programme for the Transformation of Higher Education*. Pretoria: Gazette Notice 1196 of 1997, Volume 386, No. 18207.

EduSource (2000) Edusource Data News No. 31, November, Johannesburg: The Education Foundation.

Hall, M. (2002) *The Transformation and Reconstruction of the Higher Education System*. University of Cape Town, Working Paper.

Hendricks, Natheem (2001) *The recognition of prior learning in higher education: the case of the University of Western Cape*. Unpublished Masters in Public Administration, University of Western Cape, Bellville, South Africa.

ICAE Report (2003) *Agenda for the Future – Six Years Later*. Toronto: ICAE.

Ministry of Education (2001) *National Plan for Higher Education*, February 2001, Pretoria.

Schuetze, H.G. and Slowey, M. (2000) *Higher Education and Lifelong Learners*. London: RoutledgeFalmer.

Scouffe, G. (1985) 'The assumptive world of three state policy researchers', *Peabody Journal of Education*, 62(4), 116.

Chapter 4

Looking through the kaleidoscope

Diversification, accessibility and inequality in Scottish higher education

Brenda Morgan-Klein and Mark Murphy

Introduction

This chapter explores the implications of the increasing diversification of Scottish higher education with particular reference to the issue of widening access to higher education. Widening access to post-compulsory education and training has become a central theme in lifelong learning policy in Scotland. It is argued that while these changes are perceived to be driven by an access agenda, in fact they may lead to new patterns of inequality. The discussion draws on evidence from a national study of access to higher education. We argue that higher education has diversified along a number of dimensions and that this has led to a much more complex 'configuration'. It is therefore less and less appropriate to discuss, research and analyse 'higher education' as though it were a unitary phenomenon, system or concept. For example, the diversification of higher education inevitably means that costs, benefits and risks associated with participation are less certain and likely to be highly contextually specific. This has implications for the conceptual framing and design of future research on higher education and particularly access to higher education.

The expansion of higher education in the UK and elsewhere in Europe has been well documented (e.g. Watson and Taylor 1998; Gallacher *et al.* 1997; Murphy *et al.* 2002). While this expansion is often discursively constructed as a success story in terms of the access and the lifelong learning agenda, research studies have increasingly drawn a clear distinction between increasing and widening access to previously excluded groups (Murphy *et al.* 2002). Thus in Scotland, despite significant increases in participation in higher education, participation rates of those in the lowest socio-economic groups have remained relatively static (Scottish Executive 2003a). This underlines the need to critically examine the *particular* character of increases in participation in any given system of higher education. A particularly significant feature of expansion of participation in higher education in Scotland is that it has been accompanied by institutional restructuring and diversification.

There are 21 higher education institutions (HEIs) in Scotland. These include 13 universities, the Open University in Scotland, one university college, two colleges of higher education, two art schools, a conservatoire and the Scottish Agricultural College. In addition an increasing proportion of higher education is delivered in Scotland's further education colleges (FECs) which have traditionally delivered non-advanced vocational education and training. Scotland's 13 universities developed in three phases. Four 'ancient' universities date from the fifteenth and sixteenth centuries. Four more were established in the 1960s and a further five universities were created out of Scotland's Central Institutions[1] in 1992. Therefore, each of these three groups has a distinctive legal basis and history. The clearest distinction, however, is between those institutions given university status by the Further and Higher Education Scotland Act 1992 and those already established prior to 1992. The former brought new practices and different institutional cultures to the university sector. Thus, of particular importance here is the way in which the conferment of university status on the old, and quite distinctive, Central Institutions along with the expansion of higher education in the FECs, have altered traditional ideas about the nature of higher education provision and practice itself.

The expansion of higher education in Scotland

In the ten years leading up to academic year (AY) 2000–1, participation in higher education almost doubled, increasing by 97 per cent. However, this total conceals differences in the rate of expansion over time periods, sectors and modes of study.

Table 4.1 summarises increases in entrants to higher education institutions (HEIs) and further education colleges (FECs) by mode of study and time period. There is significant growth in all instances although the increase is relatively small in the case of participation in part-time study in the first time period. The pace of growth quickened in the second time period so that in the second half of the 1990s, participation increased by 39 per cent overall as opposed to 33 per cent in the first half of the 1990s. In both periods, however, the total rate of growth was significantly faster in the FECs with the gap being largest in the first period.

These differences between the further and higher education sectors may be partly understood in the context of changes in governance in the further education

Table 4.1 Percentage increase in undergraduate entrants to higher education by year, sector and mode of attendance

Year	Total	Total		Full-time		Part-time	
		HEIs	FECs	HEIs	FECs	HEIs	FECs
1989/90–1993/4	33	27	41	32	148	4	5
1994/5–2000/1	39	36	42	14	27	163	53

sector. Following the Further and Higher Education Scotland Act (1992), colleges achieved corporate status receiving funding nationally from the Scottish Office Education and Industry Department instead of from local government. This meant that colleges became responsible to their own Boards of Management which had responsibility for strategy, management and finances, potentially giving colleges greater strategic autonomy. At the same time as these structural changes were made, national policy was *relatively* laissez-faire, reflecting an ideological belief in the ability of market mechanisms to distribute resources optimally. By the early 1990s, however, there was increasing emphasis on the need to widen access to higher education and a number of reports emphasised the important role of further education in achieving this (Garrick Committee 1997). Therefore, following incorporation, the sector embarked on a period of expansion and increased competition which was at least partly driven by increasing financial pressures. These changes encouraged institutions to seek new markets and maximise income, which resulted in the expansion of higher education provision in the shape of higher national certificates (HNCs) and diplomas (HNDs), qualifications formally equivalent to years one and two of a university degree respectively. These were higher education qualifications but they differed from traditional degrees in that they were vocationally oriented and employed competency-based methods of assessment. This diversification of provision has had a growing impact on the meaning and nature of higher education itself.

The faster rate of growth in the FE sector means that the FE sector's total share of higher education entrants has steadily increased so that over half of Scottish higher education entrants in AY 2000/1 began their studies in the FE sector. Only 3 per cent are enrolled on undergraduate degree programmes. Currently two-thirds of higher education students studying in FECs are enrolled on an HNC/D. Sixteen per cent are enrolled on a variety of certificate and diploma programmes which are for the most part professionally oriented and a further 15 per cent are enrolled on individual elements of HNC/D programmes though not for the full award itself (Gallacher 2003). Thus these students follow courses of higher education which are quite distinct from those in the universities. Table 4.2 shows the percentage share of undergraduate entrants by sector and mode in three separate years.

These data in Table 4.2 show that FE has an increasing share of higher education entrants, which underlines the growing significance of HN qualifications over

Table 4.2 Percentage share of undergraduate higher education entrants by sector, mode of attendance and academic year

Year	Total		Full-time		Part-time	
	HEIs	FECs	HEIs	FECs	HEIs	FECs
1989/90	55	45	44	11	11	34
1994/5	49	51	42	22	7	29
2000/1	48	52	35	20	14	32

the period. The data also show that entrants to the FECs are more likely to study part-time than full-time, while the reverse is true of the HEIs. This partly reflects differences between the two student groups, with FECs having higher proportions of 'non-traditional' students. These students are generally older than HE students in the HEI sector. In 2000/1 54 per cent of higher education students in FE colleges were aged 25 or older compared with 27 per cent in the HEIs. Similarly only 32 per cent of higher education students in the FECs were under 21 years of age compared with 45 per cent in the HEIs (Gallacher 2003). The growth of participation in HN study has played a major part in delivering an age participation index (API) of 50.4 per cent[2] in 2000/1. This increase in the API is often taken as evidence that policies to widen access are working. However, the overall participation statistics conceal considerable diversity of provision and patterns of participation.

In Scotland, the 2003 Scottish Executive policy document on lifelong learning (Scottish Executive 2003b) noted that the proportions of the lowest socio-economic groups in higher education have remained relatively static. However, while this is an important indicator of inequalities in access to higher education, it does not tell us about *what* is being accessed by *whom* since it does not recognise the increasing diversity of higher education practice and higher education qualifications. This means that a further dimension of inequality is often left unexamined. Researchers have increasingly distinguished between widening access (to previously excluded groups) and simply increasing access. Murphy *et al.* (2002) note for example, that differential participation by social class across different types of institution means that the oldest universities and highest status institutions have had the least success in recruiting from the lowest socio-economic groups. In Scottish higher education, lower socio-economic groups are more likely to be studying for an HN qualification in a local college while their middle class counterparts are more likely to study for a degree at university. It is noteworthy in this context that higher education places in further education colleges are less well funded than those in the universities and students in these two different sectors will have widely differing experiences of higher education. In a differentiated system it is vital, therefore, also to examine the question of *what* is being made accessible to *whom* since accessibility and equality of opportunity (and/or outcome) are not necessarily the same thing even if policy makers (and sometimes researchers) seem to think that they are.

In summary, the Scottish system of higher education has both expanded and diversified considerably over the last 15 years. This has given rise to a more differentiated system. This has implications for the accessibility of higher education in Scotland and also for equity and social justice in higher education which are not necessarily the same thing. In addition, these historically specific and politically constituted changes in higher education have implications for the way in which the issue of access is researched and theorised. The following discussion focuses on both the nature of these changes and their implications for researching access to higher education.

Diversity of institutions and provision

The granting of university status to the Central Institutions in 1992 marks a historic watershed in the provision of higher education in Scotland. These new universities laid much more emphasis on flexibility and accessibility than the pre-1992 universities.[3] This included greater diversity of delivery mode, educational pathways and curriculum including modularisation of programmes of study and semesterisation of the academic year. University status meant these institutions could now participate in the same policy fora as the pre-1992 universities as nominal equals opening the possibility that such practices could become more widespread. In terms of culture, ethos and pedagogy, the post-1992 universities were closer to the FECs than the older universities. For example, both the FECs and the post-1992 universities shared a commitment to vocational relevance in their provision – notably in HN study but also in professionally related degree programmes. This commitment included openness to stakeholders such as employers in the development of curricula. This enabled the development of articulation links of various kinds between them which had the potential to open up institutional and sectoral boundaries and to diversify educational pathways. This possibility was reinforced by the growth of higher education in the FECs and the development of a national credit accumulation and transfer framework which provided (at least theoretically) agreement between institutions on the level and weight of standard qualifications. This restructuring of higher education in the early 1990s accelerated a process of change, leading to a more diversified and differentiated higher education that was more flexible and open to change along a number of dimensions including: institutional and sectoral boundaries, curricula, delivery mode and educational pathways. These processes have been reinforced by an explosion in national policy beginning in the late 1990s which may be analysed in two distinct phases.

Policy and change

The first phase may be understood as a commitment in the UK as elsewhere in Europe to create a learning society, to improve individual employability and national economic competitiveness and to meet the demands of the knowledge economy by promoting lifelong learning. In Scotland, these aims were couched in terms of improving opportunity and access to learning. While these lifelong learning policies and discourses were criticised as economistic (e.g. Coffield 1999), they also appeared to genuinely promote the access agenda and this is reflected in the first wave of policy documents. These include, among others, *Opportunity Scotland* (Scottish Office 1998) which outlines targets for the creation of a learning society; *Opportunities and Choices* (Scottish Office 1999a) which sets out the lifelong learning agenda for 16–19-year-olds; and *Opportunity for Everyone* (Scottish Office 1999b) which sets out a strategic framework for the FE sector.

The emphasis on access, employability and vocational relevance in lifelong learning policies served to highlight the significance of the FE sector as well as practices of flexibility within the new universities. The profile of FE was raised further by the creation of the Scottish Further Education Funding Council (SFEFC) in 1998. Also of relevance here is the increasing emphasis in policy on inter-institutional collaboration, the emphasis on links with employers and employment, and the creation of new policy fora such as the regional fora for widening access to higher education. These changes significantly altered the networks of individuals and agencies involved in the practice of policy making in higher education. Significantly for this discussion, there is greater diversity along a number of dimensions including curricula, pedagogy, delivery mode, institutional ethos, institutional governance and inter-institutional links. This has resulted in greater complexity in the structure and practice of higher education and these changes have been reinforced in the second phase of policy change.

The second phase of policy development is closely bound up with Scottish devolution. While Scotland has always had separate education policy arrangements, devolution has been a watershed in the production of policy in lifelong learning. This is simply partly a result of a reinvigorated polity. Since devolution, two inquiries have reported to the Scottish Executive: the Independent Committee of Enquiry into Student Finance (2000) and the Enterprise and Lifelong Learning Committee (2002). In addition, a Review of Higher Education was launched in 2001 and reported in 2003 (Scottish Executive 2003a) and a new policy document *Life Through Learning Through Life* (Scottish Executive 2003b) was published to replace and update *Opportunity Scotland* (Scottish Office 1998). Of relevance to the issue of increasing diversity is the emergence of a highly inter-connected community of policy and practice in post-compulsory education and training in Scotland representing a *wider range* of interests. Thus, in the post-compulsory sector, policy has increasingly been framed within discourses of lifelong learning which mobilise new networks of individuals, institutions and agencies which transcend traditional boundaries and have the potential to create greater fluidity and reflexivity in practice and policy making. A clear example of this is the involvement of industry and employers in the development and planning of curricula. At the same time as the system was diversifying, in this second policy phase, one emergent theme had been the need for a more integrated system of post-compulsory education and training. For example, the Scottish Executive has taken the decision to merge SFEFC with the Scottish Higher Education Funding Council (SHEFC) as part of its aim to create a fully integrated post-compulsory education and training system. This opens the possibility of greater coherence and, not incidentally, central control in policy making. Moreover, it challenges historical notions of the distinctiveness of higher education provision.

A central theme in current policy is the reiteration of a commitment to widening access to higher education. Most famously, this has included rejection of the English policy of imposition of 'up-front' tuition fees for university students, although Scottish graduates must pay these later. A number of other policy initiatives are particularly significant. These include the intention to fully implement a new Scottish Credit and Qualifications Framework (SCQF), which will replace the previous credit framework that was applied very unevenly by institutions. Closer links between FE and HE are to be further promoted as is greater flexibility of provision. All of these initiatives are designed to create a more fully integrated system of post-compulsory education and training which includes higher education and which will be characterised by diversity of students, provision, educational pathways, modes of study, institutions and stakeholders.

Diversity and complexity

Expansion of participation, the framing of higher education policy within a lifelong learning paradigm and the restructuring of higher education have created a system that is characterised by greater diversity and potentially greater fluidity and flexibility. These changes are assumed to enhance accessibility which is in turn assumed to promote equality of educational opportunity. There is therefore very significant consensus in Scotland between the overlapping communities of policy makers, educational practitioners and educational researchers in the support for the access agenda and, therefore, for many of the changes that have been made so compellingly in the name of access. However, some significant concerns have been raised.

First, in a diversified and differentiated system, there is the potential for new patterns of inequality to develop. There is, therefore, a need for new research into the student experience of higher education. The systemic changes required to create an integrated system are promoted as enhancing accessibility but they also enhance external control of institutions via the creation of a powerful single funding council and the compulsory imposition of SCQF. This challenges the tradition of university autonomy to create and control their own curricula as they see fit. The emphasis on increasing vocational relevance and collaboration with employers and other stakeholders has the potential to further challenge institutional autonomy, as well as traditional notions about the distinctiveness of higher education and liberal values about the aims and purpose of education. In addition to these changes, education has, as with other areas of public service, been increasingly subject to control by audit via quality assessment arrangements designed to enhance accountability and efficiency. Moreover, the presumed benefits to students of the increasing flexibility of higher education provision have been questioned (Morgan-Klein and Gray 2000). In general, institutional flexibility has been criticised as primarily a matter of doing more with less rather than enhancing access (Edwards 1997).

Therefore significant changes made in the name of access and accessibility have just as significantly profoundly altered the governance of higher education. These changes reflect more general changes in the relationship between the state and the market and between the state and individuals in western capitalist democracies. For example, Scott (1995) describes how shifts in the control and funding of higher education reflect wider changes in the British welfare state which began in the late 1970s. Similarly, Taylor et al. (2003) represent these changes as the locking of higher education into the capitalist knowledge economy. Nevertheless these changes are often uncritically understood simply as dimensions of policies on access to higher education. Certainly, such changes also have the power to challenge the historical propensity for elite institutions to act in a self-interested and inegalitarian manner. However, they also give rise to a more complex system of higher education where the emergent outcomes of policies are less easy to predict and may have unintended consequences. For example, while the system has become increasingly diverse, plans to more fully integrate the diverse elements of post-compulsory education and training including implementation of SCQF are being put forward by government. These two processes of diversification and integration are potentially contradictory and the outcomes are unclear. In this way it is important that research on access recognises the highly specific (and problematic) nature of access policies in action which also means an awareness of the ways in which these are socially and politically constituted. It is simply less and less easy to make generalisations about the consequences of access policies.

A useful example here is that it is increasingly difficult to make generalisations about the student experience when higher education means different things from one sector and even one institution to another. The diversification of delivery mode means that higher education is increasingly delivered in a greater diversity of spaces (for example distance learning) and often asynchronously (as in online learning). In this way, for many students and institutions, higher education has been spatially and temporally restructured thus constructing new meanings and new experiences for higher education students. Often such delivery modes are assumed to enhance accessibility. However, it is arguable that delivery modes designed to fit with working life (for example part-time mode and online learning) may in fact offer students a more 'rushed' or 'fragmented' student experience. Moreover the ability to manage educational flexibility will be partly dependent on labour market position and the kinds of flexibility students encounter in the workplace (Morgan-Klein and Gray 2000). The impact of flexibilities in higher education on the student experience and specifically on equity issues requires further research. This research must acknowledge the greater complexity of the contemporary student experience. First, the liberal consensus on the nature of higher education is over and the issue of 'access to what' has never been more important. Second, flexible delivery has led to ever greater diversity of students' 'engagement' with learning – by this we mean the activities undertaken and the timescales and spaces in which these take place. Learning itself and students lives more generally have become more temporally complex. This reflects wider social trends including the perceived acceleration in the pace of life and the way in which boundaries of space and time have become increasingly pluralised, with teleworking being the most obvious example. In this way:

> In the sphere of production as in other areas of social life, what counts more and more is the ability to master fluid and temporal regimes and to handle their relationships with one another.
>
> (Paolucci 1996: 147)

Such changes in the student experience have too often been 'glossed' as progressively delivering flexibility and accessibility and the implications are often not specifically explored. These implications are likely to be different for different social groups (Morgan-Klein and Gray 2000).

Summary and discussion

Higher education in Scotland has diversified rapidly along a number of dimensions. This means that it is less and less appropriate to research and analyse higher education as though it was a unitary phenomenon. First there is growing diversity of provision. Different social groups appear to access different parts of the higher education system in Scotland. Therefore, the experience of higher education is differentiated by social class with students from lower socio-economic groups more likely to participate in local colleges, which are relatively poorly resourced in terms of student funding, and where facilities are relatively impoverished when compared to the university sector. Moreover, the increasing diversity of provision has accelerated the breakdown of a liberal consensus on the nature of higher education itself. This has been interpreted as a progressive challenge to academic elitism in access discourses but it has also been criticised as a conservative tilt towards vocationalism. It has never been more important, therefore, for researchers to examine closely the question of 'access to what?'. Second, higher education has diversified in terms of student character and identity since a wider range of social groups now participate. There is also greater diversity of student 'engagement' and the impact of new forms of participation on the student experience (defined broadly and not just in terms of pre-defined 'learning outcomes') requires further research. It is important, therefore, to avoid some of the assumptions contained within access policy discourses when constructing research studies. Access and even accessibility are not the same as equity. The benefits of participation cannot simply be presumed since in a differentiated system, costs and benefits are also differentiated.

A further challenge for researchers is that the system of higher education is not only more diverse but also more complex. A wider range of interests are now represented around education planning tables. This and the political changes brought by Scottish devolution mean that new and changing networks of individuals and agencies are involved in policy making in education and lifelong learning. As these networks are rapidly changing, the analysis of such policy processes becomes more complex. Changes in these more diverse networks and practices may be likened to a turn of the kaleidoscope where outcomes are less certain and consequences of actions perhaps unintended. For example, calculating the risks, costs and benefits of participation in a highly diversified system of higher education will be much more difficult for a prospective student or indeed a researcher. This clearly has implications for the way in which research is conceived and conducted. Further aspects of complexity include the likely outcomes of policies (such as the SCQF) which are designed to integrate a rapidly diversifying system. The combination of diversity and moves to integrate the system of post-compulsory education and training as a whole are likely to create complexities of management and pedagogy. At the least, this combination is likely to give rise to an increasingly dynamic system that is prone to change and perhaps more open to possibility – though not necessarily of a progressive nature. Significantly, in a more complex system, these tendencies may be more unpredictable and thus more difficult to research. At the same time, as higher education becomes less and less autonomous, there is an even greater need to be sure that the wider socio-economic and political context is not neglected. Thus there is a need for research of greater specificity that also takes account of this wider context.

Governmental funders of access research are on the other hand more interested in the general and the universally applicable, in the pragmatic and entirely understandable effort to discover 'what works' across time and place. Such contradictions and challenges for researchers are nothing new. Nevertheless, the avoidance and neglect of the more complex issues relating to access, some of which are detailed in this chapter, does not enhance the potential for long-term effectiveness in access initiatives, least of all in relation to future populations of students in Scottish higher education.

Notes

1 Central Institutions provided higher education courses which were vocationally, professionally or industrially based. They were created in the 1960s, as were polytechnics in England, in order to meet a perceived increasing need for this kind of higher education. These institutions were subject to greater public regulation than the universities. This created a binary system of higher education which was ended by the granting of university status to all of the Central Institutions in Scotland.
2 The age participation index is used to measure the number of young Scots who enter full-time higher education in a given year. Higher education includes sub-degree study. It is calculated as the number of Scots under 21 who enter higher education as a percentage of the population in Scotland aged 17.
3 While the clearest distinction can be made between the pre and post 1992 universities, it is important to note that there are significant differences between the 'ancient' and the merely 'old' universities in Scotland. In particular, the latter have in some cases a longstanding commitment to flexible delivery and accessibility.

Bibliography

Coffield, F. (1999) 'Breaking the consensus: lifelong learning as social control', *British Educational Research Journal*, 25(4), 479–99.
Edwards, R. (1997) *Changing Places? Flexibility, Lifelong Learning and a Learning Society*, London: Routledge.
Enterprise and Lifelong Learning Committee (2002) *Final Report on Lifelong Learning*, Edinburgh: Scottish Executive.
Gallacher, J., Osborne, M. and Postle, G. (1997) 'Increasing and widening access to higher education: a comparative study of policy and provision in Scotland and Australia', *International Journal of Lifelong Education*, 15(6), 418–37.

Gallacher, J. (2002) 'Parallel lines? Higher education in Scotland's colleges and higher education institutions in Centre for Research in Lifelong Learning', *Seventh Scottish Forum on Lifelong Learning: FE/HE Links*, Glasgow and Stirling: CRLL.

Gallacher, J. (2003) *The Growth of Higher Education in Scottish FE Colleges*, A Report for the Council for Industry and Higher Education.

Garrick Committee (1997) *Report of the Scottish Committee* (Garrick Report) National Committee into Higher Education, London: HMSO.

Independent Committee of Enquiry into Student Finance (2000) *Student Finance: Fairness for the Future* (Cubie Report), Edinburgh: Scottish Executive.

Morgan-Klein, B. and Gray, P. (2000) 'Flexible trends: researching part time students and flexibility in higher education', *Scottish Journal of Adult and Continuing Education*, 6, 42–57.

Murphy, M., Morgan-Klein, B., Osborne, M. and Gallacher, J. (2002) *Widening Access to Higher Education*, Glasgow and Stirling: Centre for Research in Lifelong Learning.

Paolucci, G. (1996) 'The changing dynamics of working time', *Time and Society*, 5, 145–68.

Scott, P. (1995) *The Meanings of Mass Higher Education*, Buckingham: Society for Research in Higher Education and the Open University Press.

Scottish Executive (2003a) *A Framework for Higher Education in Scotland. Higher Education Review Phase 2*, Edinburgh: HMSO.

Scottish Executive (2003b) *Life Through Learning Through Life: The Lifelong Learning Strategy for Scotland*, Edinburgh: HMSO.

Scottish Office (1998) *Opportunity Scotland*, Edinburgh: The Scottish Office.

Scottish Office (1999a) *Opportunities and Choices*, Edinburgh: The Scottish Office.

Scottish Office (1999b) *Opportunity for Everyone: The Strategic Framework for Further Education*, Edinburgh: The Scottish Office.

Taylor, R., Steele, T. and Barr, J. (2003) *For A Radical Higher Education, after post-modernism*, Buckingham: Society For Research in Higher Education and the Open University Press.

Watson, D. and Taylor, R. (1998) *Lifelong Learning and the University: A Post-Dearing Agenda*, London: Falmer Press.

Chapter 5

Discourses of access

Changing views in a changing world

David Boud

It is interesting to note how the current flood of British policy statements, papers, seminars and discussions about access are dominated by the metaphor of 'widening' (e.g. Woodrow *et al.* 2002; DfES 2003). Not deepening or extending or even 'opening', but 'widening'. In everyday usage the term 'widening' more often denotes, for example, the widening of doorways to let wheelchairs through or to meet fire regulations. Road widenings let more traffic pass. In Australia, the equivalent policy cluster has been termed 'equity and access'. While equity is clearly a large part of the concerns leading to widening access in the UK, it is not in the headline phrase.

So what exactly does the use of the 'widening access' metaphor imply and is the use of this particular metaphor significant? What is left out by focusing on the notion of widening? What else might we do to access? If we think about the metaphor of door or road widening a little further, what this suggests is 'not too wide; just a little wider'. So when we use the term 'widening access', are we implying that we want to just let a few more students through into higher education but not too many? What is very noticeable about this is that the focus here is on the point of access rather than on what occurs after entry. Clearly, making the gates wider is not necessarily going to change what goes on inside, even though we may imply that it does. Surely what happens after the student has gained entry is more important. In this chapter I argue that the discourse of widening has to be changed in order to involve all the things to which we hope it will lead. In other words, if we construct the debate differently and have a focus other than 'widening', would that change the ways in which we viewed issues of access? Would a different agenda emerge? What would be included in discussions that are not included at present?

In this chapter, I consider how the discourse of access has changed over time. I suggest that the debate is shifting rapidly and that the view which has dominated it for the past half century is insufficient for what we understand access to be today. My argument is that we need to rethink notions of access and give up the metaphor of widening. We need to find ways in which higher education can be more responsive to the diversity of needs, not just of individuals and social groups but of different purposes and roles of higher education.

Changing notions of access

Over the past 100 years we have seen the transformation of higher education from a collection of small elite institutions to a mass, and approaching a universal, system that touches on most families in most Western countries. Higher education has moved from irrelevance in public policy terms, to one of the most hotly debated topics of present times. As access has expanded, so too has scrutiny of what higher education does. For example, comments by a senior minister about a single student denied entry to one institution in the UK can hit the headlines in other English-speaking countries and reverberate in policy terms for a considerable time, as the unguarded remarks in May 2000 of the British Chancellor of the Exchequer, Gordon Brown, show.

Coexistent with these changes there appear to have been a number of key phases of the access to higher education debate. Traditionally, entry to the elite universities in the UK was either by social standing or by patronage. Children of the deserving poor were admitted through grace and favour. Later, this strategy was adopted by governments and scholarships provided for bright children from families who would not be able to support them through a course of study. In reaction to access by patronage, there was for a while a period of separate development with access to extra-mural classes distinct from the mainstream or to separate colleges (for example, various working people's colleges such as Ruskin College, Oxford). Perhaps the first major attempt to address issues of access and get a wider range of students into higher education was through the use of tests and examinations. Patronage was avoided by the use of selection tests and tests for awarding scholarships. Entry was no longer exclusively by position in society but through a particular definition of academic attainment. Class *per se* was not a barrier, but access to the schooling and resources that allowed one to excel in the examinations that led to entry was required.

The development of the idea of establishing target groups as a focus for intervention was the next major development. This was based largely on the recognition that strategies that appeared to emphasise purely academic criteria were severely limited. The notion of identifiable target groups was introduced as a way of identifying social groups who were under-represented. The Australian ministerial statement which articulated this was titled, *A Fair Chance for All* (Dawkins 1990) followed later by *Equality, Diversity and Excellence* (Higher Education Council 1996). A variety of strategies were developed to assist such groups. These included: recognising a wide range of entry qualifications, giving individuals in those groups easier entry into higher education institutions and providing individuals in target groups with bridging courses to bring their academic attainments up to an acceptable level for entry. It has also included providing financial incentives for institutions to recruit members of defined groups, or targeting funding of institutions to particular postcode areas.

Successes and failures

There have been changes in the social mix of students over time, but this has varied between countries. In all countries there are differences between social classes, with Australia being rather less unequal than the UK (Anderson 1990). Commonly, disadvantage is locked in much earlier in the process of schooling (e.g. Forsyth and Furlong 2000). With the advent of targeting strategies, generally those that have benefited have been women and the singularly disadvantaged (Marks *et al.* 2000). The extent to which women have benefited directly as a result of access policies rather than their changing status in society is, however, not clear. The main failures of policy strategies have been the inability of higher education to attract people with multiple disadvantages.

Combinations of all of these strategies can now be seen with differing emphases and differing educational and economic motivations in different countries. The limits of all of these various strategies (testing students on performance, providing scholarships, providing extra tuition, setting quotas and providing bounties for institutions) are now apparent. Economic barriers to access to higher education first decreased but more recently have increased and barriers in terms of academic achievement have generally decreased.

As the proportion of the population participating in higher education has increased, the costs to government of providing student support, and indeed even the costs of tuition, have grown. Costs have risen so much that strategies requiring large levels of financial support are in decline in most countries. There are widespread and inevitable attempts to shift the costs of higher education increasingly onto its so-called direct beneficiaries; primarily the students, through fees or new taxes, albeit sometimes deferred. This raises the question of whether we have reached the limit of subsidy or investment per head provided from government sources.

In all of these phases, the aim has been to urge students into institutions and sometimes to find ways of supporting them financially while they are there. That is to say, all of the strategies that have been tried have been concerned with widening access. Relatively little attention has been given to the nature of the experience after entry, in terms of the purposes of courses or students' experiences and outcomes. The assumption has been that additional students would experience more of the same. The new graduates would be indistinguishable from the old. This appears to have worked well for many who got in, in terms of their social mobility. However, what is less clear is the extent to which the resources of educational institutions were harnessed for the benefit of all. While such strategies have increased the numbers of students with a conventional university education, they may have done little to contribute to a learning society.

I am not arguing against the valuable achievements in improving access that have led to significant numbers of otherwise disadvantaged students benefiting from higher education. Nor am I questioning that there is still much further to go in this process. My concern is that the debate needs now to move to new ground.

The discourse of widening access through all of the phases I have described focuses on access and entry; that is, on getting in. This discourse does not emphasise the quality of educational experience that is actually accessed by the entrant. Such a discourse does not emphasise how or whether particular needs of those who gain access are met. It rests on notions of *individual* achievement within conventional educational practices. It is a discourse that does not acknowledge difference, except insofar as particular groups are excluded. It assumes that the problems prompting concerns about access are addressed by admission into the front door of the academy. It does not emphasise who or what is falling out the back. So long as those to whom new access has been provided complete their courses, the goals of widening access have supposedly been met.

It is also my contention that in the past the widening access discourse has been too concerned with quantitative measures: how many, which groups; rather than being concerned with qualitative measures: what it achieved, whether expectations were met. This neglect occurs less often nowadays, but the framing of 'widening access' rather than 'meeting needs' or 'creating opportunities' constructs the issue in a particular way. It emphasises some features at the expense of others. Ideas about utilising talents, fairness and equity, enriching institutions with a more diverse intake of students, encouraging lifelong learning and providing worthwhile educational experiences for students who would otherwise be excluded are all worthy ideals. However, too great an emphasis on widening access at a time when resources within institutions are diminishing, can lead to frustration, feelings among students of being deceived and a realisation that merely 'getting in' is not enough. So the crucial question we have to address is: 'access to what?'

New challenges to higher education

Considerations of access seem to be premised on higher education remaining the same, or at least on only making small changes to accommodate the needs of those groups newly gaining access. Meanwhile, substantial changes in higher education are shaking its very foundations, leading to a questioning of older notions of access. By the time the target groups get access to higher education, they are no longer gaining access to an elite system that at one time was so desirable. This situation poses a number of challenges.

First there is the challenge of financially supporting the increased numbers of heterogeneous students. We have gone beyond notions of mass higher education to a situation where advanced study has become a universal expectation. It is seen as a right; not a privilege. Increased levels of participation in higher education demand greater support from the public purse at a time when there is downward pressure on public expenditures in general. Governments are finding it increasingly difficult to sustain the costs of higher education. That they will provide for all the associated costs of increasing access to higher education is no longer a realistic expectation (e.g. Clarke 2003; Nelson 2003).

The second challenge is the question of relevance. It is doubtful whether higher education in its conventional forms is suitable for the much wider range of needs to which it is now subject. Even assuming higher education is suitable for the majority of society, not everyone is adequately prepared by his or her previous educational experiences for the challenges posed by advanced study. Not everyone is in a position to benefit at any given point in their lives. For example, while some may be ready and able to gain the most from their studies directly after their secondary schooling, others may be more suited to study at a later stage in their lives. There is then the added challenge that not everyone can forgo the income needed to bear the costs at any particular time. Perhaps even more challenging is the fact that not everyone desires the kind of higher education that is actually on offer; a challenge that suggests different kinds of curricula, different subjects of study and differing modes of teaching and learning might be more appropriate. While it must be recognised that higher education is unlikely to meet everyone's needs for advanced study, it is also the case that the benefits of higher education are not initially apparent to all that may be able to gain from it.

Within these challenges, a number of further questions emerge about the way in which higher education courses typically operate. More especially, serious questions must be asked about modes of operation in the future. For example, should a three-year standard undergraduate degree taken after high school continue to be regarded as the norm? Not only does this idea seem stuck in universities' collective consciousness, it has now been enshrined within the Bologna Declaration that has made this the norm for higher education across Europe. Yet is not this idea quaintly rigid? Equally rigid, but in quite different ways, could be a new norm of courses being offered online and available at any time. While actively seeking new modes of operation we need to be careful we are not replacing one arbitrary or inappropriate norm with another.

There has been an assumption in higher education institutions, as well as in society more generally, that undergraduate courses are studied by students prior to entering the workforce; that they are a preparation for the world of work. This idea is increasingly unsustainable at a time when it is being ever more strongly articulated in political statements (Clarke 2003; Nelson 2003). Students are working their way through higher education partly through necessity, but often through choice. After the Dearing Report (1997) in the UK, work experience and skills became more prominent in many courses. The preparation and delivery of courses are still more often than not based on the assumption that students have been prepared academically, for example, through school study. However, they fail to take account of the fact that many have had work experience that has prepared them in a quite different way. Changes in both of these assumptions have a profound influence on the nature of courses and what they aim to achieve.

There were moves in the 1990s (HEQC 1995) to articulate what is meant by 'graduateness' as responses to the now widespread recognition that there is no 'gold standard' for university degrees. For largely political reasons there has been an assumption of broad equivalence across degrees and across institutions. However, such equivalence has been elusive. There never has been a common academic standard even within a single institution. Indeed, there are variations between disciplines that cannot be translated from one domain to another. Articulations of notions of 'graduateness' are the beginnings of a quest to be continually pursued. It is being pursued through the increasingly dominant 'quality' agenda. Any notion, however, that this process will result in the specification of a defined set of skills, abilities, attributes and knowledge to be obtained by graduates in the future, is quite unrealistic. Increased pressure for accountability and specification of standards requires them to be documented in some form or other, but this is a partial and temporary solution. Since very different needs are being met we cannot assume a common output level. It is even unclear what this means within the current situation. So a further challenge we face is to know in what terms the outcomes of higher education should be formulated.

Perhaps the most profound challenge, however, is in the area in which universities once felt secure. It is becoming more apparent that they do not have such a central role in knowledge production and use, as once was assumed to be the case. There is increasing acknowledgement of Mode 2 knowledge (Gibbons *et al.* 1994), i.e. trans-disciplinary knowledge carried out in a context of application, the growth of highly sophisticated knowledge-intensive commercial enterprises and the wider accessibility of existing information through knowledge management and communication and information technologies. This means that universities have to reappraise their role in knowledge production and transmission. In the context of changing ideas within the context of all disciplinary areas, knowledge transmission is no longer as crucial as it once was. Developing ways to learn and cope with changing knowledge becomes much more important for students.

Beyond access to responsiveness

These wider changes and challenges within higher education suggest that there is a need to shift the frame through which the problem of access is viewed. We have to move from assuming the solution, i.e. widening, to addressing the issue: responding to changing needs in uncertain times. The current discourse of access assumes that higher education institutions already have the solution to the problem. That solution is a university education that is typically a variation on the theme of a three- or four-year full-time course more or less taught in lectures and (ever-larger) tutorials. It also now encompasses part-time and distance studies and web-based learning. It includes much greater choice of subject. This 'solution' is assumed to be a self-evident good. However, the solution of an equivalent three-year course, or perhaps now a two-year course, no matter how packaged and in what mode, cannot be the answer to all the educational demands we now face. The problem is that such a solution does not adequately engage with the challenges of our times.

I believe we now need a new emphasis on *responsiveness*. Such a new emphasis will require institutions to go beyond the moves they have already made in coping with their changing populations of students. Notions of responsive curricula conceptualise learner-managed learning in a sophisticated way avoiding the traps of the more simplistic versions of self-directed learning in common currency.

Responsiveness includes, but is not restricted to, recognising the diversity of needs of different populations: those in work as much as those preparing for work; those whose secondary education is far in the past as well as school leavers. It also means recognising that the provision of academic courses, or even courses for the new professions, is an inadequate response to student needs. The traditional distinction between the academic and vocational collapsed many years ago, but we still act as if it had not. New forms of work and new patterns of employment require new kinds of response. Responsiveness means not simply offering courses in different modes, but allowing all students to take courses in combinations of modes: face-to-face, weekly, in intensive blocks, by distance learning, using the internet, and so on.

Responsiveness is also about recognising that it is necessary to start from what students say they want but also to lead them into areas that at the start they could never have dreamt of. Being responsive also means recognising that many learners have not been well equipped by their previous educational experiences to cope with the demands that higher learning will place on them. This requires the implementation of strategies to deal with both the intellectual and emotional scars that they may have been left with from earlier learning experiences.

With the new demands from learners and the opportunities that some aspects of new technology will allow, responsiveness also means accepting that completely new forms of course will be necessary to accommodate the paucity of funding from public sources. This may mean finding new ways of utilising the population of learners more effectively as a resource for learning than we have done in the past. This could mean finding ways of more creatively linking work and learning, through new kinds of practice-based programmes, through work linked learning and through utilising the kinds of 'normal' work students do for learning purposes. Such ideas go way beyond the old notions of sandwich education that often failed through unwillingness to seriously address the tensions between learning and work.

All of these strategies pose new challenges for us. Yet as with all higher education innovations, they are all in some senses extensions of current practices. So how will we judge the extent to which our institutions are responsive? How might success be discerned?

First, our institutions, faculties, and departments would demonstrate that they are addressing a variety of needs and purposes through a range of diverse strategies (one size definitely does not fit all). Within this there would be a variety of dimensions of flexibility. Within any given programme, a variety of different modes of course offerings (for example, part-time, full-time, some intensive study, some web-based, some negotiated) will be available to learners who will be able to move freely between these. One measure of the success of this would be the extent to which the curriculum was responsive to differing student needs. The extent to which learners can adapt the course or programme as they progress to meet their changing needs and interests and accommodate their changing employment opportunities would be an indication. Responsive curricula would be those that offer more than is pre-defined by academics or by external groups.

To achieve this, there is likely to be disaggregating of programmes that can then be reassembled in new forms with the support necessary to achieve coherent patterns of study. Choice implies knowledge about what is chosen. Full descriptions of course outcomes are already in train, but choice implies that consumer reports and knowledge of consequences are available to students, not just accurate labelling.

The final criterion of responsiveness would be the extent to which other resources in society are used as part of higher education programmes: practice-based, use of practitioners, engagement with community issues. In the new context I have described, the boundaries of courses are not those of the institution but of the society in which the institution is located.

Going beyond existing institutions

If existing institutions do not engage in the radical innovations needed for the goal of responsiveness, new kinds of institutions will need to be invented. One such example is the little understood and much-maligned UK's University for Industry. This institution combines personal learning advice, online programmes and local delivery in familiar surroundings. While this institution has been criticised for not being a university, and not for industry, it has the potential to shift the way universities and industry think of learners and learning. The University for Industry, or 'Learn Direct' as it is now branded, is seeking to change the way in which the learners it serves are regarded. It has picked up some of the better elements of the vocational education and training reform agenda. It goes to learners, providing short programmes, offering educational brokerage services, and it has started to offer negotiated programmes under the banner of 'Learning Through Work'.

Another example taking us beyond the discourse of widening to embrace the discourse of responsiveness are work-based learning partnerships (Boud and Solomon 2001). These have been established within existing institutions and show how radical change may be possible from within the academy. They can be examined as a case study to point to the challenges and the needs for reconceptualisation of what access means. In work-based learning, students undertake study for a degree or diploma through activities conducted primarily in their workplace and in areas for which there may be no immediate equivalent among university subjects. The learning opportunities found in work-based learning are not contrived for study purposes, but arise from normal work. The role of the university is to equip those working to develop lifelong learning skills, not through engagement with existing disciplines or bodies of knowledge and a programme defined by university teachers, but through a curriculum that is unique for each person. In work-based learning degrees, work *is* the curriculum. Programmes are negotiated between the learner, the workplace and an academic adviser.

Many of those who participate in work-based learning degrees are those who have, in conventional terms, 'missed out' on higher education and could be seen as 'returning to study'. However, to portray work-based learning in these terms would be to ignore the very significant ways in which it confronts existing assumptions. The university does not set the curriculum. Students are not fitted into standard course units and academic staff do not define the outcomes. In many ways, work-based learning challenges all the assumptions of what constitutes a university education. What it retains is a notion of levels of achievement, an emphasis on demonstrating learning and a systematic programme of study.

Work-based learning is by no means a panacea. Like all of the innovations that will be needed within a context of responsiveness, it is good at responding to certain needs, but poor at responding to others. Work-based learning may not be good at addressing the learning needs of companies where the employers have short time-horizons and are not investing for the future. It has limited applicability where the aim is to promote learning for active citizenship. Work-based learning also does not effectively address very long-term learning needs, for example, those that are beyond the timescale of thinking of organisations, such as longer-term environmental and social issues. It is also not good at responding to learning aimed at the redistribution of privilege, for example, to directly address inequities in access to resources, and it does little to address the learning needs of the unemployed or those employed in marginal positions (whether casualised or contracted out).

Academics that have been involved in work-based learning report that it creates many tensions when working within a conventional university. In a UK context, this is argued to be more relevant in traditional rather than new universities (Caley 2001). The roles and identities of staff have to alter quite significantly. Many teaching staff in academic disciplines find the idea of responding to the actual needs of students, rather than the needs one would wish them to have, difficult to cope with. Work-based learning challenges and changes ideas of what constitutes a university education. Yet these challenges are likely to be common features of all the more substantial strategies needed to cope with responsiveness. The less they fit into the normal working patterns, career aspirations and cultural practices of existing teachers and academics, the more new kinds of practitioner and new kinds of institution need to be developed.

The challenge of responsiveness

It is easy to accept responsiveness 'as a good thing', but it has its own demands which, if it is not to degenerate into some vague notion of increasing learning opportunities, we must engage with. We need to look hard at exactly what is required for new educational forms and purposes.

Responsiveness must first and foremost acknowledge the goals of the learner. It necessarily includes a holistic view of learning while recognising that programmes may need to be modularised in a variety of ways to suit the learners' varying circumstances. It incorporates the view that learning and conceptual skills, for example new literacies, sustainable assessment, critical capacities, etc., need to be developed and avoids simplistic notions of 'skilling' without consideration of the conceptual base on which skills may need to rest. Responsiveness also relies upon an understanding of the resources to which learners have access or provision of those resources needed (e.g. utilisation of technology). There is also an emphasis on equipping learners to deal with knowledge demands rather than on the transmission of knowledge as such. In other words the emphasis is on preparing the learner to cope with their own learning needs in both the present and the future and on preparing them to be able to cope with what Barnett (2000) has termed a world of super-complexity. Finally, responsiveness means taking account of the rapidly changing nature of the world of practice and of the contexts of learners in all that this implies.

From the point of view of responsiveness, the focus of debates about access shifts from an emphasis on getting people into particular educational institutions, towards enabling them to participate in high quality learning activities wherever, and within whatever accreditation framework, they may be offered. History has taught us that the notion of the university is very robust and can adapt to changing demands. Most of what is required within a framework of access as responsiveness can be accommodated within changed notions of a university education. However, it does require us to radically reappraise what we hold dear. It may mean giving up existing patterns of work. It may involve changing our disciplinary allegiances, our conceptions of what constitutes teaching and our views about what a course should be or what students should do.

What remains is, I believe, at the core of being an academic. We are left with a commitment to notions of inquiry and with the activity of understanding and documenting our own knowledge and developing in students the skills to do the same with theirs. We are charged with the vitally important role of fostering learning. We have the challenging task of changing students' conceptions of learning and of the phenomenon of their study. Finally, we are charged with the challenge of equipping students with the personal resources to enable them to pursue their own goals. Knowledge does not disappear in this conception, but it is transformed. Teaching and learning take on new meanings.

Conclusion

The metaphors we use to describe what we do betray our intentions. In this chapter I have shown how the use of the metaphor of 'widening', when applied to notions of access to higher education, limits our ideas and aspirations. I have suggested that we need to cease to view access in simplistic quantitative terms that confine it to questions of who is entering higher education. I have argued that what is important is what happens when students have gained access. This does not mean giving up societal aspirations for wider participation in higher education. But it does mean recognising that higher education cannot do more than there are resources for. I have suggested a new metaphor to drive access agendas, that of responsiveness. In outlining some of the challenges that this new way of thinking about access poses, I have explored some newer ideas of higher education. Higher education in the future may look very different. In order to achieve this we need to give up our attachment to ideas and practices which have now outlived their usefulness. In providing for the needs of an increasingly diverse student population, our ideas of what constitutes higher education and its relationship with the world of work will change. We need to be open to and ready for this while still holding onto our key values. Responsiveness challenges us all.

References

Anderson, D. (1990) 'Access to university education in Australia 1852–1990: changes in the undergraduate social mix', *Australian Universities' Review*, 33(2), 37–50.

Barnett, R. (2000) *Realising the University: In an Age of Super-Complexity*. Buckingham: Society for Research into Higher Education and the Open University Press.

Boud, D. and Solomon, N. (eds) (2001) *Work-Based Learning: A New Higher Education?* Buckingham: Society for Research into Higher Education and the Open University Press.

Caley, L. (2001) 'The possibilities in a traditional university', in D. Boud and N. Solomon (eds) *Work-Based Learning: A New Higher Education?* Buckingham: SRHE/Open University Press.

Clarke, C. (2003) *The Future of Higher Education. Secretary of State for Education and Skills*. Cm 5735. Norwich: Her Majesty's Stationery Office.

Dawkins, J.S. (1990) *A Fair Chance for All: Higher Education That's Within Everyone's Reach*. Canberra: Australian Government Publishing Service.

Dearing Report (1997) *Higher Education in the Learning Society: The Report of the National Committee of Inquiry into Higher Education*. Norwich: Her Majesty's Stationery Office.

DfES (2003) *Widening Participation in Higher Education*. London: Department for Education and Skills.

Forsyth, A. and Furlong, A. (2000) *Socioeconomic Disadvantage and Access to Higher Education*. Bristol: The Policy Press/Joseph Rowntree Foundation.

Gibbons, M., Limoges, C., Nowotny, H., Schwartzman, S., Scott, P. and Trow, M. (1994) *The New Production of Knowledge: The Dynamics of Science and Research in Contemporary Societies*. London: Sage.

Higher Education Council (1996) *Equality, Diversity and Excellence: Advancing the National Equity Framework*. Higher Education Council, Department of Employment, Education and Training. Canberra: Australian Government Publishing Service.

HEQC (1995) *What Are Graduates? Clarifying The Attributes Of 'Graduateness'*. The Higher Education Quality Council Quality Enhancement Group. London: Higher Education Quality Council.

Marks, G., Fleming, N., Long, M. and McMillan, J. (2000) *Patterns of Participation in Year 12 and Higher Education in Australia: Trends and Issues*. LSAY Research Report No. 17, Melbourne: Australian Council for Educational Research.

Nelson, B. (2003) *Our Universities: Backing Australia's Future*. Ministerial Policy Paper. Department of Education, Science and Training. Canberra: Australian Government Publishing Service.

Woodrow, M., Yorke, M., Lee, M.F., McGrane, J., Osborne, B., Pudner, H. and Trotman, C. (2002) *Social Class and Participation: Good Practice in Widening Access to Higher Education*. London: Universities UK.

Chapter 6

Widening access and literacy

Joseph Lo Bianco

Introduction

Identifying literacy as a factor impacting on higher education access compels researchers and policy makers to address questions of post-access performance, such as retention, completion or graduation rates, as well as entry. Moreover, bringing literacy into the paradigm of widening access research will require attention to the multiple ways that literacy itself is understood and represented. These can range from the straightforward characterisations of what literacy is, how it is learned and used, that are classically found in most policy texts, to the more complex, socially situated and variable notions of literacy favoured by many academic researchers and literacy educators. These disparities suggest that access research needs to extend the range of its interests to include the quality of educational experience within higher education, and specifically teaching and learning in academic settings.

Literacy and literacies

Three interlocking notions of literacy are used in the present chapter. First, literacy is seen as the sets of '*codes, modes and meanings*' (Lo Bianco and Freebody 2001: 14) associated with reading and writing. Second, researchers' accounts of literacy as variable and socially located are regarded as persuasive in explaining the real world presence of literacy since these shed light on how individuals and various social groups relate to institutions in which communication activity, especially literacy, constitutes the dominant practice (Heath 1983; Baynham 1995; Street 1995; Prinsloo and Breier 1996; Barton and Hamilton 1998; Barton *et al.* 2000; Hornberger 2002). Third, though not extensively discussed here, is the sense that literacy should also be understood as *cultural* practice (Collins 1995; Kalman 1999), relevant in discussing cultural barriers to access.

Specific to education is Freebody and Luke's (1990) characterisation of four 'resources' that sustain effective personal literacy. These resources are an ability to *break the code* of texts; an ability to participate in the *meanings of texts*; an ability to *use texts functionally*; and an ability to *analyse texts critically*, by asking questions about the ideologies they carry. Together these resources form a general capability that literacy educators ought to aim for, far richer and more appropriate to contemporary circumstances than commonly heard appeals for a return to basics. Foregrounding critical and creative dimensions in definitions of literacy also suggests that all teaching and learning endeavours, and research on widening access to higher education, should address the specific literacy demands of subject and discipline specialisations and, possibly explicitly, conceive of all teaching as involving an extension of learners' literacy.

Literacy and policy

Examples of literacy policy in the 1990s suggest some of the conditions under which policy makers are prepared to devote attention to adult literacy education. In Australia (Wickert 2001; Falk 2001), the UK (Baynham 2003), and the US (Collins 1999; Street 2003), public policy attention has been accompanied by the imposition of bureaucratic surveillance and even control. This has involved rigid normalisation of assessment, strict centralised programme accountability, explicit criteria prioritising labour market rationales and goals over community rationales, or vernacular contexts and settings, and, often, the privileging of empirical positivistic data gathering methods over qualitative ethnographic analysis (Street 2003). Surrender of professional pedagogical autonomy is the payment demanded of literacy teachers, researchers and advocates in exchange for the allocation of public resources.

Despite their richly descriptive and powerfully explanatory findings the qualitative nature and ethnographic approaches typical of New Literacy Studies (Street 2001, 2003; Baynham 2003) have little traction in much contemporary public policy. Dominant instead are international comparative statistical collections, exemplified by the International Adult Literacy Survey of 1996, undertaken by the OECD in collaboration with Statistics Canada, and involving the participation of 20 countries (Australian Bureau of Statistics 1996; OECD 1997; Hagston 2002). Epitomising the privileging of research modes are the provisions of the No Child Left Behind Act of 2001 in the United States, which ranks acceptable research according to 'scientific' rankings that narrowly conceive acceptable practice in quantitative terms, and judge these to be the sole or dominant basis for policy formulation. This practice is labelled 'evidence-based' policy making. It is unlikely that some potentially negative effects of literacy on access to higher education will be researched by approaches that concentrate exclusively on randomised experimental, and replicable, large-scale quantitative methodologies. This will mean that overt impacts (e.g. competence barriers to access of academically powerful registers of knowledge required by the prescribed genres of various disciplines in higher education), and subtle impacts (e.g. the dissuading effects on motivation to pursue higher education induced by a culture of privileged academic literacy, functioning as elite ideology and exclusive identity), will remain outside policy influence.

Widening access requires engagement with perspectives such as those brought together in New Literacy Studies, in which out-of-school, or university, literacy events and practices are connected with the uses and values of literacy within educational institutions. Widening access also requires engagement with the pedagogical promise of perspectives from the international Multiliteracies movement (Cope and Kalantzis 2000), combining communication modality with teaching. Higher educational institutions are quintessentially literate institutions, in which most institutional events are literacy-specific, literacy-intense and defined by, and made through, literate exchange. Historically cultural barriers militating against access and participation in higher education have been erected on the basis of literacy culture; denial and negation of the range, complexity and subtlety of the literate repertoire to socially determined categories. The refinement, cultivation and display of elevated literate practice constituted, and largely still constitute, the defining character of membership of higher education and in particular the discourse communities around which its members gravitate and identify.

Many critics of the exclusionary culture of higher learning identify its norms and practices as socially and culturally repressive. Access to these practices cannot be limited simply to unqualified participation, but to diversifying the language and cultural expressive modes in which it operates. These claims are not merely for reducing barriers between abstract conceptions of the institution and class or culturally diverse populations, but between formal and institutionalised practices of education and 'ordinary life' (Hamilton 2001).

Literacy in labour market and human capital planning

In its advocacy of 'life-long learning', the OECD (1996) estimates that only one-third of all adults in the majority of 'OECD countries' have achieved 'minimum' rates of literacy and numeracy. They connect this generalisation with trends about social activity, and economic production, towards greater knowledge intensiveness, and towards deepening general links between economies and education, and more widely diffused information and communications technologies. From these connections emerge notions of the 'learning society' (OECD 1996: 37), a basic tenet of lifelong learning.

Although falling short of characterising literacy as a socially situated practice with personal and cultural meanings, the OECD nevertheless stretches the classical restricted notion of literacy as simply a psychological and motor skill, as follows: 'The very notion of literacy has evolved; in addition to reading, writing and numeracy skills, people also require technological and computer literacy, environmental literacy and social competence' (OECD 1996: 39). For the OECD signs of articulation among, or blurring of distinctions between, formal education and training, and learning in non-formal settings, and the related contraction of age boundaries between secondary and higher education, motivate what is ultimately a strong tie between 'culture' and literacy, viz., 'Raising a country's literacy profile requires a change in its culture' (OECD 1997: 85).

It is often stated within policy contexts that investing in literacy education offers a large number of 'quiet' contributions to the economy. The claimed quiet contributions are many and powerful: that workers become more productive, that private income levels increase, that government revenues rise, that individuals attain a better quality of life, that poverty is reduced, that unemployment decreases, that crime rates decline, that public assistance is reduced, that indicators of good health increase and that child-rearing practices improve. As if this roll-call were not impressive enough, other 'quiet' contributions include increased participation rates in community activities and the bolstering of various measures of citizenship.

Repeatedly the conviction that literacy is an unproblematic contributor to boosting economic competitiveness is expressed. While literacy researchers are committed to explicit language and literacy provision for adults, there is scepticism (Graff 2001; Olson and Torrance 2001) about the unproblematic, confident, basis of such claims. According to Baynham (2003) only bilingual education seems to excite as much controversy as adult literacy, citing in particular the repeated claim of governments that standards of literacy have declined, and that such declines threaten the competitiveness of national economies, with the optional, but frequently encountered rider, that these declines are attributable to 'modern' or 'experimental' or 'faddish/trendy' teaching methodologies.

Adult literacy policy investigations are replete with heady tones of newly discovered public neglect and curative policy evangelism, in extremis primary schools will be punished for laxity, teachers for incompetence, and adults saved from lives of imminent criminality, destitution or marginalisation. A cursory examination of what policy inquiries actually produce, however, reveals only regimes for testing literacy standards, usually in rigidly and narrowly normalising ways, accompanied by public declarations demanding improvement. Inquiries are often entrusted to well-meaning public notables whose pronouncements, sometimes featuring shocked earnestness, contribute to what Graff (2001: 2) calls the 'tireless but tiresome' constitution of literacy in crisis. As a historian of literacy Graff also notes in the elevated significance attributed to literacy, and its standards, continual crises: '... I cannot recall a time when literacy was not in a crisis' (p. 3); finding that in public panics about educational crisis literacy standards are 'symptoms and symbols, causes and consequences' (p. 3); and he cites Searle that higher education is 'essentially and continuously contested territory' (p. 4).

Reform

Western education and training systems have been subjected to almost relentless reform over recent decades. This has been due to policy settings that associate educational activity closely with labour market and wider economic phenomena. The inconclusive results of these policies have produced much chopping and changing in policy moves. Degree level higher education is one of the sites in which educational planners have aimed to negotiate policy settings to give governments greater leverage. This has meant increased numbers of participating mature age and part-time candidates in higher education. Driving these changes have been conceptualisations of access to higher education that are structural and financial in origin, locating policy initiatives to enhance participation and success rates in higher education within the financial means available to hesitant participants, or within needed reforms to the structural operations of institutions. These changes accommodate life-circumstances, competing occupational demands and financial restraints on candidates. The present chapter argues that alongside these necessary concerns we need to add attention to cultural, and specifically literacy, reforms; literacy itself understood both structurally (that is, the quantum and nature of literate capability that learners require to access higher education and succeed there) and as culture (that is, literate practice as indexical of values and producer of social identities, particularly those that higher education presumes, creates and communicates).

Structural articulations among education providers have modified the traditional pathways from secondary schooling to higher education via post-compulsory level examinations, supplementing these with age and alternative-mode entry arrangements and schemes. These more flexible routes are an expression of public sector calculations that access to higher education is an investment in wider economic competitiveness at a time of rapid transfer of economic attention from protective measures for national economies to 'defensive' investments in education and training, though it must be noted that despite this sense of the economic power of higher education English-speaking countries have not been prone to 'invest' in general education. These changes have in turn coincided with a greater commodification of higher education, introducing much greater numbers of international students, in the main of non-English-speaking background, into English medium education.

Flexibility in access pathways has extended to award and certification structures, including cross-institutional credit transfers, to encouragement of corporate sector investment in courses, designated research priority, including patent and copyright control arrangements that modify traditional academic patterns. Open access provision, including online and flexible delivery modalities, have further enriched these institution-based provisions. In this context the notion of lifelong learning has been elevated to prominence, partly under the auspices and leadership of the Organisation for Economic Cooperation and Development. It has also been under the influence of the OECD that literacy, adult literacy specifically, and elaborated kinds of non-prose literacy (e.g. 'information' or 'document' literacy, 'quantitative' literacy, or numeracy) have been given attention in policy discussions in developed societies. Many of these societies had until relatively recently regarded literacy as a phenomenon that had been 'dealt with' in earlier eras of social development, relevant now only to primary schooling, and having few public policy implications beyond the occasional remedial programme for newly arrived immigrants or for some disadvantaged mainstream sections of the population. The 1996 International Adult Literacy Survey marked the presence of the OECD within this field of education policy making, made statistical data collection the principal means for this work, and connected literacy education closely to economic competitiveness of nations and to 'social cohesion' (OECD 1997). The data from the IALS measures literacy on three axes of performance – prose, document and quantitative literacy – along five levels.

One manifestation of the above changes in access to higher degree studies has been the rise in academic support centres, sometimes called study support centres or student learning support units, in higher education institutions. These aim to support what is increasingly called the 'tertiary literacy' development of new cohorts of students, often not studying in their native language, but are also a reflection that what counts as literate capability has itself changed and can no longer be reliably predicted as a linear extension to school-gained literacy. This, in turn, reflects a much wider understanding of literacy as a contingent practice, in which literacy is seen less as an autonomously and endlessly transferable skill but rather as a variable set of practices influenced by setting and purpose. This shift of attention and understanding in the nature of literacy, its ethnographic and 'ideological' characteristics (Street 1995, 2001), was decisive in explaining why literacy programmes designed in developed countries and transposed to aid contexts sometimes failed to achieve the anticipated results by focusing on the local meaning and relevance of literacy. As part of this new regard for a more complex literacy, a notion of literacy sensitive to its differences, is the emergent sense that academic disciplines operate with distinctive literacies, evident in the particular literacy demands their prescribed texts require and how the displaying and demonstration of learning are assessed in that discipline. In some higher degree settings there is growing awareness that knowledge of such disciplinary literacies cannot always be taken for granted and that academic teaching includes induction into such literacies.

In recent decades there has been growing government concern about the changing structure of employment and the perceived need for new training strategies to promote global competitiveness. The decline of manufacturing and the rapid shift of economic power towards post-industrial services and information-based operations combine with sometimes radical changes in workplace relations and operations, and a number of other reinforcing factors, such as the decline in job access and preparation modes, such as the traditional apprenticeship system. The dominant way that new employment is characterised emphasises worker flexibility, adaptability and mobility, in work settings with flatter job hierarchies, comprising fewer sharply demarcated occupational categories and generally less rigid and vertical structures of operation. Labour is now expected to be more mobile in response to market driven shifts in location or occupational content. These changes tend to reinforce communication, and communication effectiveness, as factors in labour market selection, success and operations.

These kinds of communication issues, reinforced by immigration patterns which have made workforces multilingual and multi-literate, are represented in vocational education and training policies, including basic skills for employment, as key questions on the agenda of public policy making. Key target groups in these policy aspirations have been school leavers, especially 16 to 19-year-olds, the long-term unemployed, targeted minorities, and designated disadvantaged regional areas, typically zones undergoing de-industrialisation. As a result, in Australia, the UK and the US new organisational formations which link industry with education and training providers have emerged. Examples have been the Training and Enterprise Councils in the UK, the Private Industry Councils in the US and the Industry Training Advisory Bodies in Australia.

One function of such cross-sectoral organisational arrangements has been to establish local initiatives in training associated with local industrial (or post-industrial) employment generating and sustaining intervention policies. Some such bodies conduct skills training; others coordinate it, and attract or generate investments on the basis of various kinds of schemes. The ITABs in Australia are directly responsible for devising Industry Training Packages comprising complex curricula, assessment and qualifications frameworks, attempting to specify stocks of knowledge, skills, contexts and settings for application. These partnerships forged across government, business and employee organisations with education and training providers also aim to establish occupationally relevant standards of training, accreditation and recognition. Australia has been moving towards a unified national vocational qualifications framework, comprising targets, modes of quality assurance and mechanisms for determining equivalence across jurisdictions and systems. When it is separately identified, literacy is seen as either an add-on training component in these schemes, or an integral, infused aspect of all teaching content. One implication of these initiatives in the provision of post-school training in institutionalised vocational and training systems, or adult basic education schemes and initiatives, is a notion of 'widening access' where literacy is critically important in all professional and vocational disciplines.

Literacy mediates cultural and academic barriers

The present authorisation of the United States Higher Education Act of 1965 expires in September 2004. A recent report (Wolanin 2003) aiming to extend authorisation for a further four years was conducted by the Washington DC based Institute of Higher Education Policy (IHEP) (online at www.ihep.org). The IHEP report refers to US Census data showing that disparities between college participation rates of high and low-income groups, and between selected minority groups and Whites, have been remarkably persistent for the past 30 years. Family income remains a major predictor of college access today, having narrowed only about 10 per cent since the 1970s, while some comparisons, Whites–Blacks and Whites–Hispanics, have actually widened. These disparities persist within an overall pattern of increase in participation rates for all groups, and projected significant further rises over the next 15–20 years.

The approach advocated in Wolanin's study is to discuss widening access within a wide remit addressing higher education persistence, or post-access performance, especially for first-generation admissions to higher education, that is those whose parents had not attended higher education. This policy challenge goes considerably beyond removing institutional and structural barriers, or financial and academic barriers, to participation. Social and cultural barriers, exemplified in identity remarks such as 'People like us don't go to College' (p. 9), require that access research extend beyond entry facilitation by means of structural or financial policy to encompass research and policy-oriented data sensitive to the cultural consequences and challenges of intergenerational changes in family education patterns.

Similarly, addressing 'cultural competence' and 'English language acquisition history' is recent Australian research by Borland and Pearce (2002). This work identifies student language and cultural background factors that institutions can address to understand their readiness to study. Also discussed are the processes of pre-enrolment information gathering that institutions undertake to provide improved learning experiences for students from diverse language, cultural and social backgrounds, mainly by offering 'targeted academic support in language and learning' (p. 123). Both of these studies point to various kinds of 'academic adjustment' challenges that students from under-represented backgrounds may encounter, and suggest that such cultural and social barriers be embraced within a thorough and comprehensive widening access commitment.

Social and cultural barriers are many and variable, linking to parental education attainment, migration history, family income, race, ethnicity and various social identities, and the compounding effects of aggregations of these factors. Social and cultural barriers to access are also, often and deeply, manifested and mediated by academic English proficiency, and especially literate English capability, which in turn forms links to various academic barriers.

This wide array of background variables supports Absalom and Golebiowski's (2002) argument that the 'massification' of higher education has produced major changes in teaching and learning in higher education, shaped by extra-institutional forces of multiculturalism, economic rationalism and computerisation. These forces have elevated the importance of tertiary literacy as a field of research and as a practice important in assisting undergraduate and even graduate students, and in response call for ongoing professional dialogue between tertiary literacy specialists and academics from other fields of study. This idea is considered from a reinforcing but different angle by Bock and Gough (2002) who, specifically discussing groups previously excluded from South African higher education, call for teaching and assessment practices in undergraduate courses to explore the inclusion of tasks in the narrative and creative modalities of expression. They point to powerful traditions of both primary and secondary oral discourse types among traditional Xhosa, including rhetoric and genres of narrative oral literature, and suggest strong implications for teaching and assessment if policies of widening access are to be crowned with success.

According to Bock and Gough, teaching in higher education needs to accommodate wider learner characteristics, and explore conventional modes for how knowledge mastery is displayed and assessed, drawing on genres of a narrative and creative character in addition to the more academically conventional ones. In any case distinctive disciplinary literacies are a longstanding feature of conventional academic work, as Kirkpatrick and Mulligan (2002) show by reference to the amounts and kinds of reading required between social science and engineering academic programmes. The volume and character of reading is radically different, requiring a critical, personally engaged, occasionally sceptical, opinion forming disposition in the former and an information absorbing and accumulating tradition in the latter.

Cultural barriers and their connection with literacy are often well perceived by policy makers who might, however, name the policy goal in different ways. Widening access research needs to be sensitive to the different ways in which the task is named and constituted in different settings. For example, South African policy on the education of adults in the post-apartheid period has specifically targeted low-literacy adults. Some researchers note a 'disturbing' gap between what policy makers determine as a 'problem', and the likely effectiveness of the proposed solution. Literacy is particularly prone to this kind of gap. Policy attention comes at a price, sometimes in the form of 'illiteracy eradication campaigns' of the kind that literacy ethnographers consider unlikely to succeed, stigmatising of learners and simplistic. The claims, perhaps the aspirations, of policy makers for payoff from investment of public resources in literacy campaigns are high levels of politicisation and contestation around the claims for and results from such investments. Many researchers interested in literacy education lament the deleterious effects of literacy policy, to the extent that the interest of public policy makers seems to always be accompanied by restrictions to the kinds of research that are supported and to the professional latitude that literacy professionals are conceded.

Working with such dilemmas in South Africa's complex multilingual reality, and its history of extreme educational exclusion, Janks (2000) has devised an analytical framework for connecting critical social analysis with four dimensions of needed education and language action, Access, Diversity, Domination and Design. This framework is characterised by an education policy aiming to over-come past language oppression. While forthrightly naming and dealing with the history of language domination Janks' approach still acknowledges the universal esteem and demand for English literacy, realised through the notion of access. However, English medium higher education access is pedagogically difficult to implement, and ultimately problematical, if it is predicated upon cultural assimilation, and therefore in Janks' pedagogical framework principles of diversity accompany access. Design is a principle that acknowledges that codes, and modes, of literacy, though often employing literacy elements (such as text genres, or academic rhetorical modes, and computer multi-modality) that are 'extra-local', are not imposed and therefore culturally alienating but negotiated and re-made according to local meanings, and the socially situated literacy practices of students.

Higher education language and literacy policies

An immediate consequence of an awareness of the deeper cultural meanings for widening access is to see higher education institutions as quintessentially literacy-dependent entities, where by far the single greatest conventionalised activity is literate practice. In effect, higher education institutions are aggregations of interrelated intellectual communities whose primary practice and principal instrument is literate behaviour. The varying literate practices of the diverse disciplinary fields that comprise higher education institutions mediate admission or exclusion, determine knowledge acquisition, govern performance and signify identity and professional culture.

The implications of this centrality of literacy to admission, success, and membership of higher education, within a policy project of widening access, require measures to facilitate the admission of greater numbers to the literacy-dependent scholarly life of the institution, but also to attend to the progressively more complex literate demands of teaching and learning. Institution-wide and institution-specific language policies are required. These should be formulated around the language conventions of general academic performance, subject specific genres and discourses, and how learning is demonstrated, assessed and displayed. The globalisation of higher education, combined with the growing treatment of higher education certification as a traded commodity, require that the increasingly diverse language characteristics, problems and needs of learners, more and more often not first language users of English, sometimes from second dialect backgrounds, should be given prominence in such policies.

Higher education institutions need to regard language and literacy as a resource, a social and intellectual resource, whose explicit management and cultivation they undertake as part of their mainstream operations. The development of literacy policies should be the principal means for cultivating and extending literacy resources. These policies would ideally be based on informing research audits of teaching, and would aim to raise awareness among academic staff of the language and literacy dimensions of all academic activity, as they support learners' literacy development. An important goal would be to clarify the performance standards that are expected of students in oral and written communication.

Reid and Parker (2002) cite a fourteen-country survey of 20,000 academics in which two-thirds expressed dissatisfaction with the written language skills of their students, ample justification for including communication issues within formal institutional policies. The increasing language and cultural diversity of student populations, and indeed of faculty, induce Borland and Pearce to argue, 'a major shortcoming of the modern multicultural university has been the failure to adequately understand the implications of diversity in relation to students' language, literacy and cultural understanding' (2002: 103).

Literacy, understood as an expression of a wider analysis of communication issues in general, needs to be addressed in addition to access research and theory development for higher education. Theorising widening access needs to foreground literacy as the principal practice of higher learning, the mediator of knowledge and skill, and the identity marker of the communities of practice that constitute both institutional life and the professional destinations of graduates.

References

Absalom, D. and Golebiowski, Z. (2002) 'Tertiary literacy on the cusp', *Australian Review of Applied Linguistics*, 25(2), 5–18.

Australian Bureau of Statistics (1996) *Aspects of Literacy: Assessed Skill Levels, Australia*, Canberra: Australian Bureau of Statistics.

Barton, D. and Hamilton, M. (1998) *Local Literacies: Reading and Writing in one Community*, London: Routledge.

Barton, D., Hamilton, M. and Ivanic, R. (2000) *Situated Literacies: Reading and Writing in Context*, London: Routledge.

Baynham, M. (1995) *Literacy Practices: Investigating Literacy in Social Contexts*, London: Routledge.

Baynham, M. (2003) 'Adult literacy', in J. Bourne and E. Reid (eds) *Language Education, World Yearbook of Education*, London: Kogan Page.

Bock, Z. and Gough, D. (2002) 'Social literacies and students in tertiary settings: lessons from South Africa', *Australian Review of Applied Linguistics*, 25(2), 49–58.

Borland, H. and Pearce, A. (2002) 'Identifying key dimensions of language and cultural disadvantage at university', *Australian Review of Applied Linguistics*, 25(2), 101–28.

Collins, J. (1995) 'Literacy and literacies', *Annual Review of Anthropology*, 24, 75–93.

Collins, J. (1999) 'The Ebonics controversy in context: literacies, subjectivities, and language ideologies in the United States', in J. Blommaert (ed.) *Language Ideological Debates*, The Hague: Mouton de Gruyter.

Cope, B. and Kalantzis, M. (2000) *Multiliteracies: Literacy Learning and the Design of Social Futures*, London: Routledge.

Falk, I. (2001) 'Sleight of hand: job myths, literacy and social capital', in J. Lo Bianco and R. Wickert (eds) *Australian Policy Activism in Language and Literacy*, Melbourne: Language Australia Publications.

Freebody, P. and Luke, A. (1990) 'Literacy programs: debates and demands in cultural context', *Prospect*, 5, 7–16.

Graff, H. (2001) 'Literacy's myths and legacies: from lessons from the history of literacy, to the question of critical literacy', in P. Freebody, S. Muspratt and B. Dyer (eds) *Difference, Silence, and Textual Practice. Studies in Critical Literacy*, Cresskill, NJ: Hampton Press.

Hagston, J. (2002) *Exploring the International Adult Literacy Survey Data: Implications for Australian Research and Policy*, Melbourne: ARIS and Language Australia Publications.

Hamilton, M. (2001) 'Privileged literacies: policy, institutional process and the life of the IALS', *Language and Education*, 15(2–3), 178–96.

Heath, S.B. (1983) *Ways with Words*, Cambridge: Cambridge University Press.

Hornberger, N. (ed.) (2002) *The Continua of Biliteracy: a Framework for Educational Policy, Research and Practice in Multiple Settings*, Bristol: Multilingual Matters.

Janks, H. (2000) 'Domination, access, diversity and design: a synthesis for critical literacy education', *Educational Review*, 52(2), 175–86.

Kalman, J. (1999) *Writing on the Plaza: Mediated Literacy Practices among Scribes and Clients in Mexico City*, Cresskill, NJ: Hampton Press.

Kirkpatrick, A. and Mulligan, D. (2002) 'Cultures of learning: critical reading in the social and applied sciences', *Australian Review of Applied Linguistics*, 25(2), 73–100.

Lo Bianco, J. and Freebody, P. (2001) *Australian Literacies: Informing National Policy on Literacy Education*, Melbourne: Language Australia Publications.

OECD (1996) *Lifelong Learning For All*, Paris: OECD.

OECD (1997) *Literacy Skill for the Knowledge Society (Further Results of the International Adult Literacy Survey)*, Paris: OECD.

Olson, D.R. and Torrance, N. (2001) 'Conceptualizing literacy as a personal skill and as a social practice', in D.R. Olson and N. Torrance (eds) *The Making of Literate Societies*, Malden, MA: Blackwell.

Prinsloo, M. and Breier, M. (1996) *The Social Uses of Literacy*, Amsterdam: Benjamins.

Reid, I. and Parker, L. (2002) 'Framing institutional policies on literacies', *Australian Review of Applied Linguistics*, 25(2), 19–28.

Street, B. (1995) *Social Literacies*, London: Longman.

Street, B. (ed.) (2001) *Literacy and Development: Ethnographic Perspectives*, London: Routledge.

Street, B. (2003) 'What's "new" in New Literacy Studies? Critical approaches to literacy in theory and practice', *Current Issues in Comparative Education*, 5(2), 1–19.

Wickert, R. (2001) 'Politics, activism and processes of policy production: adult literacy in Australia', in J. Lo Bianco and R. Wickert (eds) *Australian Policy Activism in Language and Literacy*, Melbourne: Language Australia Publications.

Wolanin, T. (2003) *HEA: Reauthorizing the Higher Education Act, Issues and Options*, Washington DC: The Institute for Higher Education Policy.

Chapter 7

Widening access for the education of adults in the United States

Juanita Johnson-Bailey and
Ronald M. Cervero

Adult education, like all areas of education, mirrors and in part reproduces the world in which we live. US society is a place replete with hierarchical systems that privilege some and deny others. The stated goals of adult education have consistently been set forth as helping adults, especially those lacking in basic skills, to fully participate as American citizens and to avail themselves of all aspects of American citizenry (Cunningham, 1988). In contrast to the desired mission, adult education studies reveal the direct opposite: adult education programmes typically serve middle-class Whites who are continuing a family tradition of educational attainment (Cross, 1981; Merriam and Caffarella, 1999). Adult education in the United States encompasses the standard areas of continuing education, basic education, programme development, adult development, and human resource development. By definition, each of these major areas are about maintaining and reproducing what already exists in society. Primarily they are devoted to future learning in the workplace and managing and maximizing the human potential. The education of adults occurs along many lines of demarcation that confine, define, and/or exclude a disenfranchised populace by race, class, gender, ethnicity, and sexual orientation.

As adult educators in the United States, the ways in which we have constructed our practices around race have ordered our communities locally and globally with real consequences accorded along queues of privilege and disadvantage. An understanding of race invariably situates and permeates our everyday lives. Therefore, our classes, practices, programmes, and research reflect what we have experienced and what we believe about race. Although we have chosen to discuss race in this chapter, we do not imply that it is the only salient issue affecting attempts to widen access. However, it is our contention that race can serve as a consequential lens through which to view other oppressive systems. This chapter is framed by two points about race (Johnson-Bailey and Cervero, 2000). First, race is a social construct that has a tenuous grounding in biology (Gregory and Sanjek, 1994). Anthropologists and biologists have long recognized that the human form cannot be examined through visual inspection to definitively determine a person's race. It is, at best, a fleeting notion established by an arguable set of physical characteristics. Second, although race is a social construct, its effects are real in terms of social power and privilege (Giroux, 1997). Race is an invisible presence that helps to determine how society functions. This ordering of the world occurs because, as a person is categorized as belonging to a race, that person is also accorded all the privileges and baggage that accompanies the classification (McIntosh, 1995). To be White in the United States is to be the norm and this ability to blend in is the currency of access to all things better in society. The President's Commission on Race (One America, 1998, p. 46) defined this currency as the 'institutional advantages based on historic factors that have given an advantage to white Americans. … we as a nation need to understand that whites tend to benefit, either unknowingly or consciously, from this country's history of white privilege'.

Race interlocks with other forces such as gender, age, and sexual orientation, all of which order our world. When race is discussed the implied assumption is that race means otherness, brown, black, yellow, or red, but not white. Our position is that to discuss race in adult education, we must recognize the ever-absent concept of whiteness (Giroux, 1997). The purpose of this chapter is to discuss issues of widening access in the United States by examining two perspectives: 1) how the field's representative literature has historically presented the issues of race in adult education and 2) how issues of inclusion have been dealt with relative to students and faculty from under-represented groups. We end our chapter with suggestions for widening access for adults in higher education.

Race and adult education: a historical perspective of the literature

The ways in which the field defines itself through its literature is a window through which one can view how the field regards race and how the field makes a place or fails to make a place for those who are not members of the dominant White race. We therefore begin our analysis by exploring the Handbooks of Adult Education published from 1934 through 2000. We take the Handbooks as representative of how leaders define what matters in the field and what the field considers to be key issues. As historical documents that were written to define the field of adult education in the United States, the Handbooks of Adult Education tell a surprisingly contemporary story about how issues of race have continued to intersect with the practice of adult education in the United States.

Although race is a central location for the negotiation of power and privilege in education and in Western society, it has never formed the focal point of a single chapter in the entire corpus of nine Handbooks until the 2000 edition with the inclusion of 'the Invisible Politics of Race in Adult Education' (Johnson-Bailey and Cervero, 2000). Other than this most recent discussion of race, the way that race has been socially constructed in the literature over the past half-century has been remarkably stable and invisible. This view is that the White race is the norm against which all other races are to be compared. This perspective is so deeply embedded in the social fabric and language of US culture that there has been little discussion of adult education for Whites even though the White race has constituted the vast majority of the population for adult education. The other exception was one brief mention made by Rowden (1934) in her article, 'Adult Education for Negroes' in the 1934 Handbook in which she compared the adult education efforts for Negroes as lacking when contrasted to that provided for White students. In subsequent editions there is no mention of race at all (1960, 1980), while the rest discuss adult education for Negroes (1934, 1936), American Indians (1948), and racial and ethnic minorities (1989), meaning Blacks, Hispanics, and Native Americans. Whenever race is discussed in the Handbooks, then, it is conceptualized as non-White. Of course when one group is normative, the others are viewed as abnormal. This leads to the obvious conclusion that separate chapters would be needed to discuss the specific educational efforts being made to address the needs of these 'special' populations.

Although race is a social construct, there is no doubt that its effects are real in terms of the distribution of power and privilege in society. The authors who spoke to issues of race throughout the 66 years covered in the Handbooks support the view that non-White groups have disproportionally little power and access to material and cultural resources. In an early Handbook, Locke (1936a, p. 126) argued that adult education for Negroes was being driven by the 'idea that it is important as a special corrective for the Negro's handicaps (underprivilege and social maladjustment)'. A similar view is expressed in the 1989 Handbook (Briscoe and Ross, 1989, p. 583), which selected Blacks, Native Americans, and Hispanics because 'all three groups have experienced inequality in educational opportunity and participation', largely because of racial discrimination, economic disadvantage, and de jure and de facto segregation. While the Handbooks are clear that discrimination against non-White groups is an important social problem, three different educational solutions were proposed.

The first proposed educational response is what we now term 'multicultural education'. In the 1948 Handbook, Locke noted (p. ix) that: 'Group education for social, intercultural, and international understanding looms up from the context of today's living to become the paramount problem and primary concern of the educator'. This education was to serve the interest in producing a 'sound society', by providing all people with 'training for citizenship and for full and willing participation in a democratic society' (p. ix). This group education for democracy would come from an education that stressed a knowledge and understanding of all groups that make up society: 'It would seem that a much better chance of promoting unity and understanding is promised through the cultivation of respect for differences and intelligent interest in group achievements and backgrounds, and through preaching and practicing reciprocity instead of regimentation' (Locke, 1936b, p. 226). This multicultural theme has carried through to a recent Handbook with Rachal (1989, pp. 5–6), who says that: 'Adult education's greatest responsibility may well be a fostering of social tolerance and interdependence'.

Kotinsky proposed a second practical educational response to discrimination, which she argues results from prejudice: '... a mounting threat is abroad in the land, irrational hate among persons and groups, a problem which, it would appear, is ultimately soluble by educational means alone' (1948, p. 101). Like Locke, she supports intercultural education that seeks to develop 'attitudes of understanding and respect among groups and individuals of different backgrounds, whether racial, religious, nationality, or socio-economic' (p. 101). Unlike Locke, she does not believe that knowledge is sufficient to develop this understanding. She believes that educators must see that 'race prejudice is closely related to the emotional needs of the individual … For some it provides compensation, making up for severe inferiority feelings. … others find in a minority a target on which they can release their rancour without suffering too much social disapproval' (p. 106). Thus, she calls for the need for 'emotional re-education' for those in the dominant racial group, which she implies but does not name as Whites.

London echoes a third theme of discrimination by concluding from census data that: 'Negroes and other minorities are subject to many disadvantages which have their roots in discriminatory practices, inferior education and the particular occupational distribution that reflects inferior status and limited opportunity' (London, 1970, p. 13). However, unlike other authors, London specifically locates the problem in the 'insidious character of white racism that infects our society' (ibid., p. 13), using the famous quote from the 1968 Kerner Report that: 'What white Americans have never fully understood – but what the Negro can never forget – is that white society is deeply implicated in the ghetto. White institutions created it, white institutions maintain it, and white society condones it' (ibid., pp. 13–14). London believes that 'Adult education can have a significant role to play in the attack upon racism and discrimination' (ibid., p. 15). However, unlike Locke and Kotinsky, London argues that: 'providing improved educational opportunities … is not sufficient to deal with the unequal distribution of life chances in our society [because] piecemeal attack upon the problem of discrimination is insufficient to influence the drastic changes that we must secure if this problem is to be reduced or eventually eliminated' (ibid., p. 15). Thus, in a third form of educational response to discrimination, London pushes for a comprehensive social and political effort, alongside the educational opportunities, 'supported by our government, our major institutions and the responsible leadership in our society' (ibid., p. 15).

Current educational responses to issues of race

We have divided the many contemporary perspectives on race in adult education into three broad categories that are associated with different forms of practical action by adult educators.

Colour-blind perspective

Although not named in the literature as a formal educational response, the most widely used approach to race in adult education is a perspective that we refer to as the colour-blind perspective. This perspective is one in which race is not discussed directly in the adult education literature and where it is therefore assumed that race is not a significant topic or one that impacts the field in any serious way. However, we contend that the missing discussion on race means the exact opposite. Since race is of such consequence to our world and to our adult education practice, by omitting the topic we are simultaneously denying the existence of race and setting forth that there is universality around the issue of race – assuming that there is a normative race.

Colour-blind perspectives are manifested in two ways. First, most of the literature on theory, research, and praxis sets forth norms that appear not to be based on any one group. However, educational sociologists (Sleeter and Grant, 1987) agree that most of these norms are based in middle-class White Protestant values that are considered the foundation of US culture. These values emphasize individual merit and rights, competition, and freedoms (including democratic ideals). Examples of agreed upon norms are abundant in the literature. For example, most of the praxis literature, which discusses how to use small group activities, is predicated on the idea that individuals, as learners and teachers, will speak and act freely in sharing their opinions. But what happens when the learner's culture places more emphasis on the community than on the individual and therefore encourages the individual to refrain from sharing personal ideas or concerns? If the group contained Hispanics, African Americans, and Native Americans whose group cultural values are community based (Banks, 1997), climate setting could be compromised. The second way that the colour-blind perspective is manifested is in its prescriptions for adult education practice. Nearly all discussions of teaching in adult education simply avoid the racial dynamics that are omnipresent in the real world (Johnson-Bailey and Cervero, 1997). Such a script presents the view that all students are equal and all teachers are unbiased. By stripping learners and teachers of their place in the hierarchies of social life, this view assumes that we stage adult education where the politics of everyday life do not operate.

Multicultural education

A central idea that is shared by all types of multiculturalism is that one culture is seen as dominant and therefore the educational need is to teach the importance of values and beliefs that are held by other cultures. Therefore from its inception multicultural education has called for recognition and inclusion of the contributions of other cultures in the literature, research, and praxis. According to Guy (1996), the idea of multicultural education was first introduced in the adult education literature by Kallen in 1915 and expanded on by Locke in 1925. Locke represents a segment of the field that champions the multicultural argument by making known the causes and worth of certain groups. He expressed a belief in the redemptive powers of multiculturalism (Locke, 1936b), a view that remains constant in contemporary adult education.

Martin (1994) describes five types of multicultural education (assimilation/

acculturation, cultural awareness, multicultural, ethno-centrist, anti-racist) that are present in the adult education literature. Guy (1999) expresses a cultural awareness viewpoint in setting forth the belief that recognizing and valuing African American vernacular English is one way of improving delivery of literacy services. Another frequently held position calls for making changes based on the anticipated population increases of people of colour. Ross-Gordon (1990) suggests that we examine the cultural underpinnings of our field and begin to keep pace with the changing face of society. Another multicultural perspective, ethno-centrism, which asks for the recognition of non-dominant groups is widespread in current literature (Hayes and Colin, 1994; Martin, 1994) and is predicated on the belief that if the merit of the group and the significance of their contributions is known then attitudes toward the group will be favourable. While this quid pro quo relationship is not overtly stated, the notion that the expected outcome will improve inter-group relations seems obvious.

Social justice: issues of power and privilege

The social justice perspective asks adult educators to live by the mission of the field, which is to democratize the citizenry (Cunningham, 1996). Addressing not only the difference between groups, but highlighting how power is exercised in favour of one group and to the detriment of another, are the foci of the literature that addresses power and privilege (Johnson-Bailey and Cervero, 1997, 1998; Rocco and West, 1998). When the discourse on whiteness or privilege occurs in the literature, it usually involves the following: a recognition of privilege (Cunningham, 1996), an examination of classroom practices (Johnson-Bailey and Cervero, 1997, 1998), and examples of curriculum and/or texts that reproduce privilege. A large segment of the literature in this category deals with the interlocking nature of race, gender, and class (Flannery, 1994; Tisdell, 1995). Cunningham (1996) states that until we act on what we know to be right and fair, '... adult educators are complicit with these political and economic arrangements' (p. 157) that keep the current system in place. Tisdell (1995) also discusses and critiques the interlocking nature of systems of power and asks that adult educators deal with these issues through curriculum design and praxis. Her recommendations call for direct involvement and action on the individual level. This view is also expressed by Flannery in 'Changing Dominant Understandings of Adults as Learners' where she critiques existing adult education theories as androcentric and hegemonic and calls for alternatives with more inclusive viewpoints (1994, p. 22): 'The valuing of the universal in adult education must be changed. New perspectives must be developed to overcome the racism and sexism inherent in universal understandings of adults as learners. As adult educators, we must engage in an honest critique of our theories and our practices.'

In concluding this section on the perspective from the adult education literature and the resulting educational responses, what we have noted is that the literature has been duplicitous in that it continues to set forth the mantra of democratization as the mission of the field, while simultaneously avoiding any substantive discussion of race. While the infusion of multiculturalism has somewhat broadened the lens of many students and practitioners and has become perhaps the most popular trend espoused in the literature, multiculturalism fails to call for or demand change. It simply informs. If the field is to be judged by its literature base, then adult education as a discipline is sorely lacking in laying a foundation of change through its representative literature.

Issues of struggle and inclusion in the United States

A second important component of widening access in adult education concerns how the field makes space for students and faculty who are not a part of the dominant White group or what Osborne refers to as the concept of 'in reach' (Osborne, 2003). We next offer a discussion of how essential it is to open the doors of the academy to make space for students and faculty who were previously excluded. It is necessary to make the adult education field, which holds democratization as a core value, stop duplicating other areas of education where Black students are systemically locked out.

Efforts to change the academy must begin with a look at how students and faculty function in the academy and so we centre our discussion on teaching and learning – the formal and hidden curriculum. The ways in which school administrators, professors, and students act in school settings are indicative of how power operates in our society. Black students are not seen as capable scholars because of the stereotypical ways in which Blacks are regarded as intellectually inferior. Such historically and still prevalent beliefs translate into policies and subtle actions that lock Black students out of adult education programmes. The operation of the formal and hidden curriculum offers an informative look into the operations of adult education. Through our formal and informal curriculums we send a powerful message that is heard by Black students who are disenfranchised within the system: 1) you do not belong and you are not wanted; 2) if admitted, you will be treated unfairly, with different standards and expectations; 3) you must find your own means of survival; and 4) your degree if achieved, will be considered inferior or unearned (Johnson-Bailey, 2001).

Our definition of the formal curriculum includes not only the texts and research materials used, but also includes the policies and practices that set the tone of a student's educational environment. For example, over-dependence by a programme on test scores to determine a student's acceptance into the programme or to determine who receives financial assistance when such requirements have been shown to have a disparate and unfair impact on minority students sends a message to potential applicants. In addition, the actual interview process could further screen out applicants as the literature shows that a programme's intake officer is often the gatekeeper who helps or hinders the application process. The literature notes that minority students consistently report negative experiences when completing paperwork, paying fees and attempting to join or become oriented to the academic setting (Broach, 1984; Johnson-Bailey, 2000, 2001; Margolis and Romero, 1998).

While we consider the policies and practices of the entire educational environment to be components of the formal curriculum in that they affect and establish the parameters of the formal curriculum, we locate our discussion on the routine issues that occur in adult education classrooms relative to course curriculums. The recorded history of our adult education texts reflects a Eurocentric perspective that excludes the contributions of Black US adult educators (Neufeldt and McGee, 1990; Peterson, 1996). Moreover as referenced in the previous section that examined the literature, adult education handbooks have failed to examine the relevance of race in relation to how race affects the context of adult education – its programmes, learners, and instructors.

In addition, the adult education classroom practices such as small group work, Socratic discourse, and classroom facilitations are based on the values of competition and individualism which are highly valued in the dominant White culture (Banks, 1997; Sleeter and Grant, 1987). Such classroom practices and negotiations exclude or devalue the community based cultural practices of cooperation and consensus, which are endemic to African-based cultures like the Black US culture.

Overall, the formal curriculum of exclusionary texts and Eurocentric classroom practices does not present a welcoming environment to Black students in that it does not locate them in its history or functioning. Such issues may seem benign to members of the White culture, but that is because it allows Whites to continue to build on the invisibility offered by the privilege of dominance. However, to Black students it sends the message that they had no place of importance in adult education history and that their cultural practices play no significant role in shaping the daily classroom practices.

Admittedly the formal curriculum is evident in the ways in which it functions to affect the academic environment, but it is hidden curriculum that offers the most tangible examples of how power works in the adult education environment to affect the participation and retention of minority students. Once Black students are enrolled in programmes, it is the functioning of the hidden curriculum – student and professor and student/student interactions and classroom policies – that works to negatively impact retention. It is our contention, that the hidden curriculum is more influential than the formal curriculum as regards the experiences of adult education students. Examples of how the hidden curriculum operates to determine the success of Black students is seen in student groups that organize for projects or study, assignments of research opportunities, and graduate research assistantships. Often minority students are locked out of the well established and hierarchically arranged student network that mediates such matters. Although these opportunities are said to be available to all students, when they are not controlled by a formal process it is the 'anointed students' who arbitrate these opportunities by informally controlling information and through the use of sponsorship to determine who will be accepted and who will be excluded. To examine the hidden curriculum is tantamount to opening the doors of our minds and the portals of the academy. Doing so involves abandoning a falsely claimed neutral position that only disguises favouritism toward the dominant group and Eurocentric knowledge. We must understand that our students are cast in roles assigned them by Western society and that those students who are over-privileged and those who are underprivileged are likely to maintain those same positions in the learning environment.

If adult education programmes are to be successful in recruiting and maintaining Black students we must examine the hidden curriculum, which thwarts efforts to be inclusive and democratic. To demonstrate ways in which this can be accomplished we examine a specific programme at a research university and how this programme dealt with increasing the numbers of Black students, a historically under-represented group at the university. In 1994 the Adult Education Department at the University of Georgia, the largest in the United States, had over 100 graduate students and a meagre total of two Black students – two Black women enrolled in doctoral degree programmes. Located in the Southeastern state of Georgia where Blacks compose 29 per cent of the population, the public land grant institution has a mission to serve its population. Yet the university had banned Blacks from enrolling until federal courts forced the desegregation. Moreover, the university fought a lengthy court battle to keep Blacks out and members of the university student body rioted in protest of the presence of the first Black students who enrolled in 1962.

Against this backdrop, in 1995 the faculty of the Department of Adult Education made a commitment to increase the enrollment of Black students. In consultation with the currently enrolled Black students and former Black graduates, three faculty members, the department chair, the graduate coordinator, and a newly hired Black faculty member, developed an aggressive student recruitment and retention plan. The outreach effort which was designed to increase the numbers of Black students encouraged faculty and students to make personal contacts with potential Black students. Faculty was expected to commit to recruiting students from this under-represented group. Over a period of seven years the numbers of Blacks increased from a previous high of two students to a current number of forty-two.

A second important component of this 'in reach' effort was the establishment of a support group called the Students of African Descent. This self-mentoring and departmentally sponsored group became a strong student network that helped students negotiate the structured inequalities that existed in the system to discourage the participation and the retention of Black students: hostile faculty, hostile White students, a non-inclusive official curriculum, and a chilly hidden curriculum (Johnson-Bailey, 2000, 2001; Margolis and Romero, 1998).

The student-led and faculty-advised group, which met on a regular basis, was deliberate in their approach to changing the environment and developed the following as goals: establishing study circles, identifying friendly areas and faculty across the university community, increasing research opportunities for Black student scholars, increasing graduate assistantships for Black students, increasing the number of Black students who attended research conferences, and founding a research conference where Black students could present their Afrocentric research agendas. The group, which was established in 1995, continues through the present and has an active listserv that includes the Department's forty-two Black students.

The rise in the numbers of ethnic and racial minorities in adult education graduate programmes began in the 1980s. This expansion followed the national trend that also saw a swell in the numbers of women and all ethnic and racial groups in the ranks of higher education classrooms as the numbers of traditional students declined (Evangelauf, 1992; US Census, 1990). This trend has been apparent not only among students, but also with faculty of colour. In confirmation of this assessment the directory of the Commission of Professors of Adult Education corroborates the growth of people of colour in the field. For most of the 1980s the directory had a maximum of three professors who were members of ethnic and minority groups – three Black professors. In sharp contrast, the 2002 directory lists eighteen Black professors in the field of adult education. Of that number there are two Black professors in the department at the University of Georgia.

Therefore in addition to establishing a better environment for Black students, the department was proactive in recruiting and retaining minority faculty for its own programme and throughout the larger college environment. A review of adult education graduate programmes across the United States sets the university in question apart as being singular in having a stated plan to increase hiring and retention of minority faculty. A tenured White male full professor of adult education led workshops and held lunch meetings for newly hired Black faculty to acquaint them with the intricacies and pitfalls in the academy. The gatherings also functioned as a way to encourage the faculty to form a support network with other Black faculty across the College of Education. Mentoring committees were established for all minority faculty members and this successful approach was later extended to all new faculty hires. The committees, which met with the protégé each term, examined course syllabi, course evaluations, research agendas, and manuscripts. The committees were maintained through the process of promotion and tenure in an effort to ensure that the faculty member was successfully retained.

In summary, the formation of a planned means to affect the recruitment and retention of Black students and faculty positively impacted the learning and teaching environment. Not only did the numbers of students increase in the seven year period examined from two to forty-two, but the numbers of tenured minority faculty in the college increased from four in 1995 to twenty-five in 2003. The presence of Black students and faculty has affected the type of research conducted in the College of Education and in the field of adult education. More projects that represent and examine issues of race have been conducted and the programme discourse has grown to make space for 'other' voices.

A vision and strategies for widening access to higher education

An essential question, as yet unanswered, is how will the increase in discourse and the presence and recognition of other races in the field of adult education affect the quality of the lives of the participants, the practitioners, the researchers, and the literature? Our conviction is that educational institutions cannot continue to follow a colour-blind or multicultural perspective. These views suggest that if we act as if there are no socially organized barriers, the barriers will somehow disappear or that if we learn to truly appreciate each culture, parity will be achieved between all peoples. In contrast to these two beliefs, we are most aligned with the social justice perspective, which asks us to see teachers and learners not as generic individuals but rather as people who have differential capacities to act based on their place in the hierarchies of our social world. Our educational practice must be based on an understanding that the power relationships that structure our social lives cannot possibly be checked at the classroom door. There is no magical transformation that occurs as teachers and learners step across the threshold of the classroom. We need to name the racial barriers that cause some learners to be over-privileged and others to be underprivileged. Thus, we believe that rather than a no-barrier thinking, we need barrier thinking so that we may construct a future where race does not matter.

The most important manifestation of this barrier thinking would recognize that the power and politics of the academy convey a powerful message that appears unheard or unacknowledged by most enfranchised students, but seems obvious to racial minority students. How can we address the politics that shape the experiences of racial minorities who participate in higher education? A three-part strategy is set forth for consideration. First, an examination of the hidden curriculum is tantamount to opening the doors of our minds and the portals of the academy. This involves abandoning a falsely claimed neutral position that only belies favouritism towards certain types of knowledge and groups. It must be understood that students are cast in roles assigned by the positions they occupy in life. If a student has consistently experienced privilege in their life, then the assumption of privilege will be accorded and expected in the classroom. Such a stance of power will advantage them in the classroom environment, encouraging them to participate and negotiate their needs. The student will expect to be respected, listened to, and treated fairly. In direct contrast, a student who has been underprivileged in our society will expect the direct opposite. In our American hierarchical society, the benefactors of abundance and the recipients of dearth are likely to be prescribed by their life positions. Are they of White, Hispanic, Asian, African, or Native American ancestry? Are their families of origin middle-class, working-class, or working-poor? Are they able-bodied? Do they fit in or stand out?

Second, as students and practitioners we must negotiate for a new educational structure that does not reproduce the existing system. Such action requires a commitment to struggle where we stand, as practitioners, administrators, students, and programme directors. This mediation involves an active involvement in all aspects of our academic settings. Instructors must be aware of students' networks and must analyse how their actions as teachers influence those interactions. This negotiation must not remain passive, but should be an active method for changing the political vista. The power inherent in our positions as learners and educators gives us varied platforms from which to effect change. Whatever our positions, we can find ways to work within them to make a difference. Either as a practitioner or a student, we can attempt to find ways to be more inclusive. We can reach beyond the established barriers, whether physical, psychological, or social, by realizing why and by whom they were established.

Finally, in our vision of widening access it is imperative to resist the comfort of acceptance into that inner circle or to resist our exclusion from it. A bi-directional resistant force can be effective in restructuring our educational setting. Being enfranchised makes resistance difficult. It commands rigorous introspection. How do you know if you are part of the problem? If things are comfortable, then your position may be an encumbrance for others. How do you resist from within? Actively resisting from this perspective can involve substantial risks that could result in expulsion from the inner circle, loss of status, and a turbulent praxis. Resisting from the outside entails less risk because the only risk is the distant possibility of acceptance and the possibility of being labelled a troublemaker, a position already in proximity to one's pre-existing marginality.

There are many benefits to be derived from refusing to be silent, from negotiating for change and equity, and for resisting conformity or resisting marginalization. In enacting these strategies, higher education institutions can make a stride towards social justice. Additionally, such actions would establish an inclusive setting that would benefit groups historically excluded and would in turn have a domino effect on changing the spirit of the formal and informal curriculum. Admitting new participants benefits all students by invigorating the educational setting – classroom discussion will change, research agendas will broaden, and the knowledge base will be enhanced. These actions of speaking out, negotiation and resistance are a necessary foray into new territory if we are to effect a welcoming climate for all of those involved.

References

Banks, J. (1997) *Teaching Strategies for Ethnic Studies*, 6th edn, Boston: Allyn and Bacon.

Briscoe, D.B. and Ross, J.M. (1989) 'Racial and ethnic minorities and adult education', in S. Merriam and P. Cunningham (eds) *Handbook of Adult and Continuing Education*, San Francisco: Jossey-Bass.

Broach, T.J. (1984) 'Concerns of Black women and White women returning to school', doctoral dissertation, University of Florida, 1984. Dissertation Abstracts International, 46–03A:0611.

Cross, K.P. (1981) *Adults as Learners*, San Francisco: Jossey Bass.

Cunningham, P.M. (1988) 'The adult educator and social responsibility', in R. Brockett (ed.) *Ethical Issues in Adult Education*, New York: Teachers College Press.

Cunningham, P.M. (1996) 'Race, gender, class, and the practice of adult education in the United States', in P. Wangoola and F. Youngman (eds) *Towards a Transformative Political Economy of Adult Education: Theoretical and Practical Challenges*, DeKalb, IL: LEPS Press.

Evangelauf, J. (1992) 'Separate studies list top disciplines, big producers of minority graduates: earned degrees', *Chronicle of Higher Education*, 38(36), A36–7.

Flannery, D. (1994) 'Changing dominant understandings of adults as learners', in E. Hayes, and S. Colin (eds) *Confronting Racism and Sexism*, San Francisco: Jossey-Bass.

Giroux, H.A. (1997) 'Rewriting the discourse of racial identity: towards a pedagogy and politics of whiteness', *Harvard Educational Review*, 67, 285–320.

Gregory, S. and Sanjek, R. (eds) (1994) *Race*, New Brunswick: Rutgers University Press.

Guy, T. (1996) 'Alain Locke and the AAAE movement: cultural pluralism and Negro adult education', *Adult Education Quarterly*, 46, 209–23.

Guy, T. (1999) 'Culturally relevant instruction for African American adults: African American English (AAE) as an instructional resource for teachers of African American adults', in D. Nitri (ed.) *Instructional Strategies to Enhance Adult Learning*, Detroit, MI: Wayne State University.

Hayes, E. and Colin, S. (eds) (1994) *Confronting Racism and Sexism*, San Francisco: Jossey-Bass.

Johnson-Bailey, J. (2000) *Sistahs in College: Making a Way Out of No Way*, Malabar, FL: Krieger Publishing Company..

Johnson-Bailey, J. (2001) 'The power of race and gender', in R. Cervero, A. Wilson and Associates (eds) *Power in Practice: Adult Education and Struggle for Knowledge and Power in Society*, San Francisco: Jossey-Bass.

Johnson-Bailey, J. and Cervero, R.M. (1997) 'Negotiating power dynamics in workshops', in J. Fleming (ed.) *New Perspectives on Designing and Implementing Effective Workshops*, San Francisco: Jossey-Bass.

Johnson-Bailey, J. and Cervero, R.M. (1998) 'Power dynamics in teaching and learning practices: an examination of two adult education classrooms', *International Journal of Lifelong Education*, 17, 389–99.

Johnson-Bailey, J. and Cervero, R. (2000) 'The invisible politics of race in adult education', in A. Wilson and E. Hayes (eds), *Handbook of Adult and Continuing Education: New Edition*, San Francisco: Jossey-Bass.

Kotinsky, R. (1948) 'Intercultural education', in M. Ely (ed.) *Handbook of Adult Education in the United States*, New York: Teachers College Press.

Locke, A. (1936a) 'Adult education for Negroes', in D. Rowden (ed.) *Handbook of Adult Education in the United States, 1936*, New York: George Grady Press.

Locke, A. (1936b) 'Lessons of Negro adult education', in M. Ely (ed.), *Adult Education in Action*, New York: George Grady Press.

Locke, A. (1948) 'Foreword', in M. Ely (ed.) *Handbook of Adult Education in the United States*, New York: Teachers College Press.

London, J. (1970) 'The social setting for adult education', in R. Smith, G. Aker and J. Kidd (eds) *Handbook of Adult Education*, London: Macmillan.

Margolis, E. and Romero, M. (1998) '"The department is very male, very White, very old, and very conservative": the functioning of the hidden curriculum in graduate Sociology departments', *Harvard Educational Review*, 68(1), 1–32.

Martin, L. G. (1994) 'Ethnicity-related adult education cultural diversity programmes: a typology', in *Proceedings of the 35th Annual Adult Education Research Conference*, Knoxville: University of Tennessee.

McIntosh, P. (1995) 'White privilege and male privilege: a personal accounting of coming to see correspondences through work in women's studies', in M. Anderson and P.H. Collins (eds) *Race, Class, and Gender*, Belmont, CA: Wadsworth.

Merriam, S.B. and Caffarella, R. (1999) *Learning in Adulthood: A Comprehensive Guide*, 2nd edn, San Francisco: Jossey-Bass.

Neufeldt, H.G. and McGee, L. (eds) (1990) *Education of the African American Adult: An Historical Overview*, New York: Greenwood Press.

Osborne, M. (2003) 'Policy and practice in widening participation – a six country comparative study', *International Journal of Lifelong Education*, 22(1), 45–58.

One America in the 21st Century: Forging a New Future (1998) The President's Initiative on Race: The Advisory Board's Report to the President, Washington, DC.

Peterson, E.A. (ed.) (1996) *Freedom Road: Adult Education of African Americans*, Malabar, FL: Krieger Publishing Company.

Rachal, J.R. (1989) 'The social context of adult and continuing education', in S. Merriam, and P. Cunningham (eds) *Handbook of Adult and Continuing Education*, San Francisco: Jossey-Bass.

Rocco, T. and West, G. (1998) 'Deconstructing privilege: an examination of privilege in adult education', *Adult Education Quarterly*, 48, 171–84.

Ross-Gordon, J. (1990) 'Serving culturally diverse populations: a social imperative for adult and continuing education', in J. Ross-Gordon, L. Martin and D. Briscoe (eds) *Serving Culturally Diverse Populations*, San Francisco: Jossey-Bass.

Rowden, D. (1934) 'Adult education for Negroes', in D. Rowden (ed.) *Handbook of Adult Education in the United States*, New York: Adult Education Association.

Sleeter, C.E. and Grant, C.A. (1987) 'An analysis of multicultural education in the United States', *Harvard Educational Review*, 57, 421–44.

Tisdell, E. (1995) *Creating Inclusive Adult Learning Environments: Insights from Multicultural Education and Feminist Pedagogy*, Columbus, OH: ERIC Clearinghouse on Adult, Career, and Vocational Education.

US Government Department of Commerce, Bureau of Census (1990) *Educational Attainment*, Washington, DC: US Government Printing.

Chapter 8

E-learning and access

Getting behind the hype

Jo Barraket[1]

Introduction

Rapid advances in information and communications technology (ICT) – particularly the development of online technologies – have transformed the nature of economic, social and cultural relations across the globe. In the context of higher education in post-industrial societies, technological change has had a significant impact on university operating environments. In a broad sense, technological advancement has contributed significantly to the increasing complexity of global economies and societies, which is reflected in the rise of lifelong learning discourses with which universities are engaging. More specifically, the ever-expanding array of ICT available within the university sector has generated new management and pedagogical imperatives for higher education in the information age.

In recent years, we have seen a simultaneous rise in public discussions around educational access and equity in a number of developed nations. As has been observed, the discourse of lifelong learning has popularised the human capital argument in support of access and equity initiatives. That is, the promotion of access initiatives is now invoked at least in part, in order to maximise developed nations' human capital in the global economy. In the context of higher education in post-industrial nations, then, facilitating accessible use of online technologies through e-learning may be seen as serving two functions. First, it potentially supports entry into education to those for whom geographical or physical impediments limit traditional face to face participation. Second, as tools which potentially enhance students' technological literacy, e-learning may be viewed as equipping them with the skills critical to flexible labour market participation in the information age.

As discussed by Selwyn *et al.* (2001), the rise of technology and lifelong learning discourses in education has provided new impetus for policy makers to address the relationships between social exclusion, technology and education. The growing use of ICT to support learning and teaching in higher education offers both new possibilities and new challenges for facilitating access and equity for all students. The most commonly cited advantages of online learning technologies, for example, are that they overcome the tyranny of distance by providing remotely accessible learning opportunities and new ways of interacting with fellow students and staff, and the tyranny of fixed class times by providing greater opportunities for students to 'learn in their own time'. However, a key concern is the widely recognised division between the information rich and information poor – the so-called 'digital divide' – which has the potential to create disadvantage that mirrors traditional socio-economic inequalities. With regard to online technologies, the digital divide includes issues of physical access to ICT, the technological literacy skills to utilise it effectively, and the relevance and appropriateness of online content.

The discussion contained in this chapter is based on the findings of a federally funded research study conducted at the University of Technology, Sydney (Barraket *et al.* 2000) in 1999–2000. The principal objective of the research was to investigate the access and equity issues associated with the increasing use of ICT in learning programmes at the University. Specifically, the study sought to identify differences in access to, and use of, ICT between students from government targeted equity groups and a control group. While the research explored students' use of both 'old' and 'new' technologies, respondents focused overwhelmingly on their experiences of online learning and information access, and it is these experiences which are the focus of this chapter. The study's findings have implications for conceptualising and researching educational access in the information age. These implications are discussed in detail in the latter part of the chapter.

Methodology

The research was conducted in two phases. In the first phase, a series of focus groups was conducted, in which students from all equity groups and a control group were represented. Student equity groups, as defined by the Australian government are: students of low socio-economic status; Aboriginal and Torres Strait Islander students; students with a disability; students from non-English speaking backgrounds; rural and isolated students; and women in non-traditional areas of study. The control group comprised students who were not part of any equity group.

Twenty-seven students participated in the focus group phase. The information from the focus group study was used to develop an effective survey instrument for phase two, and to provide rich 'snapshot' information on the ICT experiences of a small number of students.

In phase two, a detailed survey was administered to students in 44 classes, representing all faculties and levels of study. The subjects from which classes were selected included those making limited use of online technologies, those using online technologies to supplement face to face learning, and subjects being delivered completely online.

A total of 1,323 completed questionnaires were returned, with an overall response rate of 78 per cent. It is notable that there was a zero response rate from

36 surveyed students participating in subjects delivered solely online. Of the total respondents, 825 were from the control group, 36 were rural and isolated students, 39 were Aboriginal and Torres Strait Islander students, 103 were from a non-English speaking background, 118 were of low socio-economic status, 74 were students with a disability, and 128 were women in non-traditional areas of study. The sampling method used did not ensure representation of every group as a proportion of the UTS student population.

The analysis of the quantitative survey results was based on an interpretation of the descriptive statistics, and unpaired t-tests to determine significant differences between mean responses of students from equity groups and the control group. Qualitative results were subjected to thematic analysis, conducted separately by two members of the research team. Synergies and contradictions between the qualitative and quantitative results were considered.

A significant dilemma in researching the effects of online technologies is the rapidity with which these technologies change and the implications of this for the relevance of research findings over time. It should be noted that, some 12 months after the conclusion of this study, a broad consultation (Aynsley, 2001) was conducted to identify significant organisational changes in the use and management of ICT for teaching and learning purposes. No significant changes were identified at this time.

Conceptualising effective e-learning

As with traditional teaching and learning methods, successful learning using online technologies is contingent on a range of factors which operate in complex interaction with each other. On the basis of the existing literature on ICT use for learning, and current understandings of what characterises high quality learning programmes in higher education (see Alexander and Blight, 1996; Alexander and McKenzie, 1998; Scott, 1999), the research team developed a conceptual framework which predicted that effective ICT use for learning requires the efficient interaction of three elements: ready access to 'front end' infrastructure; appropriate use of ICT as part of a broader learning design; and effective support for these uses by the staff, systems, infrastructure and procedures of the institution. The research findings discussed below supported the validity of this conceptual framework, indicating that access, use and support are all significant, and inter-dependent, determinants of the quality of students' online learning experiences.

Infrastructure and beyond: factors affecting access

The research identified a range of physical, experiential, social, economic, and institutional influences on respondents' access to online learning. The findings indicated that, compared with the control group, students from some equity groups are disadvantaged in their access to ICT for use in their learning programmes.

Some of the key access issues identified by respondents as impacting upon them were: a need for reliable access to on-campus facilities, particularly for students with no other access options; a lack of adaptive technology and modified equipment in mainstream campus facilities for students with particular disabilities; the cost of purchasing, maintaining, and upgrading equipment for students of low socio-economic status; the high costs of internet service providers and dial up fees for rural and isolated students. It was also found that poor levels of information literacy led to a lack of confidence to access available resources by women, older students, students of low socio-economic status, Aboriginal and Torres Strait Islander students, and rural and isolated students. The issue of information literacy is discussed in further detail in a later section of this chapter.

The economic costs of maintaining personal ICT equipment with online capabilities remain considerable in the current Australian context. Our findings that cost was a significant barrier to ICT access and use for students from some equity groups – particularly students of low socio-economic status – are supported by the limited body of empirical work in this area. Costs are also magnified for students with particular disabilities, due to the added expense of purchasing modified hardware and/or adaptive software. Fichten *et al.*'s comprehensive study of the ICT needs for post secondary students with a disability in Canada found that:

> Regardless of what question was asked or how it was formulated, the high cost of acquiring and maintaining computer technologies was the single most important and common issue noted by computer users and non-users alike.
>
> (Fichten *et al.*, 1999: 177)

Proponents of ICT as a means of expanding educational access for students from traditionally disadvantaged groups have tended to skate over this issue, interpreting it simply as a small problem to be overcome, rather than a significant access constraint which disproportionately affects students from some equity groups.

A significant methodological finding of the research described here was that low socio-economic status was most effectively measured as those students who were first in their families to attend university, and who were on a federal government recognised low income. The disadvantages reported by these students were significantly greater than those students who conformed to the measure of socio-economic disadvantage used by the Australian Government (that is, a measure of regional disadvantage via postcode). While this has particular implications for the way in which this equity group is defined by policy makers and researchers, it also illuminates the intergenerational disadvantage faced by students who have limited family and social networks experienced in higher education. For many of these students, reliance upon the services and staff of the university is crucial to educational success, as they lack access to experiential knowledge through their family and social support networks.

Anecdotal information from equity practitioners indicates that Australian universities have sought to respond to the cost barriers to personal ICT use through negotiations with financial institutions to offer low interest student loans, and computer companies to offer long-term lease or repayment schemes. The University researched in this case study has an in-house interest free loan scheme specifically available to students from equity groups for the purchase of computer equipment. However, the low uptake of this scheme suggests that, for those most economically disadvantaged, even interest-free long-term loans are not feasible. In the words of one survey respondent, 'My family lives on government benefits at the moment and it is a real chore just to provide our basic needs such as home, food, clothing, etc.' (26–40-year-old male Aboriginal student of low socio-economic status with a disability).

The issue of equipment costs has significant implications for institutions, as well as the individuals studying within them. It is clear that, currently, the provision and maintenance of ICT is a necessary and spiralling infrastructure cost to universities. Despite ongoing debates about the potential of 'online universities' to expand educational access while dramatically reducing physical participation at university campuses, students are not vacating campuses in droves, and traditional infrastructure requirements remain. Further, the anticipated cost savings of online learning in terms of teaching costs have not been uniformly realised. Many Australian institutions have introduced ICT-based flexible learning options without weighing up the full cost implications, including the skills development required to accommodate shifting roles for academic and general staff, and the real benefits to students.

In Australia, policy makers have acknowledged, but not systematically responded to, the increased costs associated with the effective use of ICT in education (see West, 1998; McCann et al., 1998), and universities have yet to take a unified stand with government on this issue. Our research indicates that, on the ground, lack of reliable and sufficient 'front end' infrastructure is most likely to disadvantage students who need it the most – that is, students with limited or no other access options. Given the rapid advances of ICT, and associated societal expectations of taking up new ICT options, it is unlikely that these inequities will be resolved without the implementation of deliberate and appropriately resourced policy responses.

While economic cost remains a key barrier to equitable ICT access, it is important to note that the cost of home-based technology alone does not determine students' preferences with regard to where they access ICT. Another important issue raised by students from some equity groups – particularly students of low socio-economic status and students with a disability – was the quality of home study conditions. Qualitatively, several students from these groups clarified their responses by explaining that they found university facilities, including the library, more productive study spaces as they did not need to contend with cramped study conditions and/or household demands. For some students with disabilities, the university facilities provided access to adaptive technologies not available in their homes.

A significant implication of the research for university support services (including libraries and other common facilities) is that those students most disadvantaged in relation to ICT are also most reliant on common facilities and support services. Students from equity groups – particularly Aboriginal and Torres Strait Islander students and students of low socio-economic status – also reported significantly greater reliance on public library ICT facilities than the control group. However, these students reported a range of problems with this access option, including high costs of printing in public libraries, insufficient time allocations for computer use, and the need to book computer time days in advance. Qualitatively, these students indicated a greater preference for use of university library facilities, where available and reliable. For Indigenous students who were on block release study programmes and lived in communities remote from the university, regular physical access to the university library was simply not possible.

Information literacy: issues of use and support

While access to front end infrastructure was identified as a significant issue in itself, another key factor affecting students' use of ICT for educational purposes was levels of information literacy. Rigmor and Luke (1995: 1) have defined information literacy as an awareness of the 'kinds of information available, possible sources of this information, and the means of locating and retrieving it', linked to a deeper understanding of the information required in relation to existing knowledge. They point out that information literacy is an important enabler, essential to the pursuit of knowledge, both within and outside formal educational spheres, in the information age. In this sense, the traditional role of librarian as information specialist has shifted, with librarians increasingly being required to teach users their craft in order to facilitate the development of information literacy.

Our research found that students from some equity groups were significantly more likely than other students to enter university with highly limited information literacy skills, and that this lack of information literacy acts as both a deterrent to accessing available ICT resources and a limitation on ICT use. These students reported variously that their experiences of ICT had been constrained by educational disadvantage prior to entering university, by limited exposure to such technologies in their family or social networks and/or by time spent out of the educational system and labour market, where day to day exposure to these technologies is not common.

A number of respondents, particularly older students and women students, and some students of low socio-economic status, commented that they did not use available facilities due to lack of confidence. These students indicated a number of concerns about accessing common ICT facilities, including those housed within the library. These concerns included: embarrassment about having to ask for technical assistance from staff; negative experiences of asking technical and support staff for help; and concern about tying up resources needed by other students for long periods while trying to improve skills. It is clear that poor information literacy limits students' motivations and capacity to access available resources. This creates a 'catch 22' dilemma, as students are deterred from using

ICT due to poor information literacy skills, and cannot improve those skills without regular use of ICT or access to training on it.

There was considerable evidence in the study's results that flexible learning mechanisms, such as 'just-in-time', 'just-for-me' technical training, were crucial in determining students' experiences of online education. However, students from some equity groups noted barriers to taking advantage of the current types of support made available in this area. For example, students with family responsibilities and Indigenous students who study on block release programmes noted the difficulties of accessing training at times appropriate to their study schedules. The experiences of Indigenous students on block release programmes, in particular, illustrated the need for effective integration between course provision and ancillary services for students who are studying in non-traditional modes. Some of these students reported particular concerns about using common computing facilities after hours, which was the only time available to them due to the 'nine to five' intensive nature of their classes. These students were particularly concerned about personal safety issues; particularly, having to negotiate an unfamiliar ICT environment at night.

Another specific issue raised by students from non-English speaking backgrounds and Aboriginal and Torres Strait Islander students was the lack of culturally appropriate training available to them. While not the dominant trend in the research findings, several students from these groups commented qualitatively on negative experiences of culturally insensitive training, which had deterred them from seeking further support. While there are support units within the University studied which are targeted at meeting the specific needs of these two groups, there is no systematic ICT training offered through these units. To the extent that the library is a key provider of such training, and the target units are the source of expertise on culturally appropriate educational support, it is clear that an integrated service model coordinated by these areas could enhance the ICT experiences of some students from these groups.

Knowledge of existing services

As has been discussed above, the effective use of ICT is predicated upon students having adequate access to ICT infrastructure and appropriate levels of information literacy to use the tools available. A related factor which emerged in the research is that there appears to be a correlation between those who are 'information literacy poor' and those who are information poor, generally. That is, students who identified poor information literacy as a barrier to ICT use were also less likely to be aware of the resources available to them within the university or how to access them. This particularly affected students with a disability and Indigenous students. One explanation for this is that students with particular disabilities are proportionately more likely to be studying on a part-time basis, while the majority of Indigenous students at this University study on block release programmes, which involve 'campus intensives', rather than day to day interaction with the

University. These factors negatively impact on students' exposure to informal information networks and university 'information loops'.

The relationship between equity status and lack of knowledge of existing services is not unique to this study. Indeed, effective marketing of services to students from equity groups is an ongoing issue for equity practitioners. The finding does, however, reinforce the need for all support units to address student diversity when marketing their services. A 'trickle up' approach which is targeted at the needs of those most disadvantaged is likely to be the most effective strategy in achieving equitable access for all students.

Policy and research implications for widening access

The findings of this project raise a number of significant implications for researching widening access to e-learning specifically and higher education more generally. These include: recognising the access impacts of University service provision structures; reconceptualising our definitions of 'access'; and the challenges of promoting accessible lifelong learning opportunities to an increasingly diverse student population.

Access impacts of service provision structures

A recurring theme across the research findings was that the equity impacts of online technology use in higher education are significantly affected by the division between 'technology services' and 'access and equity services'. Within the case study University, there was evidence of a range of student support services seeking to address the equity implications of increased ICT use in learning programmes. However, students from specific equity groups reported a number of problems associated with these approaches. One specific example is a small, but qualitatively significant number of respondents commenting on culturally inappropriate technological training from those support services within the University that had high levels of technological expertise, but limited understanding of access and equity issues. Conversely, a number of Aboriginal and Torres Strait Islander students commented on the fact that they felt more comfortable learning within their cultural support unit, but that this was hampered by the lack of technological expertise of staff in this unit (which is, itself, reflective of inequities at the staff level within this University).

Both of these examples reinforce the importance of an integrated service delivery approach to access and equity within the University environment. That is, equity initiatives are most likely to be effective where they are integrated into all support functions within the University, rather than seen as an 'add-on' or designated to the specific realm of equity practitioners.

Reconceptualising 'access'

The research findings emphasise the complexity of access issues affecting online technology use by students from designated equity groups. As discussed above, student experiences reported in this study suggest that effective access to e-learning is not limited to physical access to the necessary technology, but is constituted in a diversity of physical, experiential, social, economic and institutional factors. In addition to the obvious cost barriers associated with regular ICT use, the key obstacle to effective ICT use identified by students from specific equity groups was limited access to technologically competent support networks, both within and outside the university. This illuminates the significance of the intergenerational effects of educational exclusion, which is anecdotally supported by higher education equity practitioners in Australia.

It is important also to note the more general finding that research participants were generally happy with the level of ICT supported learning available, and did not wish to have reduced access to face to face learning opportunities. This has particular significance for students from some equity groups, for whom broader social participation may be limited due to disability or language barriers. In the words of one respondent:

> I wouldn't like there to be much more computer-based learning. It's really important that study is a social event as well as a learning event. I like the balance we have at the moment – where you can come into uni[versity] and study with your friends and get inspired, but also go home and have resources there to do work on your own.
>
> (16–24-year-old female undergraduate from a non-English speaking background)

As mentioned in the methodology section above, it is significant that there was a zero response rate from students participating in subjects that were being delivered solely online. Whilst it is possible that there was a methodological concern which limited responses from this group (for example, concern that online return of surveys would reduce anonymity), the complete absence of responses does seem to suggest a lack of affective ties between this student group and the broader university.

While not a central focus of the project, these findings suggest that social capital – that is, 'those features of social organization, such as trust, norms and networks, that can improve the efficiency of society by facilitating coordinated actions' (Putnam, 1993: 167) – is an important feature of educational participation. Specifically, the research suggests that social capital is both an important determinant of effective educational access and a critical non-tangible asset that university education provides. The research is particularly suggestive of the importance of bridging social capital, or networks between diverse individuals, firms, and groups, in overcoming the sustained effects of intergenerational educational exclusion. As Brown and Duguid have observed more generally:

> People leave [university] not just knowing things but knowing people, and knowing not just academic facts but knowing social strategies for dealing with the world. Reliable friendships and complex social strategies can't be delivered and aren't picked up in classroom hours alone, but they can give a degree much of its exchange value.
>
> (Brown and Duguid, 1996: 10)

It would appear that social capital may be a useful conceptual tool in developing a rigorous research programme in this area. With regard to policy development, the research findings suggest that better understanding the relationship between social capital and educational participation is important if we are to truly progress beyond the 'revolving door' approach to university access and equity in the information age.

Lifelong learning and diversity: challenges to universities

The findings from this research reflect the increasing diversity of university student needs in the information age. This diversity is not limited to the access needs of students from designated equity groups, but encompasses the range of needs of all students who are participating in university education in increasingly flexible modes at different stages of their personal and professional lives. At the same time, student expectations of appropriate access to changing technologies as part of their learning programmes has grown in line with demands for such knowledge in the labour market and the broader society. All of these factors pose significant resource implications for universities, and suggest a growing need for greater flexibility in resource allocation, staff skills and knowledge, and pedagogical development. This case study provides no simple answers, but illuminates in one university environment the growing complexity of organisational and cultural challenges which universities face in the global era.

Conclusion

In a policy analysis of the equity implications of a virtual university in the United States, Gladieux and Swail conclude that:

> there is evidence that the students with the greatest need get the least access [and that] … the most advantaged are most able to benefit from cutting edge technology. Advantage magnifies advantage.
>
> (Gladieux and Swail, 1999: 20)

The research discussed in this chapter aligns with this conclusion. The research findings suggest that it is essential for active steps to be taken to ensure that those who can most benefit from higher education are not further marginalised as they seek to access, use and receive support for ICT-enabled learning in universities. As the digital age unfolds, the central challenge for Australian higher education is to develop the total intellectual, cultural and creative capital of the country. A crucial element of this challenge is to ensure that technology-based flexible delivery serves the diversity of our university communities, so that all may benefit from the opportunities of the information age.

Note

1   This chapter is based on research conducted with Ann Maree Payne, Geoff Scott and Lucy Cameron. Parts of this chapter have been previously published in Barraket, J. and Scott, G. (2001) 'Virtual equality? Equity and the use of information technology in higher education', in *Australian Academic and Research Libraries Journal*, 32(2): 204–12.

References

Alexander, S. and Blight, D. (1996) 'Technology in international education', International Education Conference, Adelaide, South Australia, October.

Alexander, S. and McKenzie, J. (1998) *An Evaluation of Information Technology Projects for University Learning*, Committee for University Teaching and Staff Development and Department of Education, Training and Youth Affairs, Canberra: Australian Government Publishing Service.

Aynsley, D. (2001) *Equity and the use of information and communication technology at UTS: A Follow Up Report*, Equity and Diversity Unit, University of Technology, Sydney.

Barraket, J., Payne, A.M., Scott, G. with Cameron, L. (2000) *Equity and the Use of Communications and Information Technology in Higher Education: A UTS Case Study*, DETYA Evaluations and Investigations Programme (00/7), Canberra: Australian Government Publishing Service.

Brown, J.S. and Duguid, P. (1996) *Universities in the Digital Age* at http://www.parc.xerox.com/ops/members/brown/papers/university.html.

Fichten, C.S., Barile, M. and Jennison, V.A. (1999) *Learning Technologies: Students with Disabilities in Post-Secondary Education*, Office of Learning Technologies at http://www.olt-bta.hrdc-drhc.gc.ca/download/Dawson79160.pdf (accessed May 2003).

Gladieux, L.E. and Swail, W.S. (1999) *The Virtual University Educational Opportunity: Issues of Equity and Access for the Next Generation*, Washington, DC: The College Board.

McCann, D., Nicholson, P. and Stuparich, J. (1998) *Educational Technology in Higher Education*, Department of Education, Training and Youth Affairs Occasional Paper Series, Canberra: Australian Government Publishing Service.

Putnam, R.D. (1993) *Making Democracy Work: Civic Traditions in Modern Italy*, Princeton, NJ: Princeton University Press.

Rigmor, G. and Luke, R. (1995) 'The critical place of information literacy in the trend towards flexible delivery in higher education contexts', Learning for Life Conference, Adelaide, November.

Scott, G. (1999) *Change Matters: Making a Difference in Adult Education and Training*, Sydney: Allen and Unwin.

Selwyn, N., Gorard, S. and Williams, S. (2001) 'Digital divide or digital opportunity? The role of technology in overcoming social exclusion in US education', in *Educational Policy*, 15(2), 258–77.

West, R. (1998) *Learning for Life: Review of Higher Education Financing and Policy*, Canberra: Australian Government Publishing Service.

Chapter 9

Access as more

Issues of student performance, retention, and institutional change

Hunter R. Boylan

Introduction

The major premise of this chapter is that current higher education research in the United States has been shaped by the events that broadened higher education access in the decade of the 1960s. Much of what we do today and much of the research we conduct today in US higher education has its origin in the social unrest and political upheavals that characterized the 1960s. These events brought about legislation that changed the course of American higher education and made access a priority.

A secondary premise of this chapter is that results of higher education research have contributed to making broadened access more meaningful. If educational opportunity is to have meaning for individuals and provide benefits for society, those who take advantage of this opportunity must have a reasonable chance of success. Much of the research that grew out of the 1960s and continues today was designed to provide those who have attained opportunity with the support necessary to become successful in that opportunity.

A tertiary premise is that broadening access has not only changed the research agenda in US higher education, it has also changed what we do in our colleges and universities. When access is broadened, new groups with new voices enter the higher education discussion. The combination of broadened access and research resulting from this access then causes us to revise the way we organize and deliver US higher education.

This chapter begins with an exploration of the impact of desegregation on US institutions of higher education. It continues with a discussion of efforts to make access meaningful by improving the learning skills of nontraditional students. The chapter concludes by exploring the ways in which granting access for nontraditional students has also changed US higher education.

The impact of desegregation

Until the 1960s, higher education in the United States was not only segregated by color it was also segregated by gender and class. The decade of the 1960s witnessed the desegregation of US higher education as well as the redistribution of higher education opportunities. Although people of color in the US were occasionally admitted to colleges and universities in some regions of the country, higher education was still strictly segregated in the south and parts of the southwest until the 1960s. Furthermore, women and the poor of any color were greatly under-represented in US higher education. For most of the twentieth century US higher education was dominated by white males of the middle and upper classes. But social unrest and civil rights advocacy in the 1960s were to bring about federal legislation that would change this situation (Brubacher and Rudy 1976; Cross 1971).

The Civil Rights Act of 1964 and the Higher Education Act of 1965 effectively ended the segregation of American higher education. These acts represented the classic "carrot and stick" approach to solving social problems. The Civil Rights Act made segregation by color or gender illegal. It required colleges and universities to admit applicants without regard to race, gender, age, or religion or suffer the loss of all federal funding to their institution. Because colleges and universities received substantial amounts of federal money from research grants, financial aid, and other subsidies through the Higher Education Act, the potential loss of these funds offered a serious threat. The loss of funding represented the "stick." The Higher Education Act of 1965 provided huge amounts of financial aid to enable the poor to participate in higher education. This provided a substantial pool of funding that higher education institutions could only obtain by increasing access for minorities and the poor. The provision of funding represented the "carrot."

The act also provided money for colleges and universities to offer academic support programmes for minorities and the poor, the very students who had previously been denied access to higher education. The initial Higher Education Act funded the establishment of Upward Bound, Talent Search, and Student Support Services Programmes. The Upward Bound Programme recruited first generation and minority students at the high school level to participate in special academic and cultural programmes that would prepare them for college. The Talent Search Programme identified students with potential who were no longer in a school setting and attempted to place them in an appropriate educational experience. The Student Support Services Programme provided counseling, tutoring, and other support services to first generation and minority students once they arrived in college. Initially, only these three programmes were funded by the Higher Education Act. Because there were only three programmes funded they were generally referred to as "TRIO Programmes." As a result of these and other programmes minorities, the poor, and first generation college students became a valuable commodity in US higher education.

As a consequence of legislation, eliminating discrimination in admission, providing financial aid for the poor, and funding academic support services, enrolment in US colleges and universities not only increased, but it became more diversified. Not only did ethnic minorities represent an increasing percentage of students seeking higher education but the percentage of older adults, women, and poor white students applying to colleges also increased (Cross 1976; Cohen and Brawer 1989). According to Cross (1971) the result was an influx of the so-called new or "nontraditional" college students. In essence, these were students who, previously, had little hope of ever attending college. They were often students who had inadequate high school preparation, who had been out of school for a decade or more, who were the first in their families to seek higher education, or who had performed poorly on standardized tests.

Inadequate social or academic preparation for college was also a factor, which contributed to high attrition rates among nontraditional students in the late 1960s and early 1970s. As Cross pointed out, "open door" admissions policies soon led to the "revolving door" in which nontraditional students were easily admitted and quickly failed (1971). The experience of US higher education in the 1960s and 1970s was that the promise of educational opportunity was not met by access alone.

From access to success

By the end of the 1960s, it became apparent that federal legislation had, indeed, broadened access to higher education in the US. What it failed to do was guarantee that those who had attained access to it would be successful in college. Consequently, although legislation resulted in a more egalitarian higher education system in the US, it also generated a number of policy, teaching and learning, and cultural issues that continue to dominate higher education research. Primary among these issues were activities that promote retention, particularly for nontraditional college students. In order for higher education access to be meaningful, those who have attained access must have a reasonable opportunity to also attain a degree. This is a critical and often overlooked component of access education. The goals of access are poorly served when huge numbers of those who have entered through access programmes fail to complete any portion of higher education.

Although many nontraditional students flourished in higher education as a result of their newly won access, many others failed. As Lavin and Hyllegard (1995) point out, it was not unusual for students entering college through educational opportunity programmes in the 1960s to have attrition rates of 60 per cent or higher. The National Study of Developmental Education found that only 10 per cent of the underprepared minority students entering community colleges had either attained a two-year degree or transferred to a four-year institution within six years (Boylan et al. 1992).

These high attrition rates among nontraditional college students led to increased research interest in the areas of teaching and learning and student retention. The community of higher education scholars and policy makers believed that attrition could be reduced if teaching techniques more appropriate to nontraditional students were discovered and employed. The higher education community also believed that academic and student services could be organized and delivered in ways that would reduce attrition. These beliefs, coupled with the realization that retaining students led to additional institutional profits stimulated considerable research on teaching and learning and student retention. After all, retaining more students simply represented good business practice. It was far more cost effective to retain students who were already on campus than to have to replace those who dropped out with new students (Noel et al. 1985). Furthermore, at public colleges and universities, state subsidies for junior and senior level students were usually higher than for freshmen and sophomores (second year students).

Surprisingly enough, there was very little research on college teaching until the 1960s. Jerome Bruner's 1966 work, Toward a Theory of Instruction, was one of the first to articulate a theoretical approach to college teaching. This was followed by a literal deluge of scholarly work attempting to explain how students learn and how college professors might promote that learning. These works were all part of a chain of scholarly research exploring issues of teaching and learning in an effort to improve the quality of instruction.

A number of other authors were to use this work as a basis for identifying successful techniques for teaching and retaining nontraditional students. As a result of their efforts, we are now aware of a variety of teaching techniques that can promote meaningful access by increasing the likelihood that nontraditional students will be academically successful.

By the beginning of the twenty-first century, this research had solidified into a body of knowledge providing working guidelines for all those involved in educating the nontraditional students who had recently attained access to higher education. It was no longer necessary for personnel in these programmes to have to guess what methods and techniques might be most helpful. There was a substantial amount of research available to guide their efforts on behalf of nontraditional students. Examples of research based approaches to successful instruction for nontraditional students include:

- An emphasis on mastery learning (Bloom 1976; Cross 1976; Roueche and Snow 1977),
- The use of supplemental instruction to support "problem courses" (McCabe and Day 1998; Martin and Arendale 1994; Ramirez 1997),
- The use of frequent testing (Boylan et al. 1992; Kulik and Kulik 1991; Roueche 1973),
- The use of diverse instructional techniques (Casazza and Silverman 1996; Cross 1976; Grubb and associates 1999),
- The teaching of critical thinking skills in the content areas (Chaffee 1992; Halpern 1999; Weinstein et al. 1998),
- The integration of classrooms and laboratories (Boylan et al. 1992; Keimig 1983; Roueche and Roueche 1999),
- The use of holistic learning strategies (Casazza and Silverman 1996; Cross 1976; Higbee and Thomas 1999),

- The use of learning strategies instruction, particularly metacognition (Boylan 2002; Young and Ley 2001; Weinstein *et al.* 1998),
- The integration of study strategies into instruction (Boylan *et al.* 1992; Nist and Holschuh 2000),
- The use of learning communities (Tinto 1997; Tinto 1998; Roueche and Roueche 1999).

The use of these instructional techniques contributes to both higher student grades and higher retention for nontraditional students (Boylan *et al.* 1992; Boylan 2002).

Research in higher education was also directed toward programme organization and policy issues that contribute to the success of nontraditional students. Two generations of research have identified a number of programme components and policies that contribute to the success of nontraditional students. Examples of these include:

- The use of mandatory assessment and placement (Boylan *et al.* 1997; McCabe 2000; McCabe and Day 1998; Roueche and Roueche 1999),
- The establishment of clearly specified programme goals and objectives (Casazza and Silverman 1996; Donovan 1974; Roueche and Snow 1977),
- An emphasis on the orientation of students to the expectations of the institution (McCabe and Day 1998; McCabe 2000; Upcraft and Gardner 1989),
- The centralization of services designed to assist nontraditional students (Boylan *et al.* 1992; McCabe and Day 1998; Roueche and Snow 1977),
- The evaluation of programmes, with particular emphasis on formative evaluation (Boylan *et al.* 1997; Casazza and Silverman 1996; Maxwell 1997),
- The integration of programmes into the mainstream of institutional activity (Keimig 1983; McCabe 2000; Roueche and Roueche 1999),
- An emphasis on professional development for programme staff (Casazza and Silverman 1996; McCabe and Day 1998; Maxwell 1997),
- The adoption of a developmental philosophy to guide programme and institutional activities (Boylan 2002; Casazza and Silverman 1996: Keimig 1983),
- The provision of tutoring by well-trained tutors (Boylan *et al.* 1997; Casazza and Silverman 1996; Maxwell 1997).

Research has demonstrated that the application of these components contributes to the retention of underprepared and nontraditional students (Kulik *et al.* 1983; Boylan 2002).

In the past decade, this research-based knowledge of teaching and learning issues as well as organizational and policy issues has formed the basis of practice for access education in US higher education. Most programmes involved with access education in US colleges and universities rely, at least partly, on the available research to guide their actions and the design of their programmes.

This body of research has, as a result, also transformed the way in which courses are taught, programmes are organized, and services are delivered.

The impact of access on institutional change

The shift to a more egalitarian form of higher education taking place in the 1960s not only impacted upon research on teaching, learning, organizational, and policy issues, it also had an impact on the very nature of US higher education. As higher education became more diverse institutions began to change to accommodate this diversity. This change was not always welcomed by traditional academicians. It was usually accomplished only following frequent and often bitter debates. Nevertheless, by the end of the twentieth century, most colleges and universities in the US had highly diverse populations and engaged in a variety of activities to promote the success of these populations (Cohen and Brawer 1989; Chaney et al. 1998).

The broadening of access brought more diverse students and these students also brought diverse cultures to US higher education. This resulted in the proliferation of student clubs and organizations designed to serve minority interests. Organizations such as Asian, Latino, and African-American student associations, gospel choirs, and multicultural clubs began to appear on college and university campuses and spread throughout US higher education. Alternative student activities in music, art, and culture also became more prevalent (Fleming 1984).

Nontraditional students brought their cultures with them to academe and these cultures often conflicted with that of their institutions. After all, the types of music listened to by middle aged white college professors were dramatically different from those listened to by African-Americans from the ghettos or Hispanics from the barrios. So, too, the visual and performing arts, recreation, and social activities. Minority and other nontraditional access students were often confronted with a choice of abandoning their own culture or becoming isolated within their institutions. This difference in culture and the consequences of this difference was seen as one of the primary reasons for the attrition of minority and access students. The higher education research community responded to this situation with increased research designed to understand how institutions could accommodate nontraditional students. This research suggested that institutions needed to:

- place greater emphasis on multicultural awareness throughout the college campus (Fleming 1984; Richardson and Skinner 1991; Smith 1997),
- maintain data on the performance of minority students (Astin 1992; Richardson and Skinner 1991; Richardson et al. 1992),
- include multicultural materials in the curriculum (Astin 1993; Vilalpando 1994),
- provide specific support services designed to assist ethnic minorities (Nora and Cabrera 1996; Richardson and Skinner 1991; Smith 1997),

- promote the mentoring of minority students (Pope 2002; Lavant *et al.* 1997),
- use noncognitive assessment to improve understanding of the academic needs of minority students (Anderson 1989; Higher Education Extension Service 1992; Sedlacek 1986), and
- develop specific plans for improving the quality of campus life for minorities (Richardson and Skinner 1991; Richardson *et al.* 1992; Smith 1997).

As a consequence of these research findings, higher education institutions began to place greater emphasis on multiculturalism, revise the content of the curriculum, and develop more services designed to assist minority and nontraditional access students. The resulting efforts enabled US higher education to become increasingly multicultural not only in the students it served but also in the services provided and in what was taught in the curriculum. It was also to become more diverse in terms of its faculty, staff, and administrators.

As the US undergraduate population became more diverse in the 1960s and 1970s, so too did the graduate population in the 1970s and 1980s. In spite of high attrition rates among nontraditional students, many of them still completed their undergraduate work and went on to earn doctoral degrees. As more nontraditional college students graduated and pursued advanced degrees, more of them also joined the American professoriate. Between 1990 and 1997, for instance, the percentage of minority faculty in US higher education institutions increased from 11.3 per cent to 13.4 per cent (Chronicle of Higher Education 2000). Their presence in academic departments and institutional governing bodies provided an expanded base of support for changes in academe designed to accommodate women, minorities, and other nontraditional students.

As faculty in US higher education became more diverse nontraditional voices entered the discussion of research in higher education. As women became more prevalent among faculty members, feminist perspectives became more influential in the research community. Not only did women's issues become legitimate subjects of higher education research but the way in which these issues were studied was also influenced by the feminist perspectives (Banks and Banks 1993; Donato and Lazerson 2000).

Ethnic minorities also joined the ranks of faculty, establishing and legitimizing research interest in ethnic and cultural studies. Women's studies, ethnic studies, and African-American or Latino studies programmes proliferated on the campuses of US universities (Banks 1993). This not only led to more diversification in research topics, it also added a new perspective to the way in which research was viewed. The influence of women and minority scholars led to a debate over the very methodology to be employed in research (Grant and Sleeter 1986; Glazer-Raymo and Shepard 2000; Tayak 2000).

The traditional research paradigm of US higher education and in higher education throughout the world in the twentieth century had been quantitative. It emphasized the use of experimental design, control and comparison groups, and statistical analysis of data to make predictions or validate theories (Campbell and Stanley 1966). In the 1970s and 1980s, new voices in the research community argued that quantitative research had limitations that often caused researchers to draw the wrong conclusions from their data (MacMillan 1996). These voices argued for increased use of qualitative research methodology. Qualitative methodology emphasized the use of oral histories, interviews, observation, and case studies to enhance understanding and provide contextual meaning (Boylan et al. 2000).

For much of the 1980s and 1990s, debate over these two research methodologies flourished at conferences, in the academic literature, and even in the popular media. For the most part and with few exceptions, at US institutions, this debate had white male faculty on one side and women and minority faculty on the other. The debate in the higher education research community was often referred to as the "paradigm wars" as both sides attempted to establish the supremacy of their methodological approaches. Eventually, the paradigm wars were resolved with what seemed to all a reasonable compromise. Researchers began to agree that both quantitative and qualitative methods were necessary to provide a complete understanding of any issue under exploration. Quantitative methodology could be profitably used to define and describe phenomena. Qualitative methodology could be equally profitably used to assign meaning and enhance understanding of these phenomena.

This led to a dramatic increase in the number of qualitative studies attempted and also in the number of such studies published in the literature. The result is that contemporary research in US higher education has become about evenly mixed between the two methods. Furthermore, researchers often collaborate to apply both methods in exploring issues in higher education.

A further result of the presence of nontraditional voices in the US higher education research community has been the proliferation of revisionism, particularly in historical, sociological, and psychological research. This history is now being revised to include the views of women, Hispanics, African-Americans, as well as the impact of policies implemented by the predominant (white) culture (Tayak 2000). The revisionist perspective has engendered a new debate about the nature and purpose of higher education in the US. It is likely that this perspective will continue to influence the higher education debate in the twenty-first century.

Conclusion

Higher education in the US has journeyed toward access and diversity as a result of social, political, and legislative events taking place in the 1960s. That journey shifted the dominant perspective of US higher education from the traditional philosophy of elitism toward a philosophy of egalitarianism. In essence, US higher education moved from a model for exclusion of women, minorities, and other nontraditional students to a model for inclusion. In the process, the research agenda of higher education changed to support this shift in philosophy and promote inclusion through access.

A great deal of higher education research in the US has served as a tool to promote access and diversity. Instruction for nontraditional students and the organization of programmes serving them has been greatly advanced through research. In many ways, higher education research has become a driving force in broadening access. It also helped make access meaningful by ensuring that we know how to help access students take advantage of the opportunities provided to them.

An unexpected result of broadening access to higher education, however, has been a change in the very nature of the higher education endeavor in the US. The research originally designed to improve instruction for nontraditional students has improved instruction for all students. The research originally designed to improve the retention of nontraditional students has improved retention for all students. The research originally designed to help us understand the cultures of nontraditional groups has established their cultures as a permanent fixture in the landscape of US higher education. In the process, US higher education has changed and with this change has come a change in the topics, issues, and methodologies employed in research.

As a result of all these factors, higher education professionals in the US have discovered that access invites change. When the student body we serve changes, the ways in which we serve the students must also change. When we change the way we serve students, we also frequently make fundamental changes in the nature of our higher education institutions.

References

Anderson, J. (1989) 'How to teach across cultures', paper presented at the Conference on Cultural Literacy in Professional Education, Sea Island, GA.

Astin, A. (1992) *Assessment for Excellence*, San Francisco, CA: Jossey-Bass.

Astin, A. (1993) *What Matters in College: Four Critical Years Revisited*, San Francisco, CA: Jossey-Bass.

Banks, J. (1993) 'Multicultural education: historical development, dimensions, and practice', *Review of Research in Education*, 19(1), 3–49.

Banks, J. and Banks, C. (1993) *Multicultural Education: Issues and Perspectives*, Boston, MA: Allyn and Bacon.

Bloom, B. (1976) *Human Characteristics and School Learning*, New York: McGraw-Hill.

Boylan, H.R. (2002) *What Works: Research-based Best Practices in Developmental Education*, Boone, NC: Continuous Quality Improvement Network/National Center for Developmental Education.

Boylan, H., Bliss, L. and Bonham, B. (1997) 'Programme components and their relationship to student performance', *Journal of Developmental Education*, 20(3), 2–9.

Boylan, H., Bonham, B., Claxton, C. and Bliss, L. (1992) 'The state of the art in developmental education', paper presented at the First National Conference on Research in Developmental Education, November, Charlotte, NC.

Boylan, H., Bonham, B., White, J. and George, A. (2000) 'Evaluation of college reading and study strategy programmes', in R. Flippo and D. Caverly (eds) *Handbook of College Reading and Study Strategy Research*, Mahwah, NJ: Lawrence Erlbaum Associates.

Brubacher, J. and Rudy, W. (1976) *Higher Educational Transition: A History of American Colleges and Universities, 1636–1976*, New York: HarperCollins.

Bruner, J. (1966) *Toward a Theory of Instruction*, New York: McGraw-Hill.

Campbell, D. and Stanley, J. (1966) *Experimental and Quasi-experimental Designs in Research*, Chicago, IL: Rand-McNally.

Casazza, M. and Silverman, S. (1996) *Learning Assistance and Developmental Education*, San Francisco, CA: Jossey-Bass.

Chaffee, J. (1992) 'Critical thinking skills: the cornerstone of developmental education', *Journal of Developmental Education*, 15(3), 2–8.

Chaney, B., Muraskin, L., Calahan, M. and Goodwin, D. (1998) 'Helping the progress of disadvantaged students in higher education: the federal student support services programme', *Educational Evaluation and Policy Analysis*, 20(3), 197–216.

Chronicle of Higher Education (2000) 'The Nation: employment in colleges and universities', 1 September, 38.

Cohen, A. and Brawer, F. (1989) *The American Community College*, San Francisco, CA: Jossey-Bass.

Cross, K.P. (1971) *Beyond the Open Door*, San Francisco, CA: Jossey-Bass.

Cross, K.P. (1976) *Accent on Learning*, San Francisco, CA: Jossey-Bass.

Donato, R. and Lazerson, M. (2000) 'New directions in American educational history: problems and prospects', *Educational Researcher*, 29(8), 4–15.

Donovan, R. (1974) *Alternatives to the Revolving Door: Report of FIPSE National Project II*, Bronx, NY: Bronx Community College.

Fleming, J. (1984) *Blacks in College*, San Francisco, CA: Jossey-Bass.

Glazer-Raymo, J. and Shepard, L. (2000, December) 'Representation, voice, and inclusion: AERA in the year 2000', *Educational Researcher*, 29(9), 15–20.

Grant, C. and Sleeter, C. (1986) 'Race, class, and gender in education research: an argument for integrative analysis', *Review of Educational Research*, 56(2), 195–211.

Grubb, N. and associates (1999) *Honored but Invisible: An Inside Look at Teaching in the Community College*, New York: Routledge.

Halpern, D. (1999) 'Teaching for critical thinking: helping college students develop the skills and dispositions of a critical thinker', in M. Svinicki (ed.) *Teaching and Learning on the Edge of the Millennium: Building on What We Have Learned, New Directions in Teaching and Learning*, No. 80, San Francisco, CA: Jossey-Bass.

Higbee, J. and Thomas, P. (1999) 'Affective and cognitive factors related to mathematics achievement', *Journal of Developmental Education*, 23(1), 8–17.

Higher Education Extension Service (1992) *The Academic Performance of College Students: A Handbook on Research, Exemplary Programming, Policies and Practices*, New York: Teachers College, Columbia University, Higher Education Extension Service.

Keimig, R.T. (1983) *Raising Academic Standards: A Guide to Learning Improvement*, ASHE/ERIC Report # 3, Washington, DC: Association for the Study of Higher Education.

Kulik, J. and Kulik, C.-L. (1991) *Developmental Instruction: An Analysis of the Research*, Boone, NC: National Center for Developmental Education.

Kulik, J., Kulik, C.-L. and Schwalb, B. (1983) 'College programmes for high risk and disadvantaged students: a meta-analysis of findings', *Review of Educational Research*, 53(3), 397–414.

Lavant, B.D., Anderson, J.L. and Tiggs, J.W. (1997) 'Retaining African-American men through mentoring initiatives', in M.J. Cuyjet (ed.) *Helping African-American Men*

Succeed in College (43–54). New Directions for Student Services, Number 80, San Francisco, CA: Jossey-Bass.

Lavin, D. and Hyllegard, G. (1995) *Changing the Odds: Open-admissions and the Life Changes of the Disadvantaged*, New Haven, CT: Yale University Press.

MacMillan, J. (1996) *Educational Research: Fundamentals for the Consumer*, New York: Harper-Collins.

McCabe, R. (2000) *No One to Waste: A Report to Public Decision-makers and Community College Leaders*, Washington, DC: Community College Press.

McCabe, R. and Day, P. (1998) *Developmental Education: A 21st Century Social and Economic Imperative*, Mission Viejo, CA: League for Innovation.

Martin, D. and Arendale, D. (1994, Winter) *Supplemental Instruction: Increasing Achievement and Retention*, New Directions for Teaching and Learning, Number 60, San Francisco, CA: Jossey-Bass.

Maxwell, M. (1997) *Improving Student Learning Skills*, Clearwater, FL: H. and H. Publishing.

Nist, S. and Holschuh, J.P. (2000) *College Rules: How to Study, Survive, and Succeed in College*, Toronto: Ten Speed Press.

Noel, L., Levitz, R. and Saluri, R. (1985) *Increasing Student Retention*, San Francisco, CA: Jossey-Bass.

Nora, A. and Cabrera, A. (1996) 'The role of perceptions of prejudice and discrimination on the adjustment of minority students to college', *Journal of Higher Education*, 67(2), 119–48.

Pope, M.L. (2002) 'Community college mentoring: minority student perceptions', *Community College Review*, 30(3), 31–45.

Ramirez, G. (1997) 'Supplemental instruction: the long-term effect', *Journal of Developmental Education*, 21(1), 2–10.

Richardson, R. and Skinner, E. (1991) *Achieving Quality and Diversity: Universities in a Multicultural Society*, New York: Macmillan Publishing Company.

Richardson, R., Mathews, D. and Finney, J. (1992, June) *Improving State and Campus Environments for Quality and Diversity: A Self-assessment*, Denver, CO: Education Commission of the States.

Roueche, J. (1973) *A Modest Proposal: Students Can Learn*, San Francisco, CA: Jossey-Bass.

Roueche, J. and Roueche, S. (1999) *Remedial Education: High Stakes, High Performance*, Washington, DC: Community College Press.

Roueche, J. and Snow, G. (1977) *Overcoming Learning Problems*, San Francisco, CA: Jossey-Bass.

Sedlacek, W. (1986) 'Black students on white campuses: 20 years of research', *Journal of College Student Personnel*, 19(3), 242–8.

Smith, D. (1997) *Diversity Works: The Emerging Picture of How Students Benefit*, Washington, DC: Association of American Colleges and Universities.

Tayak, D. (2000) 'Reflections on histories of US education', *Educational Researcher*, 29(8), 19–20.

Tinto, V. (1997) 'Classrooms as communities: exploring the educational character of student persistence', *Journal of Higher Education*, 68(6), 599–623.

Tinto, V. (1998) 'Learning communities and the reconstruction of remedial education in higher education', paper presented at the Conference on Replacing Remediation in Higher Education, January, Palo Alto, CA: Stanford University.

Upcraft, P. and Gardner, J. (1989) *The Freshmen Year Experience*, San Francisco, CA: Jossey-Bass.

Vilalpando, O. (1994) 'Comparing the effects of multiculturalism and diversity on minority and white students satisfaction in college', paper presented at the Association for the Study of Higher Education Conference, November, Tucson, AZ.

Weinstein, C., Dierking, D., Husman, J., Roska, L. and Powdrill, L. (1998) 'The impact of a course in strategic learning on the long-term retention of college students', in J. Higbee and P. Dwinnel (eds) *Preparing Successful College Students*, Columbia, SC: National Center for the First-Year Experience and Students in Transition.

Young, D. and Ley, K. (2001) 'Developmental students don't know that they don't know: bridging the gap', *Journal of College Reading and Learning*, 31(2), 171–8.

Chapter 10

After access

Researching labour market issues

Ewart Keep

Introduction

The function of this chapter is to review the main bodies of evidence on economic demand for graduates and what returns accrue to investments in higher education (HE), the strengths and weaknesses of these different strands of research, and the somewhat different stories that they tell. The bulk of the research covered here relates to England or the UK as a whole, but where relevant, mention is made of distinctive research relating to the other three nations that make up the UK.

Two points need to be made at the outset. First, given the vast body of material that is now available on this topic, this chapter can only review representative examples of the main categories of research. It cannot hope to be encyclopedic in coverage, nor to engage with many of the more detailed aspects of the debates that surround this research.

Second, it is important to note the centrality of labour market data to the case for expansion of the higher education system in the UK. The stated reasons given by governments for more graduates are twofold: to boost international economic competitiveness/productivity; and to promote social inclusion/justice/mobility. The second reason only has force if there is a labour market payoff from obtaining a degree. Therefore, if the demand is not there, or does not meet expected levels, the implications for all the actors – government, employers, students and their families, teachers and academics, schools, colleges, and universities – will be serious and unpleasant.

A third reason is sometimes deployed (though in the UK usually not by government or policy makers). This revolves around the need for better-educated citizens and the benefits of education as an end in itself. The English Secretary of State for Education and Employment has offered his view that such wider non-economic benefits are 'over-rated', and the Department for Education and Skills (DfES) has claimed that, 'universities exist to enable the British economy and society to deal with the challenges posed by the increasingly rapid process of global change' (*The Guardian*, 9 May 2003). Plainly this type of argument thus carries limited weight with the present government, and for it to have greater force it is probable that a very different pattern and type of HE provision would be required.

In terms of structure, what follows reviews in turn the following bodies of research on labour market issues: international comparisons, rate of return analysis (private and public), labour market demand (current and projected), surveys of graduate career trajectories, and evidence on graduate utilisation in employment.

International comparisons

There is a long-standing tradition of undertaking international comparisons of workforce qualification levels. Such research can then be deployed to underpin the case for greater investment in skills in order that we match our international competitors.

There are a number of problems with this type of evidence. Comparing like with like in terms of qualifications across countries is difficult. Second, comparing stocks of qualifications in national workforces tells one very little about the economic effect to which they are being put. Simple comparisons of this type fall into the 'arms race' trap whereby having a higher qualification stock than other countries is, like having more Dreadnaughts or ICBMs, argued to be a good thing in itself (Keep and Mayhew, 1996). The counter-argument is that skills only matter if they can be put to productive use.

The evidence on the linkages between stocks of skill and economic performance is extremely complex (see Keep *et al.*, 2002). At best, higher levels of skill may be a necessary but not sufficient precondition for improved performance. Thus, in the 1980s Japan's high levels of participation in higher education and the success of its economy were often adduced in support of improvements in UK participation rates. Rather less is heard from policy makers these days about Japan. It still has a very high participation rate, but its economy is no longer a model to be copied.

The second set of problems with international comparisons is that the different surveys and forms of comparison produce widely varying figures even for the UK in terms of the proportion of the population or workforce that have reached Level 4. Thus O'Mahoney and deBoer (2002) arrive at a figure of 15.4 per cent of the UK workforce for the year 1999, whereas data from the Labour Force Survey used by Wilson (2001) suggest 24 per cent of the UK workforce possessed a Level 4 qualification by 2001.

In making international comparisons, the focus is often on participation rather than completion rates. The latter produces a very different overall ranking for the UK's performance than the former. In the white paper *The Future of Higher Education* (DfES, 2003), the claim is made that English participation rates in HE are lower than in many other developed countries (Sweden, Norway, Australia, the Netherlands, and Finland are cited), though no mention is made of the fact that English rates are still well above the OECD average. However, as Westwood and Jones (2003) point out, in terms of graduation rates Office of National Statistics figures suggest that, in 1999, the UK as a whole had the highest graduate rate from first degrees of any European Union country, at 37 per cent (ONS, 2002) – a fact confirmed by IES/OECD, 2002. Given these variations, different official reports have in the recent past concluded that our stock of Level 4 skills a) exceeds, b) equals, or c) is lower than that of rivals such as Germany and France.

There is also a tendency by policy makers to focus on qualification gaps between England/UK and competitors at one level, while not mentioning England/UK's superior performance at another. For example, the UK is often compared unfavourably with the USA in terms of proportions of the workforce which have achieved degrees/Level 4, while ignoring our superior relative performance at Level 3. In comparisons with Germany, we are shown to trail in craft and technician training at Level 3, without mention being made of our (at least according to some figures) much better performance at Level 4.

Rates of return

Rates of return have been the main tool by which economists have chosen to illuminate the benefits that accrue to those who gain access to HE. There are two forms of analysis: that which relates to the returns that accrue to the individual (private), and that which relates to society at large (social returns). These are dealt with in turn below.

Rates of return (private)

Individual rates of return are calculated by comparing earnings foregone (and other costs incurred) in undertaking study with the extra lifetime earnings that the student obtains over and above what s/he would have earned if they had not gone into HE. Sometimes non-wage benefits (such as the cultural benefit of having studied a degree) are factored in.

All recent major UK studies show individual rates of return to be positive, and to be holding up well despite the expanding supply of graduates. Dearden *et al.* (2000) suggested a 28 per cent return to male graduates and a 25 per cent return to females. However, although the average rate of return appears to remain high, the dispersion of earnings benefits across the graduate population also appears to be growing – some degrees, for some people, appear to produce much better returns than others. Returns appear to vary (often quite considerably) according to gender, subject, class of degree and institution (Conlon and Chevalier, 2002). Average figures are hence misleading.

Unfortunately, there are a number of difficulties with and limitations upon the evidence on private rates of return. Many of these are technical and complex, and readers with an interest in these issues are directed to Keep *et al.* (2002) and Aston (2003). To begin with the data produced is backward looking, and past performance is not a guarantee of future returns, particularly in the longer term and with reference to what will increasingly be a fundamentally different labour market. High levels of participation have been with us for only a relatively short time. The likely cumulative impact of entry to the labour market by successive large cohorts of graduates is hard to read (see below for details).

Second, there is a fundamental problem in calculating rates of return because of the lack of an adequate comparator or control group. Put simply, the earnings of graduates may not be being compared with those of non-graduates of similar ability. Given that nearly all of those who attain two A levels (or their equivalent) now proceed into HE, the control group available is rather small. One oft-quoted DfES statistic compares the earnings of all graduates with those of all non-graduates and announces that a degree is worth an extra £400,000 over a working lifetime (see Aston, 2003 for details). This may not be a particularly useful comparison.

The other two difficulties relate to the fact that the higher earnings of graduates may (in part) reflect the use of HE as a screening or signalling device, whereby employers use a degree as a sign that people have ability and are willing to work and learn in a structured fashion. HE may not be adding to an individual's store of useful skill, merely signalling that they have certain characteristics (that one could argue were really certified by their achieving two A levels (or their equivalent) in order to get into HE in the first place).

Credentialism is simply the possibility that, all other factors being equal, employers, given the choice, will tend to choose the best qualified candidates that present themselves, irrespective of whether the job really requires that level of qualification. As people with higher levels of credential occupy the better jobs they tend to earn more than those with lower levels of credential who come to be confined to lower level employment. In this respect it is interesting to note that in the USA the relatively high rates of return recorded on a college education reflected not rising wages for college graduates (these remained more or less static), but falling real wages among blue collar workers lower down the job ladder (Lafer, 2002).

Finally, rate of return analysis provides no direct data to support the English government's latest emphasis on Foundation Degrees as the main focus for the future expansion of HE. As Foundation Degrees are new, there is no longitudinal data available to indicate what return they might generate. Evidence on the returns to the most likely comparator qualifications (HNDs/HNCs) suggests a much lower likely return than on a three-year honours degree – 15 per cent for men, 9 per cent for women (Dearden et al., 2000). Perhaps rather unsurprisingly, enthusiasm among prospective students for Foundation Degrees appears somewhat muted.

Rates of return (social)

These can be dealt with more briefly. The social rate of return to producing a graduate is held to be the social value of the extra output that a graduate produces as a result of being made more productive by virtue of their education, plus a range of less tangible benefits (social externalities), such as the notion that better educated people make better citizens. Some economists go further on the intangible benefits of education, arguing that it produces endogenous growth in the economy (for a useful review of this literature, see Gemmell, 1997).

The theory is relatively straightforward. The problem comes in producing credible and accurate measures of social returns. The value of extra productivity cannot be simply observed and something has to act as a proxy. The something is normally wages. Thus, for calculations of social rates of return to have much utility, wages need to directly reflect individual productivity and to be influenced by no other factors. This is rarely the case. Years of industrial relations research has indicated that, irrespective of skill level, other factors, such as age, gender, and occupation, have a very significant impact. Even within the same occupation there are often large disparities of income that do not appear to be related to the individuals' levels of qualification or human capital (Lafer, 2002). Relative wages may not directly reflect relative productivity.

Social returns are normally used to help justify additional state expenditure on HE. As Keep *et al.* (2002) point out, leaving aside whether the figures arrived at have much meaning or are accurate, there is an unfortunate tendency to consider the rate of return to investment in HE in isolation from similar rates of return analysis for other forms of education (for example, adult basic skills). As they note, 'set against such criteria it is far from clear that spending on higher education would come out as well as spending, for example, in junior schools or sub-degree post-16 education' (Keep *et al.*, 2002: 10).

Labour market demand – estimates and projections

One strand of labour market focused research has sought to investigate the existence of shortages and mismatches in the supply of graduates in particular sectors or disciplines (usually science-based). Mason's work on chemistry graduates (1998) and engineering, science and IT graduates (1999) are good examples. His research suggests that many of the problems employers are reporting stem from problems with the quality rather than the quantity of graduates leaving the HE system.

There is also a well-established body of research that examines current labour market demand for various levels and types of qualification, often via very large-scale surveys of employers, and which also tries to forecast future demand. These forecasts are generally based on complex economic models of growth in the economy, the trends of occupational and sectoral growth or decline, and factors such as technical change. Major examples of this approach include *Skills In England 2001* (Campbell, 2001; and Campbell *et al.*, 2001).

In seeking to make a case for further expansion, the English government has placed a heavy reliance on a particular reading of elements of the data generated by this type of research. Thus, the DfES in its white paper on *The Future of Higher Education*, pronounced that, 'demand for graduates is very strong, and research shows that 80 per cent of the 1.7 million new jobs which are expected to be created by the end of the decade will be in occupations which normally recruit those with higher education qualifications' (DfES, 2003: 16).

Unfortunately, this is not what the research shows. The oft-quoted 80 per cent figure (which comes from *Skills in England, 2001* – Campbell, 2001) actually relates to, '4 in 5 of the new jobs being at least at NVQ level 3, or equivalent, by the end of the decade' (Campbell, 2001: 7). In other words, the projections suggest that there might be a need to expand Level 3 (craft/technician/associate professional) education and training, rather than more degrees. There is a huge difference (the difference between A levels and an honours degree) between Level 3 and Level 4 (with associated implications for the costs of appropriate provision).

The other side of the picture is that the figures endlessly quoted by ministers are for new jobs. They do not count in the people who will be needed to fill jobs from which incumbents leave or retire. Campbell notes:

> The volume of replacement demand that is likely to be required, and thus the relevant skills that go with them, may well be around 5 times as great as the volume of 'new' jobs and the skills that go with them.
>
> (Campbell, 2001: 9)

As Table 10.1 indicates, once replacement demand is factored in the picture on future labour market growth in terms of the five largest growing occupations looks somewhat different.

Three other points might be noted about these forecasts of employer demand. First, insofar as these forecasts are influenced by employer statements about what they would want to recruit, they reflect 'cost-free' demand whereby employers can require an ever more highly qualified set of new workers at no direct cost to themselves. Would employers' projections of future recruitment remain the same if they were told that for each new graduate they recruited they had to pay the state £2,000 as a contribution towards the cost of HE? Employers, rather than train, may be seeking to pass more and more skill formation costs onto the state via the education system.

Second, survey evidence suggests that individuals' perceptions of the qualifications needed to do their current jobs are much lower than one might expect.

Table 10.1 Projected demand by SOC sub-major group 1999–2010

Occupations	Replacement Demand	Expansion Demand	Net Requirement
Elementary occupations (clerical and services related)	+ 1,327	– 154	+ 1,172
Administrative and clerical occupations	+ 1,178	+ 160	+ 1,338
Sales occupations	+ 939	+ 172	+ 1,111
Caring personal service occupations	+ 673	+ 471	+ 1,144
Managers/proprietors in agric/services	+ 649	– 151	+ 498

Source: Wilson (2001)

The second Skills Survey (Felstead et al., 2002) found that in 2001 only 13.4 per cent of respondents from a representative sample of the UK labour force felt that they were using a degree level qualification in their current job (i.e. they needed it to get the job and it was essential or fairly essential to carry out the work competently). If non-degree Level 4 qualifications were added in, the figure rose to 22.7 per cent of the sample, as compared to 16.2 per cent in 1986.

Finally, it is interesting to note that, despite being held up as both *the* leading knowledge driven economy and as the country from which our model of 'massified' HE is largely being borrowed, official US forecasts of future demand for graduates are lower than perhaps might be imagined (particularly by UK commentators and policy makers). Hecker's projections (2001) indicate that by 2010, no more than 21.8 per cent of jobs in the US labour market will require a bachelor's or higher degree.

These figures are less surprising when trends in occupational change in the US labour market are taken into account. While seven out of the ten fastest growing occupations in the US between 2000 and 2010 will require a degree or associate degree (nearly all these occupations are bound up with ICT), they are growing from a low base. Of the ten occupations showing the largest projected growth over the same period there are just three that will require a degree or associate degree. Of the others, six will need short-term on-the-job training and one medium-term on-the-job training. The fastest growing of these jobs will be 'combined food preparation and serving workers, including fast food' (see Brown, 2003: 172–3 and Brown et al., forthcoming, for a much fuller exposition).

Surveys of graduates' career trajectories

One of the most influential approaches to researching this area has been a series of survey-based studies that examine graduates' early career histories and trajectories since leaving HE, and which provide data on a range of topics, including employment status (employed/unemployed), earnings, employment type, job satisfaction, progression, and participation in further education and training (Elias and Purcell, 1999; Purcell et al., 1999). A separate study covering Scottish graduates has been produced (Elias and Purcell, 2001). A recent follow-up study is currently being prepared for publication.

This approach provides a very useful supplement to the rather narrow economic data that individual rate of return analyses generate. Although backward looking, the studies suggest that, to date, most graduates are extracting a premium in the labour market from their skills and that graduates are moving out of initial jobs that might be non-graduate type employment, into 'traditional' graduate jobs. For example, among a sample of graduates from Scottish HEIs, over the period July 1995 to November 1998, the proportion of the sample in 'traditional' jobs increased from under 30 per cent to around 60 per cent (Elias and Purcell, 2001). Three and a half years into employment, about 52 per cent of English and Welsh graduates in the sample considered themselves to be in jobs where a degree was required and used, and a further 17 per cent in jobs where the qualification was not required but being used.

More generally, the *Moving On* studies suggest that the boundaries between graduate and non-graduate employment opportunities is, at least in the eyes of young graduates, relatively fuzzy and indistinct. Over time, the research suggests that there tends to be a general convergence of career paths, as careers are established and graduates are able to move up and out of first or second jobs that may not have required a degree towards jobs that have a higher skill content.

Studies of graduate usage by employers

The survey approach focusing on the perceptions of young graduate labour market entrants themselves (as used by the *Moving On* studies) has been complemented by a range of other attempts to see how graduates are recruited, what kinds of jobs they enter, and what impact their employment has on their own earnings and progression and on the performance of the firms and sectors that employ them. Overall, what this research demonstrates are massive variations in the penetration by occupation and sector of graduates within the UK labour market and very different approaches by firms to how they use a more highly qualified workforce.

Mason's investigation of graduate usage in the steel industry, banking, retail, computer services, and transport and communications (Mason, 1995 and 2001) is one of the best examples of this type of approach. In some sectors (e.g. steel and computer services) Mason found that employers were making good use of the skills of graduates (in both traditional graduate jobs and non-traditional ones), with signs that graduates in non-traditional jobs could 'grow the job' in order to add value. In other sectors, particularly retailing, some graduates appeared to occupy jobs that did not require their skills. Job upgrading, where it was taking place, appeared to be of two types. First, a one-off, permanent upgrade of some types of job (such as customer service, clerical and admin posts); and second, temporary job upgrades largely instigated by the job holder as a way of securing internal promotion or getting out into the wider labour market.

Both the *Moving On* studies and Mason (2001: 55) suggest that, over time, graduates entering jobs that do not really require degrees are able to move upwards and outwards, into jobs that do. However, there may be a question mark over whether this trend can be sustained if underlying growth in the labour market of jobs that require graduate skills or can use them to add competitive advantage do not expand as fast as the supply of graduates. It could be argued that most professions, and some sectors and occupations have reached saturation point, and that graduates will not be able to move up into them, but instead will spend their entire working lives in much lower level occupations.

This is a point explored in Hepworth and Spencer's (2002) extremely useful study of the regional dispersion of knowledge-intensive employment within Great Britain. In illuminating the oft-forgotten spatial inequalities within and between

British regions in terms of the types of employment on offer, the study has some interesting examples of regions where the supply of graduates is massively outstripping the local demand for new graduate labour. Graduates either migrate out of the region, or take jobs that would previously have been occupied by school leavers.

Hepworth and Spencer argue that this problem will not vanish. Outside of lowland Scotland, London and the South East of England, the private sector knowledge-intensive economy is small and often growing slowly. For example, between 1994 and 2000 knowledge-intensive employment in the North East grew by between 1 and 2 per cent, while the proportion of graduates in the workforce rose by 17 per cent (2002: 18). In a world of 50 per cent age cohort participation, the outputs of HE will have to move into the less knowledge-intensive sectors, sectors in which in 2000 graduates made up less than 15 per cent of the workforce but which accounted for 49.5 per cent of all GB private sector employment (e.g. hotels, restaurants, retailing). It is open to question how graduates will be used productively or to add value in shopfloor jobs in, for example, mass market retailing given the product market strategies, job design and management hierarchies that often pertain there.

Some of these difficulties are illustrated in Rodgers and Waters' (2001) study of graduates entering associate professional occupations (insurance underwriters, legal executives, estate agents, market researchers and personnel officers). Associate professionals represent 14 per cent of expected employment growth to 2010 (Wilson, 2001) but as Rodgers and Waters report:

> The growth in the number of graduates employed in associate professional occupations has been driven largely by the increase in the supply of graduates … rather than being caused by an increase in demand from employers for graduate type skills. There was no significant evidence to suggest that employers now require new entrants into associate professional positions to possess graduate level types of skills – there are incidences of under-utilisation of graduate skills … graduates often enter associate professional occupations as an interim measure whilst trying to secure 'graduate' employment. There is no direct evidence to suggest that graduates are getting work experience that then allows them to progress into traditional graduate roles either in the firm in which they are currently employed or elsewhere in the labour market.
> (Rodgers and Waters, 2001: 3–4)

Finally, research into the process of graduate recruitment has tended to be thin on the ground. A major forthcoming study by Brown et al. helps to remedy this lacuna, at least in terms of how large, 'blue chip' organisations seek to select entrants to their 'fast track' graduate training schemes. These jobs represent the 'glittering prizes' of early twenty-first century employment in the UK, and are consequently highly sought after – one organisation in Brown et al.'s study received over 14,000 applicants for just 400 places.

Besides exploring how and why recruitment systems are structured to try and winnow the 'wheat' from the 'chaff', the research argues that in a world where the supply of suitably qualified and employable candidates far exceeds the number of good jobs the result is massive and increasing positional competition among candidates, and that this in turn has a major impact on how individuals perceive themselves, their skills and their own identities. Many of the consequences are far from benign. For example, competition tends to encourage acquisitive learning (learning in order to collect qualifications in order to enter the competition for good jobs) rather than inquisitive learning (learning out of interest and for its own sake). The rules of the contest are also heavily skewed against 'outsiders' as a range of types of social capital play an increasingly important part in differentiating between equally well-qualified candidates. Thus, Brown *et al.* found that candidates applying from Oxford University were 29 times more likely to be appointed to a job than someone applying from a 'new' (post-1992) university.

Conclusions

The fate of those for whom access is impossible

One of the greatest weaknesses of research into the interaction between graduate supply and labour markets and the economy, indeed of more general research and debates on access in a mass higher education system, is the scant regard that is often paid to the wider impact of expansion on other forms of education and training provision, and upon those who will not be destined, even in an expanded system, to enter degree or sub-degree level study. If education qualifications act as positional goods in a zero-sum game form of competition for a limited supply of 'better/good' jobs in the labour market (Brown, 2003), expanding the supply of graduates may both intensify competition between them for access to a finite stock of good opportunities, and, at the same time, further reduce the opportunities (not least for progression) for those who do not possess degrees. Expanding access to HE may create new winners, it may also create new losers (those who do not get in). Visions of what will be on offer to the 'bottom half' – the 50 per cent not destined for HE – remain very vague.

Different strands, different stories

As this chapter has sought to outline, the different strands of research on the prospects for and returns to graduates who enter the labour market reach very different conclusions. Some elements, such as those on rates of return, and the *Moving On* studies, are optimistic about the future and suggest that further expansion is both relatively unproblematic and beneficial (to individuals and the economy). Other strands, such as future labour market projections, work on graduate recruitment systems for elite graduate jobs, and assessments of how different sectors and localities are absorbing and utilising graduate labour, offer a much more varied, nuanced and less rosy picture. As with so many other areas of academic research on education and training, the tendency is for the different research traditions to pursue parallel courses, with remarkably little attempt at dialogue and synthesis between the different strands. This is an enormous missed opportunity. In the short to medium term probably the single most useful step the research community could take would be to try to bring together the different bodies of evidence and thrash out what they can and cannot tell us, and to attempt to reconcile their widely varying conclusions about the utility of mass HE and who stands to gain and to lose from it.

The impact of research on policy

The evidence base for current policies of yet further expansion of higher education is, at best, patchy. For example, there are many factors and areas for which no evidence is available (for example, the returns to Foundation Degrees). Moreover, some of what evidence is available is weak, partial or open to a wide range of very different interpretations from which no one simple, consistent picture emerges.

Unfortunately, policy makers have chosen to disregard evidence that contradicts or undermines simple participation targets, and to fixate on getting people into the HE system, rather than asking harder questions about how this relates to underlying demand in the labour market, and what expansion may achieve in the long term, both for those who go through HE and, perhaps more importantly, for those who do not. The evidence base for current policies is thin. Given what we know, there are grounds for thinking that a serious debate about the real benefits of a 50 per cent target might be justified. Instead, the debate is about how to achieve the target, not whether it makes any real sense.

References

Aston, L. (2003) *Demand for Graduates: A Review of the Economic Evidence*, Oxford: Higher Education Policy Institute.

Brown, P. (2003) 'The opportunity trap: education and employment in a global economy', *European Educational Research Journal*, 2(1), 142–80.

Brown, P., Hesketh, A. and Williams, S. (forthcoming) *The MisManagement of Talent: Employability, Competition and Careers in the Knowledge-Driven Economy*, Oxford: Oxford University Press.

Campbell, M. (2001) *Skills in England 2001 – The Key Messages*, Nottingham: DfES.

Campbell, M., Baldwin, S., Johnson, S., Chapman, R., Upton, A. and Walton, F. (2001) *Skills in England 2001 – Research Report*, Nottingham: DfES.

Conlon, G. and Chevalier, A. (2002) *Rates of Return to Qualifications: a Summary of Recent Evidence*, London: London School of Economics, Centre for the Economics of Education.

Dearden, L., MacIntosh, S., Myck, M. and Vignoles, A. (2000) 'The returns to academic, vocational and basic skills in Britain', *DfEE Research Report*, RR192, Nottingham: DfEE.

Department for Education and Skills (2003) *The Future of Higher Education*, London: DfES.

Elias, P. and Purcell, K. (1999) *Moving On: Graduate Careers Three Years After Graduation*, Manchester: Careers Service Unit.

Elias, P. and Purcell, K. (2001) *Scotland's Graduates ... Moving On (A New Horizon Report)*, Glasgow: University of Strathclyde and the Industrial Society.

Felstead, A., Gallie, D. and Green, F. (2002) *Work Skills In Britain 1986–2001*, Nottingham: DfES.

Gemmell, N. (1997) 'Externalities to higher education: a review of the new growth literature', *NCIHE Report*, No. 8, London: National Committee of Inquiry into Higher Education.

Hecker, D. (2001) 'Occupational employment projections to 2010', *Monthly Labor Review*, 124(11, November), 57–84.

Hepworth, M. and Spencer, G. (2002) *A Regional Perspective on the Knowledge Economy in Great Britain*, London: Department of Trade and Industry.

Institute of Employment Studies/Organisation for Economic Cooperation and Development. (2002) *Education at a Glance 2002*, Paris: OECD.

Keep, E. and Mayhew, K. (1996) 'Economic demand for higher education – a sound foundation for further expansion?', *Higher Education Quarterly*, 50(2), 89–109.

Keep, E., Mayhew, K. and Corney, M. (2002) 'Review of the evidence on the rate of return to employers of investment in training and employer training measures', *SKOPE Research Paper*, No. 34, Coventry: University of Warwick (SKOPE).

Lafer, G. (2002) *The Job Training Charade*, Ithaca: Cornell University Press.

Mason, G. (1995) 'The new graduate supply-shock: recruitment and utilisation of graduates in British industry', *NIESR Research Report*, No. 9, London: National Institute of Economics and Statistics.

Mason, G. (1998) *Change and Diversity: The Challenges Facing Chemistry Higher Education*, London: Royal Society of Chemistry and the Council for Industry and Higher Education.

Mason, G. (1999) 'The labour market for engineering, science and IT graduates: are there mismatches between supply and demand?', *Department for Education and Employment Research Report 112*, Sudbury: DfEE.

Mason, G. (2001) 'Mixed fortunes: graduate utilisation in service industries', *NIESR Discussion Paper*, No. 182, London: National Institute of Economic and Social Research.

Office of National Statistics (2002) *Social Trends*, London: ONS.

O'Mahoney, M. and deBoer, W. (2002) *Britain's Relative Productivity Performance: Updates to 1999 – Final Report to DTI/Treasury/ONS*, London: National Institute of Economic and Social Research.

Purcell, K., Pitcher, J. and Simm, C. (1999) *Working Out? Graduates' Early Experiences of the Labour Market*, Manchester: Careers Services Unit.

Rodgers, R. and Waters, R. (2001) 'The skill dynamics of business and public service associate professionals', *Department for Education and Skills Research Report 302*, Nottingham: DfES.

Westwood, A. and Jones, A. (2003) *FE UK: Productivity, Social Inclusion and Public Sector Reform*, London: Work Foundation.

Wilson, R. (ed.) (2001) *Projections and Qualifications and Occupations 2000/2001*, Coventry: University of Warwick (Institute of Employment Research).

Part II

Methodological issues

Chapter 11

Participatory paradigms

Researching 'with' rather than 'on'

Ramón Flecha and Jesús Gómez

Introduction

In this chapter we will discuss communicative-dialogic social research. Dialogic research goes beyond both the positivist theories of early modernity and the post-structuralist 'theories' of postmodern perspectives, as it is based on dialogue and information exchange among researchers and researched social agents. It arises from the dialogic turn in our societies, in which dialogue becomes a critical ingredient in helping to define our lives. Family and personal relations, the crisis in traditional organisations, the search for new and more direct ways of participation and the pursuit for the international implementation of human rights are increasingly being approached through dialogue.

The shift towards a more dialogic and communicative society has been identified by the most referenced authors in contemporary social sciences (Habermas 1984, 1987; Beck 1992; Touraine 1997). This orientation, which places human agency at the core of social action, is increasingly shaping the processes of knowledge creation within the social and educational sciences. By the same token, research into these fields is also turning towards dialogue, with social scientists such as Beck *et al.* (1994) calling for the de-monopolisation of expert knowledge.

Dialogic societies need dialogic research investigations that are able to analyse the changes that are taking place. In this chapter, we present the communicative paradigm and methodology developed in CREA (Centre for Social and Educational Research), of the University of Barcelona, as a research paradigm that responds to the increasing importance of dialogue in today's societies.

Dialogic research for dialogic societies

Our societies are becoming increasingly more dialogic. This refers to practices that are based on communication and reaching agreement among people in order to understand given aspects of our lives and societies and to co-ordinate strategic actions (Beck-Gernsheim *et al.* 2003). While people have always had and continue to have such communicative and dialogic skills, today's Information Societies offer the opportunity to extend these practices to broader social environments.

Dialogue is permeating social relations. In different social spheres, within the public and private, it is used as a form of resolving problems and decision making. An analysis of these dialogic dynamics, and how they help generate dialogic theories, has been considered as the 'fundamental task of sociological theories for the 21st century' (Flecha et al. 2003).

This new reality appears in diverse contexts. The new types of families, for example, coincide with the practices that are transforming intimacy, which lead to the need for institutions to recognise ways of life that were formerly invisible. This creates a framework for interaction between social practices and systems. While in the first half of the twentieth century marriage was guided by strict gender roles and age, today these roles are negotiated (Beck and Beck-Gernsheim 1995). We can say, based on Giddens, that there is a system of interrelationships in the family that are based on agreement and consensus, more than the old system of rights and obligations. In this reference, our societies are generating values that are increasingly dialogic, whose transformations must be analysed (Giddens 1992).

In the business sphere, there is a trend towards a more flexible, egalitarian and democratic organisation, new forms of managerial organisation and direction. With regard to the State and public administration, the European Union, in its objectives and policies, is setting out new dimensions to add to the traditional structures of governance, which are tending towards citizen participation and active citizenship (EC 2002a). Dialectic relationships between the local and the global, the public and the private, etc. have marked profound changes in the forms of deliberation, decision making, co-operation, and, ultimately, mechanisms for dialogue. In addition, numerous groups and social movements have come on the public scene and have become new and potent contexts for public discourse, capable of organising a large percentage of the population.

The spread of the Information and Communication Technologies (ICTs), the establishment of a fully global economy and the consolidation of a process of cultural change, have resulted in a series of social structural transformations that have given rise to a new social model: the information society. In this context the ICTs present new possibilities for expression, action and the creation of social capital. The tremendous mobilising capacity that social movements are demonstrating today is directly linked with the use and extension of these ICTs, especially the Internet (as in the recent global mobilisation against the war in Iraq) (Flecha and Tortajada 1999; Flecha et al. 2003). They have an unprecedented potential for extending our dialogic societies, even on a worldwide scale, so that the democratisation of the Internet is seen to play a significant role in the move towards a more dialogic society.[1]

Dialogic dynamics in our societies affect different social spheres and are generated through very varied mechanisms (technological, intersubjective, etc.). In this way, they make up a significant exponent of the new relational, partici-patory, institutional, inclusive and dialogic paradigms, which transcend the scientific, academic, political and institutional spheres, transversally penetrating a wide social spectrum. For this reason, it is crucial for the social sciences to offer appropriate theories and proposals to the problems posed by today's social realities. In order to keep apace with these demands, social science research should be as dialogic as society is. The role of social sciences must be, precisely, to offer appropriate theories and proposals posed by today's social realities. As a result, education and a significant part of social research today are faced with a dual task: to assure equal access to knowledge for all, as well as to reflect on forms of knowledge that have remained invisible in the academic spheres, but are equally valuable and useful for resolving social problems.

The communicative paradigm in research

In a world in which globalisation and the communication and information tech-nologies make us all aware of other practices and cultural contexts, our everyday ways of living and former certainties are questioned. Thus, we face both newness and tradition in a more open, plural and reflexive way. Human agency has become aware of its role in building social reality (Habermas 1987; Giddens 1990).

On the basis of a dual conception of society, the communicative methodology puts much weight on interactions between the systems and the 'lifeworld'.[2] This conception helps to recover the situations in social practice that are a result of non-academic abilities and recognises the capacity of human agency to transform social reality, not stopping at an analysis in which individuals are victims or mere reflections of structures. Finding the mechanisms by which social subjects dialogue with structures, provides researchers with a powerful tool to promote the demo-cratisation of societies in today's globalised world. According to this perspective, we have abilities to interact with other individuals, be social subjects, using language and communication to mediate with the social structures. An analysis of the dialogic and participatory dynamics that are led by social movements and citizen participation today illustrates the extent to which this is true.

These subjects are not merely self-interested, strategic agents, as in the tradition of methodological individualism. They are social subjects capable of language and action (Habermas 1984). This helps us to understand people's capacity for transforming their lives and helping to shape history (Freire 1997). Furthermore, it also explains their demands for science to provide them with the tools to support and carry out transformations. Social movements are turning to, and calling for, theories that are socially useful, that is, theories that help in the creation of social change.

Recognising the role and potential of human agency today means radically changing the perspective of most social science research, bringing social agents back onto centre stage. The communicative methodology is based on the direct participation of the people whose reality is being studied throughout the whole research process, so that the research becomes the result of the plurality of voices, disciplines and genders that interact and interpret reality within a common framework. This makes it possible to detect problems, add precision to and compare interpretations between researchers and researched, on equal terms and with scientific rigour.

In contrast, some perspectives assert the need for some distance between the researcher and the people who are researched, in an attempt to offer a fully external and rigorous observation of social facts. These perspectives maintain that the neutrality of scientific language is the only way to approach social reality, in this way missing the richness of the human lifeworld, the space that is shared by all people and still uncharted ground by the social sciences.

Any social researcher who aims to penetrate the lifeworld needs to turn to pre-theoretical knowledge, like any other person does in a process of mutual understanding. This interaction links 'communicative' or 'dialogic' researchers and the participants in the research project. If the researcher maintains his/her interpretation of a subject's action as the objective reality, a *relevant methodological gap* is opened in the research (Habermas 1987). The absence of the subject's interpretation would make it impossible to be truly faithful to reality, given that the researcher cannot be the only one in possession of the truth with regard to the cultural and social actions carried out by people. In this reference, dialogic research overcomes this *gap* by advocating for the joint construction of objective reality by both the researcher and the researched. Therefore, this perspective lays the ground for the creation of a space for listening to the contributions, interpretations and analysis of the people who are living the reality studied in the research.

Here lies the main difference between the communicative paradigm and other participatory paradigms, for example, action research, with which it is sometimes confused. The communicative paradigm is the only one that advocates for the joint interpretation of reality by both researchers and the researched on an equal basis. Despite the fact that other approaches take into account the voices of the researched subjects, they maintain the researcher's role as expert, considering his or her interpretations more valid due to his or her position of power. On the other hand, this also means a significant difference from methodologies based on constructivist conceptions. According to constructivism, each and every researched individual builds his or her own and unique meaning of a given reality, so that meaning creation is considered to be an individual process in which the interactions among subjects are not taken into account.

Our work is based on social research that offers scientific knowledge and methodologies that incorporate people's voices, with the aim of providing elements that favour overcoming the social exclusion they face. The communicative paradigm in research takes into account the centrality of dialogue and participation in the construction of knowledge, and does not prioritise the accumulation of information, but its use and results. Drawing on people's capacity to interpret their own reality and to create culture (Flecha 2000), dialogic research provides deep and critical reflexive insights. This is in line with social scientists' observations on forms of knowledge that have been overlooked by the academic world and that, once incorporated in communicative research, allow us to reach new results in a more rigorous and socially relevant scientific process.

Researching 'with': characteristics of CREA's work

Our social research is guided by the aim of affording theories that are socially useful. That is to say, in addition to describing our social reality, we seek to contribute to the creation of elements that help to transform reality. We have been able to meet this challenge through interdisciplinary and interinstitutional research.

The dialogic research methodology allows us to hear the voices of the excluded groups and individuals that we research with, thus linking theory and practice. We recognise that it is not possible to have rigorous theories without a direct connection to practice, in the same way that it is unlikely to have good practices that are not linked with theories. Dialogic research is grounded in exchanges with different disciplines, institutions and people living the realities we are researching. Research based on the communicative perspective brings together influences that are more than the sum of the contributions. Above all, it presents a fertile ground for providing new, innovative and viable proposals for overcoming social inequalities and exclusion.

Interdisciplinarity and interinstitutionality

Our research team (CREA) at the University of Barcelona, is characterised by the many influences and experiences our members bring to the work. There are people from different disciplines from the social sciences (sociology, education, psychology, economics, political science, ...), educational experiences, cultural and ethnic backgrounds, ages, genders, sexual orientations and so forth. A closer look at the members from CREA, at the University of Barcelona, illustrates this diversity. Josep is a Professor of Sociology at the University. His experiences as a former school drop-out and his struggle to re-enter the educational system through Adult Education are as significant as those of Lucas, a Roma who is co-ordinating the Centre for Gypsy Studies. Manuel is a disabled person, who is also professor and former dean of a school. Dion is an African immigrant who is currently assistant researcher in a research investigation on immigration and the labour market in Spain. This multiplicity of views and life experiences comes together to form a rich basis from which to do research aimed at a common goal: to contribute to opening up education to all those who have traditionally been excluded and to provide elements for overcoming social inequalities.

Over the years we have also established ties with specialists from different universities, departments and disciplines, collaborating on research projects and exchanging information. These exchanges and collaborations that we maintain nationally have led to the organisation of seminars and conferences, creating spaces to share work, ideas, create joint proposals and new interdisciplinary and interdepartmental networks. Interdisciplinarity matched with interinstitutionality not only provides a rich learning process for everyone involved, but allows for the creation of complex and far reaching theories.

On the other hand, our links with entities and organisations help us to keep ourselves firmly connected to the community and to social and educational practices. Collaboration with them allows us to maintain an ongoing relationship with the groups and collectives within the community that are committed to overcoming educational and social inequalities. Three organisations in the field of adult education that CREA collaborates with on widening access are the following: CONFAPEA is the Confederation of Associations of Participants in Cultural Associations and Adult Education that has been working on gaining educational rights for all; REDA is a network of democratic adult education practitioners who exchange information and work collaboratively to promote an inclusive and social model of education; Group 90 is a group of university professors that works for developing and supporting democratic educational conditions and practices.

Working with the agents in social movements that are leading dialogic and participatory dynamics in society allows us to make specific theoretical contributions to educational and social theory that arise directly from the field of Adult Education. These have led to and support very concrete and practical actions being carried out in adult learning centres and associations today (De Botton et al. 2003). This demonstrates that the link between research and social movements provides an exchange that multiplies the possible proposals in order to transform the face of Adult Education.

What characterises our work within CREA and with all of these associations that we collaborate with is a dialogic and egalitarian way of functioning. The foundation for these collaborations is based on sincerity and solidarity around a common goal: working to provide recommendations for educational and social change (Habermas 1987; Flecha 1996). This enhances and multiplies the work that is produced. This points to the need to overcome the hierarchies of university departments in order to produce research that is relevant, viable, and cross-cutting in terms of disciplines and social factors (gender, race, socio-economic, ethnic, cultural ...).

Communicative methodology

We depart from the premise that social research must not only commit to the coherence between theory and practice in research, but also recognise that it is the most effective way of detecting and analysing specific phenomenon in society today. In many cases, communities at risk of exclusion are objects of a series of research investigations that, once they are concluded, do not benefit the community. Many of these projects do not take into account people's ability to understand their realities, to highlight the relevant information and, thus, contribute to the resolution of social problems that affect them.

Our premise is that people know their reality and have the capacity to reflect on and analyse it, as well as to formulate proposals to improve their situations. Therefore, in dialogic research, the key element of the process from the onset to the very end of the project is the egalitarian participation of the people who are the target population. In this, there is also the recognition that people carry out dialogic and communicative practices in social reality, which help them to transform their personal and social realities. In our theories and methodological approaches we attempt to identify these communicative practices, and thus promote them.

We pay close attention to the analysis of situations, phenomena and interactions that create barriers to people's inclusion in certain practices or exclusion from social benefits (exclusionary factors) as well as to those that overcome or help to overcome these barriers (transformative factors). The distinction between the notions of *factors* and *variables* helps us to provide an analysis of exclusionary factors that detect the nuances of social situations and create an opening for identifying transformative actions. Thus, we have identified variables like age, sex, ethnicity, culture or socio-economic background that have traditionally been used as justifications for setting up obstacles to people's social inclusion; that is to say, these variables have been repeatedly interpreted as exclusionary factors. However, from the communicative perspective, we have been able to establish that these same variables can be exclusionary or transformative factors, depending on how individuals interpret and deal with them in their lives.

Starting from this conceptual difference, we are able to see, for example, the Romaní family (oftentimes automatically interpreted as a burden that hinders Romi[3] from attending school) with different lenses. For certain Romi, the family represents the possibility for continuing their education, having set up arrangements in which relatives or the husband provides childcare as well as moral support. It is precisely the ongoing dialogue, shared interpretations and consensus with the participants from the target groups that help us to move away from any readings based on researchers' possible prejudices, or preconceived notions. In this case, it allows us to better understand the complexity of Romaní people's lives, and social realities in general.

The communicative methodology allows us to provide the conditions to truly collaborate with the subjects who are living the realities we are interested in researching. This is defined by intersubjective egalitarian dialogue and consensus. Furthermore, the dialogic procedures inherent to communicative research techniques reject any power claims that participants (researchers and researched) might turn to in the research. This principle permeates the whole research process from its onset to the very end. Thus, researchers and participants are equally aware of the purpose of the research and the information needed to carry it out. These factors allow all contributions, motivations, and interpretations to be represented, and for all subjects of the research, both researcher and researched, to become active agents committed to the work. The fruit of this process is a more reflexive and rigorous analysis.

The guiding principles of dialogic research are based on the following premises (Gómez 2001):

- The *universality of linguistic competencies* affirms that we all have linguistic communicative abilities, and thus, we are all capable of interacting through dialogue.

- The *person as a transformative social agent* recognises people's ability to reflect on and interpret their reality, create knowledge and build their own practices, having an impact on or modifying the social structures.

- *Communicative rationality* determines the process of understanding as well as action. There are the reasons that motivate an action and the rationality of the interpretation of these actions by the interpreter.

- *Common sense* is based on our life experience and consciousness, which is generally developed within the context we grow up in. It is essential to recognise people's common sense to be able to interpret the reasons for an action, because, people might have different interpretations.

- *Disappearance of an interpretative hierarchy* recognises that people's ontological presumptions can have just as much validity, or more than those of the research team.

- The *possibility of objective knowledge* is central to communicative research, because through an intersubjective analysis on the basis of validity claims, 'researchers' and 'researched' jointly reach an agreement on interpretations.

- In a communicative process there is *no methodological inequality*; the researcher lets go of the role of observer and interpreter participating like any other in speaking as well as listening on equal terms.

- *Objectivity as intersubjectivity* breaks with the notion that arises from the natural sciences that was adopted by the social sciences equating people with objects. Through intersubjective dialogue, researcher and researched reach agreements on what is objective, both acting as subjects in the search for answers to scientific and practical questions.

Communicative organisation

Our research with traditionally excluded groups in society is providing contributions that are helping to shape investigations on an international and national level. In Workaló,[4] the direct participation of the Gypsy Community from the onset of the project has provided rich reflections and analyses. This is also the case of AMAL,[5] but with respect to the immigrant community in Spain, especially Arab and Muslim. The needs and interests of the communities that are the target of the research are the guiding point of our joint research.

Egalitarian dialogue and consensus set the stage for bringing together all the different forms of knowledge and contributions, which arise from the multicultural composition of our research team and the research groups of the projects, our joint work with entities and associations and the spaces of interaction. The objectives and development of the research are agreed upon between the participants of the target communities and researchers. This happens in spaces where all the interpretations are valued on the strength of an argument, not the status of the speaker. Thus, an objective view of reality is reached intersubjectively from the richness of the different rational perspectives.

For this purpose, Workaló has created an 'Advisory Panel', which is made up of (individuals or members of organisations) Gypsy and non-Gypsy individuals. This Council offers its knowledge to a multicultural group of researchers, for the revision of documents, orientation and control of the development of the project in line with the objectives that were stipulated, and evaluation throughout the process, including the assessment of the social utility of its results. The Advisory Panel has provided very innovative analyses about the labour market and the Gypsy Community. A document is not considered to be complete without the agreement and contributions of these members of the research project. The results have significant implications. We have been able to incorporate the untapped potentials of this community, demonstrating that they have skills that meet the requisites of the new occupational profiles. Such results are helping to open the scope of possibilities for the labour and educational inclusion of the Gypsy Community. This process is also taking place in AMAL, where the results of the quantitative methodology were revised by immigrants, who have been contributing to new and interesting conclusions.

The organisation of research is done by creating operative work groups, that are specific and flexible. Each group has concrete tasks, which are later brought together in the plenary meetings. In these sessions there is an analysis and debate about the documents, materials are created and proposals are defined that will be presented to the Advisory Panel.

Communicative techniques

Supported by a communicative organisation and principles, communicative techniques involve an egalitarian and dialogic interaction with the agents of the target community. This implies that the researched people know the aims of the investigation and why they have been chosen to participate in it, so that they can undertake an interaction with the researcher on an equal basis. In order to assure the joint interpretation of reality by both researchers and researched, it is essential to carry out a second meeting after the implementation of any technique. In this second meeting, both parties agree on the interpretations made from the information gathered, so that they avoid biased explanations and confirm the validity to the conclusions.

Communicative or dialogic research does not deny the use of any technique, but its methodology, as we have seen, involves a concrete way of implementing them. Below, we briefly describe some of the communicative techniques that we have developed in different educational and socio-economic projects:

- In the *communicative observation*, researchers and participants share and argue meanings and interpretations of actions, events and situations on equal terms, contrasting the information obtained with the subjects that are observed. So for example, in the observation of a marketplace for the Workaló project, after each observation the researcher discussed their impressions with the person observed.

- *Communicative discussion groups* are made up of natural groups that participate jointly in an activity, in which these techniques are implemented with a trusting and comfortable exchange. In contrast to the traditional discussion groups, both the researcher and the participants adopt an attitude of speaker and listener, who dialogue about situations. Interpretations are argued with the intention of reaching a consensus.

- *Daily life stories* are conversation-narrations that the researcher maintains with the participant, about daily life and in relation to the theme of the research.

In this way, we can deepen our interpretations and understanding about people's actions and ways of resolving real and possible conflicts. The participants in the research can have diverse characteristics (different profiles, lifestyles, and so forth), depending on the objectives of the investigation. However, in the development of any communicative techniques, described earlier, there is an egalitarian dialogue established in which the importance lies in making joint interpretations through intersubjective dialogue, rather than the differences between the individuals.

In addition to these qualitative techniques, we have found that communicative quantitative techniques, like questionnaires, for example, are also very valid and useful. In the AMAL research (mentioned earlier), the questionnaires that we used were elaborated with the participation of immigrants, in order to ensure that it meets their needs, uses the appropriate vocabulary, etc. In this way, the dialogic approach does not imply a constraint on the use of particular methods. It is possible to combine quantitative and qualitative communicative techniques, or in other cases, only qualitative communicative techniques might be used, depending on the characteristics of the research that is carried out.

Conclusions

We have been able to experience that a dialogic and egalitarian way of functioning sets the ground for collaborations that are based on sincerity and solidarity in our work around a common goal: to contribute to educational and social change. Therefore, we call for a move away from the hierarchies which characterise many of our universities towards the dialogic dynamics that are helping to redefine our societies today. Our aims in widening access research demand a shift in research dynamics, in order to produce proposals that are relevant, viable, and cross-cutting in terms of disciplines and social factors (gender, race, socio-economic, ethnic, cultural, …).

On a European level the European Union (EC 2002b) is defining a series of objectives to guide the future of social research. In light of this, the research that is going to be funded is focused on European needs, interdisciplinarity, inter-institutional cooperation, emphasis on networks of excellence and a combination of basic-applied research. The dialogic approach and communicative methodology incorporate these elements, contributing to increasing participation, widening access and guaranteeing the social utility of the research.

In this sense the work developed in CREA characterised by interdisciplinarity and interinstitutionality, as well as the development of the communicative methodology, favours direct participation in the research process of people facing the issues that are the object of the study. These characteristics are also creating the conditions that favour egalitarian terms for this participation. The close collaboration with entities and social movements, and thus the link between theory and practice, contributes to the definition of effective and useful forms of identifying and analysing social phenomena in today's societies. In this way, the inclusion of the voices of groups that have traditionally been excluded from research is making it possible to guarantee the elaboration of quality scientific work aimed at social transformation. This makes it viable to respond to the new challenges of our globalised societies.

Notes

1 Learning Communities is a social and educational project developed in the Basque Country, Catalonia and Aragón which adopts as one of its priorities, preparing students and the family members involved in the community with the skills and competencies required in the information society. This aim goes hand in hand with the goal of facilitating access to the ICTs, working towards an information society for all (Elboj et al. 2002).
2 This is a concept from Schütz (Schütz and Luckmann, 1973) that was later revised by Habermas (1987). It refers to unquestioned convictions that underlie actions and co-operative interpretation processes.
3 Romi means Gypsy women. In Ramírez-Heredia, J. (2001) *Primer Manual de Conversa Romanó-Caló*, Barcelona: Unión Romaní.
4 *Workaló, The Creation of New Occupational Patterns for Cultural Minorities*. The Gypsy Case, RTD FP5. DG XII, 2001–4 (CREA 2001–4).
5 AMAL, *Inmigración y Mercado Laboral, Plan Nacional I+D+I*, 2002–5 (CREA 2002–5).

References

Beck, U. (1992) *Risk Society*, New York: Sage Publications.
Beck, U. and Beck-Gernsheim, E. (1995) *The Normal Chaos of Love*, Cambridge: Polity Press.
Beck, U., Giddens, A. and Lash, S. (1994) *Reflexive Modernization. Politics, Tradition and Aesthetics in the Modern Social Order*, Cambridge, MA: Polity Press.
Beck-Gernsheim, E., Butler, J. and Puigvert, L. (2003) *Women and Social Transformation*, New York: Peter Lang Publishing.
CREA (2001–4) *Workaló, The Creation of New Occupational Patterns for Cultural Minorities. The Gypsy Case*, RTD project. Framework Programme 5. DG XII. European Commission.
CREA (2002–5) AMAL, *Inmigración y Mercado Laboral, Plan Nacional I+D+I. Programa de Socioeconomía*, Ministerio de Ciencia y Tecnología.

De Botton, L., Puigvert, L. and Sánchez, M. (in press) *The Inclusion of Other Women: Dialogic Learning in Multicultural Societies*, Dordrecht: Kluwer.

Elboj, C., Puigdellívol, I., Soler, M. and Valls, R. (2002) *Comunidades de Aprendizaje. Transformar la Educación*, Barcelona: Graó.

European Commission (2002a) *Enhancing Democracy*, A White Paper on Governance in the European Union, http://www.europa.eu.int/comm/governance/index_en.htm (Accessed on: 27/02/02).

European Commission (2002b) *FP6 Sixth Framework Programme (2002–2006)*, http://fp6.cordis.lu/fp6/home.cfm (Accessed on: 23/10/03).

Flecha, R. (1996) 'Traditional modernity, postmodernity and communicative modernity related issues in constructing roles and learning tasks of adult education', in *International Adult & Continuing Education Conference (IACEC): Constitutive Interplay Midst Discourse of East and West: Modernity & Postmodernity Renderings in Adult & Continuing Education*, pp. 91–115, Seoul: The Institute of Industrial Studies, Chung-Ang University/Institute for International Women's Studies.

Flecha, R. (2000) *Sharing Words. Theory and Practice of Dialogic Learning*, Lanham, MD: Rowman & Littlefield.

Flecha, R. and Tortajada, I. (1999) 'Retos y salidas educativas en la entrada de siglo', in F. Imbernón (coord.) *La educación en el siglo XXI. Los retos del futuro inmediato*, Barcelona: Graó.

Flecha, R., Gómez, J. and Puigvert, L. (2003) *Contemporary Sociological Theory*, New York: Peter Lang.

Freire, P. (1997) *A la sombra de este árbol*, Barcelona: El Roure.

Giddens, A. (1990) 'Structuration theory and sociological analysis', in J. Clark, C. Modgil and S. Modgil (eds) *Anthony Giddens. Consensus and Controversy*, London: The Falmer Press.

Giddens, A. (1992) *The Transformation of Intimacy. Sexuality, Love and Eroticism in Modern Societies*, Cambridge: Polity Press.

Gómez, J. (2001) 'Hacia una perspectiva comunicativa de la investigación educativa', X Congreso Nacional de Métodos de Investigación Educativa. Asociación Internacional de Investigación Pedagógica. A Coruña.

Habermas, J. (1984) *The Theory of Communicative Action, Vol. 1: Reasons and the Rationalization of Society*, Boston, MA: Beacon Press.

Habermas, J. (1987) *The Theory of Communicative Action, Vol. 2: Lifeworld and System: A Critique of Functionalist Reason*, Boston, MA: Beacon Press.

Ramírez-Heredia, J. (2001) *Primer Manual de Conversa Romanó-Caló*, Barcelona: Unión Romaní.

Schütz, A. and Luckmann, T. (1973) *The Structure of the Life-World*, Evanston, IL: Northwestern.

Touraine, A. (1997) *Pourrons-nous vivre ensemble? Égaux et différents*, Paris: Fayard.

Websites

Sanromá, M. (1999) 'Las redes ciudadanas'. http://www.lafactoriaweb.com/articulos/sanroma.htm (Consulted on: 20/12/00).

Serra, A. (2000) 'Redes ciudadanas: construyendo nuevas sociedades de la era digital'. http://www.englobal2000.org/doc/arturpaper.doc (Consulted on: 20/12/00).

Chapter 12

Questions of access and participation

Some contributions from qualitative research

Beth Crossan and Michael Osborne

Introduction

In recent years, lifelong learning has re-emerged as a key policy focus at local, national and supranational levels (Nicoll and Edwards 2000). This policy interest has led to questions about who is participating in what types of learning, and how we can best understand issues surrounding access, participation and non-participation in greater depth. As well as focusing on participation in lifelong learning broadly, access to higher education has emerged as a key question in a world-wide context as is evident from the contributions to this book. This focuses on not just increasing access to higher education, but widening participation to non-traditional groups. Non-traditional students can be defined as those learners emanating from social groups who do not usually participate in post compulsory education or training. As Thomas (2000) argues, this work should not be premised solely on good intentions, but be supported by research, evaluation and dissemination. This chapter explores some contributions that qualitative research has made to researching access and widening participation. It focuses on qualitative studies which have expanded the conceptual and theoretical frameworks within which to understand these issues.

Research in the field of lifelong learning broadly has a well-established track record of concern with patterns of participation. Britain has been particularly well served by this tradition. A series of large scale national quantitative surveys has created a solid and cumulative body of knowledge respecting broad patterns of participation in adult learning (Sargant *et al.* 1997; Beinart and Smith 1998; La Valle and Finch 1999). Much is now understood about participation that remained intuitive or largely unknown in the 1950s. Survey data, for example, persistently show that levels of participation are generally associated with a group of social, economic and demographic factors such as educational attainment in youth, socio-economic status, family influences, region, and age (Gorard *et al.* 1999; Forsyth and Furlong 2003).

More recently, these data have been complemented by a growing number of qualitative studies. These studies have made a considerable contribution to understanding access and participation as social processes and can illuminate the anxieties and tensions experienced by, for example, adults who go back to university in later life (Merrill 1999). Qualitative studies have also highlighted the differing ways in which individuals negotiate transitions back into formal and community based learning (Gallacher *et al.* 2000).

Qualitative research

Both quantitative and qualitative approaches have contributed to building a more comprehensive picture of understanding access and widening participation. However, rather than thinking of these two approaches in dichotomous terms, it is possible and more helpful to see qualitative and quantitative methods as part of a continuum of research techniques, all of which are appropriate depending on the research objective (Casebeer and Verhoef 1997). There are strengths to both approaches and strengths to combining approaches. From the perspective of widening access research, George and Gillon (2001) argue that there is a need for wider interpretation of what counts as evidence to inform policy and practice, and that a range of qualitative as well as quantitative data must be sought.

When wanting to understand social processes and subjective experiences, qualitative approaches to research may be more appropriate. Unlike the quantitative paradigm where essentially methods can be differentiated into experiments, surveys and secondary analysis of datasets, qualitative research methods or approaches, as Cresswell (1994: 10–12) indicates, offer a range of traditions from the human and social sciences. Various authors have sought to narrow these down with their own typologies. So for example, according to Mason (1996), there are certain schools associated with the broad categories of phenomenology, ethnomethodology and symbolic interactionism and more recently post-modernism could be added to this list. Merriam and Simpson (1995: 103–17), in the context of adult education, suggest a fourfold typology of common forms of qualitative research as ethnography, case study, grounded theory and phenomenology, a classification shared by Cresswell (1994). In general terms qualitative work has a strong emphasis on exploring the nature of particular phenomena, working with unstructured or semi-structured data, and the interpretation of meanings and functions of human action.

There are numerous qualitative research studies in the field of access and widening participation. There are researchers working in this area who have been explicit as to their use of qualitative approaches as being more appropriate because of the nature of their enquiry and the questions that they seek to answer. Heeman (2002), for example, explored women's reasons for not continuing in higher education following successful completion of an access course. Ethnographic interviews were used, as the aim of the research was to enable the women to tell their own stories:

> This qualitative approach was deemed particularly suitable as it enabled the
> researcher to gain an insight into the women's views and perspectives. I felt
> this method would enable me to further develop my rapport with these

women. The loosely framed interview schedule allowed me to direct the discussion without rigidly controlling them.

(Heeman 2002: 42)

In such qualitative interviews data are not gathered or collected but are produced through interaction. Another example in the field of access research is the work of Haggis and Pouget (2002). This research focused on both pre-entry to, and experiences of, university for young people who came from families with no history of participation in higher education. A number of qualitative methods were used including reflective diaries, observation notes, individual and group writing, and interviews. This combination of data sources enabled the researchers to explore the complexity of factors involved in individuals' learning experience, which extend past discussions of approaches to study and outcomes (Haggis and Pouget 2002). This study sought to uncover the interplay of significant factors rather than produce widely generalisable findings. These are just two examples of qualitative studies in the field, of which there are many.

In relation to qualitative approaches in the field of adult education, Weil (in Merrill 1999: 47) argues that qualitative research does have a particular contribution to make. She argues:

Qualitative research helps to expose a new language – the language of genuine lived experience. It is a mode of research that does not pre-define the nature of learning and adult learners' experiences .... Research that is grounded in concern with meaning and relevance rather than measurement and typology can shift the ground from which we seek to understand the experiences of adult learners. It has the capacity to enrich – and to re-define – theory and practice related to adults learning.

(Merrill 1999: 47)

This is helpful, as researching access and participation in lifelong learning is an eclectic field, traditionally lacking a strong theoretical tradition, and is a relatively undertheorised area (Merrill 1999). Qualitative approaches can help relate this field of research to a critical and theoretical framework. This chapter therefore focuses on some contributions that qualitative approaches to access and widening participation research have made to aiding our conceptual and theoretical thinking in the field. The chapter explores three areas: *biography*; *learning careers*; and *institutional habitus*. These are three areas which have been influential in research undertaken by the Centre for Research in Lifelong Learning, where both authors work.

Biography

Biography is an approach to research which, particularly within the adult education community, is becoming more common, and is explored in greater depth by Merrill and Alheit (Chapter 13). In biographical research, interviewees are the narrators of their own story, constructing the past, present and future with the researcher as a guide. The interview is a social process and a social construction between the researcher and the researched, and the interviewee is placed central to the research process. This approach helps understanding of issues surrounding access and participation by highlighting the inter-relationships between macro, meso and micro levels, and helps to reveal the interaction between agency and structure in people's lives (Merrill 1999). The use of biographical interviews has shown that the trajectory of the life course can no longer be thought of as linear, for example, as is illustrated by the decision of adults to return to learn later in life. Biographies have also shown that life stories are always located within particular contexts that change over time.

Barbara Merrill used biographical interviews in her study of the experiences of mature women students at university (Merrill 1999). Drawing on both feminist and interactionist approaches, the research explored the women's experiences as mature students in university. In the course of the research, each woman was interviewed twice. These biographical interviews were used to understand the connection of past lives with present experiences, and the ways that private and public lives interacted. Using biographical approaches enabled the interviewees to reflect upon, interpret and give meaning to, and construct past events and experiences in social context (Merrill 1999: 55). The data produced in the interviews were used to explore the intersection of education, class and gender in the women's experiences of university life. The data generated in the qualitative interviews highlighted different learning trajectories and the ways in which identity changed over time with continued participation in learning.

Learning careers

This biographical approach to producing data discussed above was drawn on by Gallacher et al. (2000) in their study exploring widening participation, social inclusion and further education colleges[1] in Scotland. This research focused on 80 adults and young people who were either participating or not participating in learning in a main campus of a further education college, or in community based further education provision. Many of those who took part in the study had left school at the earliest possible age with few if any formal qualifications. Many of those who were participating in learning could be regarded as 'tentative learners'. Using the data generated in one to one biographical interviews, and a limited number of focus group interviews, the research explored the ways in which individual and collective biographies impacted on decisions on whether or not to take part in learning, and the ways that biography shaped different learning trajectories. The concept of learning career, previously developed by Bloomer and Hodkinson (1997), was used and extended to explore the social processes that underpinned participation and non-participation in learning.

In Bloomer and Hodkinson's work, the concept of learning career draws on symbolic interactionist theory, and the processes through which social identity is shaped and reshaped through interaction with others. The concept of 'career' refers here to the processes through which people's self-perception changes and their involvement in certain areas of activity develops as a consequence of this interaction. It became prominent initially in studies of deviance and education (Becker and Strauss 1959). In this analysis, learning career argues against the dominant positivist paradigm where learning is conceptualised as a product of input-output mechanisms, to an analysis of learning as a subjective experience and a transformatory process which cannot be separated from other life experiences.

The Bloomer and Hodkinson (1997) study focused on young people's experiences of further education to explore the ways that dispositions to learning changed over time. They argued that for the young people involved in the study, course choices, occupational aspirations, dispositions to learning and approaches to studentship all changed over time. The concept of learning career was developed to refer to the changes in a student's dispositions to learning over time. The theories of Bourdieu were used, where dispositions are part of a wider habitus (Bourdieu and Passeron 1977). Habitus refers to a set of dispositions created and shaped by the interaction between objective structures and personal histories, including past experiences. Changing dispositions to learning are influenced by what happens both outside and inside the formal learning environment. Experiences of formal education and dispositions to learning can and do change other dispositions within the habitus.

This work focused on transformations in dispositions to learning among young people who were already engaged in formal learning, mostly on a full-time basis and who had moved onto college directly from school. In contrast, the Gallacher et al. (2000) study, rather than examining continued initial education, was primarily concerned with adults who had either made a conscious choice to re-enter learning later on in life, or who had drifted into learning in an unplanned way. Many were studying on a part-time, rather than on a full-time basis. The focus was not therefore on formal education but extended to adults, many of whom took part in learning in community based settings and who would not have gone to a main college campus.

Using data produced in biographical interviews to explore changing dispositions to learning and in developing Bloomer and Hodkinson's conceptual framework, the concept of a learning career could not be understood as a linear upward progression, but much more by the analysis of career as a fluid and dynamic process (Gallacher et al. 2002; Crossan et al. 2003). Learning careers may be forged as people's dispositions to learning change, their attitudes to learning become more positive and dispositional barriers are slowly overcome. Linked to such changes are transformations of the person in terms of identity, personal relations and expectations of what is achievable. As in Merrill's (1999) work, changes in dispositions to learning are therefore bound up in a complex restructuring of the person and identity.

The research undertaken by Gallacher *et al*. (2000) found that learners identified several types of resources as key to developing an engagement with learning. These were social resources (e.g. social relationships and networks in and outside of the learning context), material resources (e.g. money, access to books and equipment), the location and environment for learning (e.g. geographical and cultural nearness, provision of childcare facilities) and symbolic resources (e.g. the wish to develop an identity different from an ascribed social role such as 'mother'). The qualitative interviews were able to explore the ways that these often interlinked in complex ways. This helped explain the ways that individuals moved in and out of learning at different times in their lives, became more committed learners with a stronger learner identity, or remained resistant to learning, or unconvinced of its merits.

This developing body of qualitative work has enabled understandings of participation in learning, which has moved beyond a focus on motives and barriers, towards an understanding of the processes through which participation can be encouraged. Here a better understanding was gained as to the complex social processes which may result in non-traditional learners taking their first steps back into learning.

Institutional habitus

The work of Bloomer and Hodkinson (1997) and Gallacher *et al*. (2000) focused on both young people and adults who were involved in learning in further education colleges. Qualitative approaches have also been used to explore the experience of non-traditional students negotiating entry into, and their experiences of, higher education. This again draws on the theories of Bourdieu. Using a multi-method approach which included one to one interviews and focus groups Thomas has used the concept of *institutional habitus*, drawing on the work of Reay *et al*. (2001). Habitus, as a set of dispositions, can refer to the norms and practices of particular social classes or groups. Although habitus can transform, change is slow, and therefore habitus both produces and confines action as the possibilities open to certain social groups may be limited (Thomas 2000). This has been developed into the concept of 'institutional habitus' which is used to refer to the impact of cultural group or social class on an individual's behaviour as it is mediated through an organisation. In relation to understanding issues of retention, when a student feels that they do not fit in, that their social and cultural practices are inappropriate and their tacit knowledge is undervalued, they may be inclined to withdraw from their studies early and drop out of university. The analogy of a 'fish out of water' is given, compared to those from the dominant social class, who at university are 'fish in water'. Habitus and institutional habitus are argued to be useful tools in researching student experience and issues of retention (Thomas 2000).

This links to the work of Forsyth and Furlong (2003) who undertook a longitudinal study exploring the experiences of higher education for young people who were academically able, but socio-economically disadvantaged. The researchers used a combination of quantitative and qualitative approaches. The rationale for using qualitative interviews was that they would help unravel why students from disadvantaged backgrounds had moved along each of the various educational pathways identified by the researchers in the quantitative stage. The interviews were also used to identify the underlying reasons why some disadvantaged students fared particularly poorly within higher education. One conclusion from the study was that often the young people had difficulty adjusting to student life and the culture of the institution, particularly the more elite and traditional universities. Here the idea of 'fish out of water' and the concept of 'institutional habitus' were again used, as the young people often reported having little in common with other students or staff (p. 54). Overall the research showed that disadvantaged young people faced numerous and inter-linking barriers when in higher education (Forsyth and Furlong 2003). This is an example of using a multi-method approach and the strengths that each method gives. When wishing to explore the ways that factors inter-linked and the social processes behind the taking of different educational pathways, qualitative approaches were used to unravel these complexities.

Discussion

Within a world-wide context where lifelong learning is high on the political and policy agenda, questions over who is participating in learning have come to the fore. As well as access to higher education, the focus is on participation in learning more broadly. There is a body of research which is helping to unpack the complexities of access and widening participation. Quantitative studies are showing that factors such as age, social class, and attainments at school all remain important factors.

Qualitative studies have been useful in exploring subjective experiences and the ways that factors can inter-link in complex ways to shape different learning trajectories. We suggest that qualitative studies have also been helpful in developing conceptual and theoretical frameworks within which to explore questions of access and participation. In this chapter we have overviewed qualitative research in three areas, biography, learning careers and institutional habitus, to highlight the ways that qualitative research is contributing to a more theoretical understanding of key issues in the field.

Recently, however, it has been suggested in the current UK context there is increasing pressure on social and educational researchers to make their work have greater impact on policymaking and practice than has previously been the case (Hammersley 2002; Hodkinson 2001). This, in turn, has implications for the kinds of research studies that are funded. In response to recent government pronouncements about educational research, Hammersley (2002) argues that these would seem to prioritise quantitative over qualitative research. For example, in a recent large funding round from one prominent grant giving body, it is suggested that qualitative research is given a subservient role to that of quantitative research, or when used should be done in combination with quantitative work. Here the implication is that qualitative research is believed unable to deliver the kind of findings which are required for evidence based policy (Hammersley 2002).

In his contribution to this book, Peter Scott (Chapter 2) takes a more positive view of current UK developments within access research. Although in the UK this field of research can in some ways be seen as being 'immature', Scott points to the development of distinctive approaches to research which are helping to shape both policy and practice. A greater spectrum of epistemologies and methodologies are drawn upon and the contribution of new approaches to the generation of knowledge and understanding is increasingly recognised, not just in access research, but more widely in society. An important challenge facing researchers in this field will be to develop approaches which are innovative and distinctive, while maintaining the rigour required if they are to make an important contribution to understanding these issues, and to the development of policy and practice.

Note

1   Further education colleges in the UK provide a range of learning opportunities, including vocational qualifications.

References

Becker, H.S. and Strauss, A. (1959) 'Careers personality and adult socialisation', in H.S. Becker (1970) *Sociological Work*, Chicago: Aldine Publishing Company.

Beinart, S. and Smith, S. (1998) *National Adult Learning Survey 1997*, Sheffield: Department for Education and Employment.

Bloomer, M. and Hodkinson, P. (1997) *Moving into FE: the Voice of the Learner*, Bristol: FEDA Publications.

Bourdieu, P. and Passeron, J.C. (1997) *Reproduction in Education, Society and Culture*, Beverly Hills, CA: Sage.

Casebeer, A.L. and Verhoef, A.J. (1997) 'Combining quantitative and qualitative research methods: considering the possibilities for enhancing the study of chronic diseases', *Chronic Diseases*, 18(3), 1–12.

Cresswell, J.W. (1994) *Research Design – Qualitative and Quantitative Approaches*, Thousand Oaks, CA: Sage Publications.

Crossan, B., Field, J., Gallacher, J. and Merrill, B. (2003) 'Understanding participation in learning for non-traditional adult learners: learning careers and the construction of learner identities', *British Journal of Educational Sociology*, 24(1), 55–67.

Forsyth, A. and Furlong, A. (2003) *Losing Out? Socio-economic Disadvantage and Experience in Further and Higher Education*, Bristol: The Policy Press.

Gallacher, J., Crossan, B., Leahy, J., Merrill, B. and Field, J. (2000) *Education for All? Further Education, Social Inclusion and Widening Access* (Report submitted to the Scottish Executive), Glasgow Caledonian University: Centre for Research in Lifelong Learning.

Gallacher, J., Field, J., Merrill, B. and Crossan, B. (2002) 'Learning careers and the social space: exploring fragile identities, adult returners and the new further education', *International Journal of Lifelong Education*, 21(6), 493–509.

George, J.W. and Gillon, E.J. (2001) 'What evidence do we need? A case study of widening participation', *Widening Participation and Lifelong Learning*, 3(2), 15–20.

Gorard, S., Fevre, R. and Rees, G. (1999) 'Two dimensions of time: the changing social context of lifelong learning', *Studies in the Education of Adults*, 31(1), 35–48.

Haggis, T. and Pouget, M. (2002) 'Trying to be motivated: perspectives on learning from younger students accessing higher education', *Teaching in Higher Education*, 7(3), 323–36.

Hammersley, M. (2002) *Educational Research Policymaking and Practice*, London: Paul Chapman Publishing.

Heeman, D. (2002) 'Women, access and progression: an examination of women's reasons for not continuing in higher education following the completion of the Certificate in Women's Studies', *Studies in Continuing Education*, 24(1), 40–55.

Hodkinson, P. (2001) 'The contested field of educational research: the new research orthodoxy and the limits of objectivity', paper presented at the British Educational Research Association Conference, University of Leeds, September 2001.

La Valle, I. and Finch, S. (1999) *Pathways in Adult Learning*, Sheffield: Department for Education and Employment.

Mason, J. (1996) *Qualitative Researching*, London: SAGE.

Merriam, S.B. and Simpson, E.L. (1995) *A Guide to Research for Educators and Trainers of Adults*, 2nd edn, Malabar: Krieger.

Merrill, B. (1999) *Gender, Change and Identity: Mature Women Students in Universities*, England: Ashgate.

Nicoll, K. and Edwards, R. (2000) 'Reading policy texts: lifelong learning as a metaphor', *International Journal of Lifelong Education*, 19(5), 459–69.

Reay, D., David, M. and Ball, S. (2001) 'Making a difference? Institutional habituses and higher education choice', *Sociological Research Online*, 5(4). Online at: http://www.socresonline.org.uk/5/4/reay.html.

Sargant, N., Field, J., Francis, H., Schuller, T. and Tuckett, A. (1997) *The Learning Divide*, Leicester: National Institute of Adult Continuing Education.

Thomas, L. (2000) 'Bums on seats or listening to voices: evaluating widening participation initiatives using participatory action research', *Studies in Continuing Education*, 22(1), 95–113.

Chapter 13

Biography and narratives
Adult returners to learning

Barbara Merrill and Peter Alheit

Introduction

Widening participation and lifelong learning in higher education is high on the
policy agenda of several European national governments and the European
Commission. Alongside this is a questioning of the purpose of universities and
the eliteness of some institutions. This chapter discusses the use of biographical
methods in adult education research through the findings of a research project
funded by the European Commission on the access policies and practices for
non-traditional adult students in universities across six European countries. Using
biographies enables us to understand these issues by highlighting the inter-
relationship between macro, meso and micro levels. The research identifies
different typologies of universities by drawing on Bourdieu's work on symbolic
capital and knowledge hierarchies which may either promote or hinder the access
of adults. The life histories of the learners revealed several educational biographies
shaped by their habitus. The relationship between biographies, social capital and
experiences of learning in HE are examined and developed in relation to the
symbolic space of a particular university using case studies from the UK and
Germany. While participating in HE is a risky business for many adults it can
also be an empowering one for others.

Using biographies in adult education research

In recent years biographical methods have returned from obscurity to become a
popular approach within the social sciences, including adult education research,
to such an extent that it is now referred to as the 'biographical turn' (see Alheit
et al. 1995). Thomas and Znaniecki's study of the Polish peasant and migration
(1958) established life histories as a methodology for understanding the social
world from micro and subjective perspectives, countering the dominant positivistic
research approaches. Sociologists at the Chicago School – starting in the 1920s –
later employed and developed life history approaches during the 1950s and 1960s
but it never became a 'mainstream' method within sociology. Feminist researchers
from the 1970s onwards embraced biographical approaches and narratives as a

means of giving 'voice' to women who had previously been hidden from history and society. Despite this it continued to remain on the margins of sociological methods until the emergence of postmodernism and its focus on subjectivity and the individual together with the development of theories of individualisation by Giddens (1991) and Beck (1992). In the UK the 'biographical turn' emerged in the 1990s although in France and Germany it occurred earlier. In 1981, for example, Bertaux referred to a 'biographical movement' in a study entitled *Biography and Society* (Bertaux 1981).

Within adult education the use of narratives and biographies has become widespread across Europe through the work of adult educators such as Bron, Alheit, Dominicé, and West as a means of understanding motivation, attitudes and experiences of adult learners. Biographical methods in many ways complement the traditions of adult education of placing the learner central to the process and taking into account the subjectivity of the learner. Interviewees are the narrators of their own story, constructing the past, present and future with the researcher as a guide. Mannheim succinctly defined narrating as 'the description of a context in relation to a particular experiential space' (1980: 231). The life history interview is a social process and a social construction between the researcher and the researched. Biographies reveal the complexities of adult learners' lives as they struggle to combine a life lived in several social spaces. The life course trajectory is no longer linear as illustrated by the decision of adults to return to learn later in life. Life stories are always located within particular contexts that change over time:

> The stories that are selected by the biographer to present her/his life history cannot be regarded as a series of isolated experiences, laid down in chronological order ...; individual experiences are always embedded in a coherent, meaningful context, a biographical construct... The present perspective determines what the subject considers biographically relevant, how she or he develops thematic and temporal links between various experiences, and how past, present, or anticipated future realities influence the personal interpretation of the meaning of life.
>
> (Rosenthal 1993: 62–3)

A person actively constructs their biography through past experiences. As Alheit *et al.* explain:

> Each biographical experience is reflected in the total biography by the way in which it is processed by the biographical subject. Experiences are not 'social inputs' that determine extraneously the overall shape of a biography. They must be understood more cogently as 'intakes', as external stimuli that do not acquire their significance until the individual imposes her or his own processual structure on them. That structure is determined for its part by a

'gestalt' of biographically layered experience that has already taken shape –
a kind of 'experiential code' into which contingent experiences have first to
be translated.

(Alheit *et al.* 2004: 5)

Biographies while appearing on the surface to be individual reveal the interaction
between agency and structure in people's lives. They are always situated within a
historical context. For Bertaux 'the biographical project' highlights the 'social,
economic, cultural, structural and historical forces that shape, distort and
otherwise alter problematic lived experiences' (1981: 4). The life stories told by
many adult learners reveal the way in which returning to learn is used as a way of
dealing with change and transition in their lives at the personal and societal
level. For some this process results in creating new identities:

The people whose lives we are researching tell stories about a process at
once more fundamental and humane: the struggle for meaning at times of
change and fragmentation ...

(Lea and West 1995: 172)

The research context

The research context of this chapter is an EU TSER funded project; (SOE2-
CT97-2021) 'University Adult Access Policies and Practices Across the European
Union and their Consequences for the Participation of Non-Traditional Students'.
It was undertaken in six European countries (Belgium, Germany, Ireland, Spain,
Sweden and the UK) and involved the following universities: Louvain,
Goettingen, Maynooth, Barcelona, Stockholm and Warwick. The focus was on
undergraduate adult students. Using biographical approaches allowed us to
connect early life experiences, such as initial schooling, with current ones and
identify a pattern, or not, of lifelong learning. Life history interviews enabled the
voices of adult learners to be heard as they reflected upon, interpreted and
constructed past experiences within a social context.

A condition of the funding, set by the EU, was to arrive at a common European
definition of a non-traditional adult student. Although words such as adult student
had different meanings amongst partners, as higher education contexts vary, the
following definition was arrived at:

A new mature student entrant (by age in respective countries) with no
previous HE qualification whose participation in HE is constrained by
structural factors additional to age.

Entry into the academy and experiences of life inside revealed a complex
interaction of structure and agency as adult undergraduates established, sometimes

through struggle, a student career and new/changed identities. The notion of biographicity is useful here. As Alheit and Dausien point out, biographicity 'can be understood as an individual knowledge resource to deal with modern reality' (1999: 401). Theoretically it links the interdependence of education, transition and biography. The life journeys of adults and their engagement in lifelong learning revealed several learner types which were lived out within different types of universities. First, we explore the various typologies of universities within Europe.

Institutional journeys of adult students

Adult learners in Europe experience different lifelong learning opportunities as pathways to universities vary from country to country. A number of obstacles often have to be faced if they decide to access university. To understand these processes more fully we looked at the interaction and inter-relationship between the macro level (national policies and educational structures), the meso level (institutional policies and practices) and the micro level (student experiences). The biographies of learners are situated at the micro level yet these had to be understood within the different contexts and types of universities. Socio-economic changes in postmodernity have led to a re-shaping and transformation of higher education systems from elite to mass-based and more diverse institutions (Trow 1973; Scott 1995). The nature and purposes of universities in postmodernity are being questioned, redefined and reconstructed. Yet despite these change processes, hierarchies continue to exist with some universities remaining elite institutions both in the UK and Germany. The more mass type universities (post-1992 institutions in the UK and reform universities in Germany) are more open to adult access. Structures and cultures vary with the different types of universities providing different experiences for adult students. The first type of university is a traditional one where adults are treated as a 'normal' student and entry is dependent upon passing an examination, for example, in Spain, France and Belgium. It is an exclusive scholastic model.

Second, the hidden elitist type of access whereby the law guarantees mature students the right to enter without a special examination but the university presents itself as a strange and unfriendly symbolic universe: an elite place. This is the case in most German universities because of their tradition as exclusive institutions, where non-traditional students often experience a clash of lifeworlds, a deep conflict of personal and institutional attitudes. Some systems like the UK have an open type. UK universities have a long tradition of connections to their community and adults have a wide range of pathways into university. However, adults are not located evenly across the system as most study in the new universities and only a minority in the elite institutions which overall still cater mainly for younger students.

Swedish universities represent the inclusive type. Access is restrictive as adults have to possess the school leaving qualification or enter through the 25+4 route.

For the latter a person has to be 25 years old, have four years work experience and pass an examination. Once in the system it is supportive to adults (sometimes even exclusive towards younger students).

'Non-traditional' biographical journeys

Adult students are not a homogeneous group as they differ by age, gender, class, ethnicity and mode of study. The majority in our study came from a working class or petty bourgeois background and most could be described as 'social upclimbers'. Many exhibited what Bourdieu (1979) calls a 'pretentious habitus'. This developed in diverging ways as participants experienced different educational journeys. From their stories we identified five types of educational biographies:

- patchworkers
- (educational) climbers
- integrators
- emancipators
- careerists.

Some of the biographies cut across the boundaries as they consisted of more than one type although there was a tendency for one type of educational biography to dominate.

Patchworkers collect several new (professional) beginnings within their biographies. Their biography is fragmented as they are virtuosos of starting courses but are never able to complete them. Their biographical reflexibility is weakly developed. The decision to start a university career is generally a link in a chain of new attempts to find a meaningful life. Often they break off and try to start a new career both inside and outside the university. This form of biography is a risk type for study.

Educational climbers do not behave like the typical career type as they are neither interested in money nor in superficial prestige. However, they want to participate in the higher symbolic universe of the university. Despite a broken educational biography, often due to structural constraints, they never abandon the idea of learning as they are intrinsically motivated. In engaging with the academic world it is necessary for them to sever their former social relationships. However, this is a biographical risk as studying in a university is not a guarantee of success and acceptance in their new social world. Often they feel homeless in the academic world as they lack 'social capital'.

Integrators are both unpretentious and pragmatists. University is used instrumentally while at the same time they maintain ties with their former social relationships and experience. They maintain a certain distance to the symbolic universe of the academic field and remain autonomous yet they have a positive attitude towards study. Integrators are mostly women.

Emancipators often look back to a biographical journey of repression or critical incident – as a child, or in adulthood. This type makes a conscious effort to break away from past experiences and create a new biography. Education is viewed as a means of liberation and empowerment. Studying for a degree fills a gap left by, for example, a broken partnership or frustrating job experiences. It represents a symbolic change in their lives and a search for a new identity. They are generally successful at university.

Careerists are usually – unlike integrators – very pretentious as they enter university for prestige or financial reasons. They are extrinsically motivated by economic factors as academic studies provide an instrument to reach a goal, such as a better job, and as a result they are successful in their studies.

These biographical journeys are all differentially represented in European universities. Careerists appear to be an Irish characteristic, whereas emancipators are found mostly in Britain. Integrators were common in Germany while educational climbers and patchworkers were found everywhere. The latter reflects the postmodern life history of people in modern societies. How do the different types of biographies fit into the symbolic universes of European universities?

'Travelling customs' in a strange environment: two case studies

The pathway to and through university for adults is characterised by obstacles as they enter an institutional environment designed for younger students. We draw on the biographies of adult undergraduates in Germany and the UK to tell the story of the risks mature students experience in university.

The clash of lifeworlds: a Bourdieuan approach to universities

Students with a working class background cannot hide the influence of a particular lifeworld. The background knowledge they are taking with them, the implicit or tacit taken for granted meanings, are usually different from academic knowledge. The traditional working class milieu is characterised by a sense of co-operation and solidarity, while the social space of universities consists of hierarchies and status in relation to faculties and disciplines. Bourdieu's study of French universities (*Homo Academicus*, 1984) and the social space of the academic field as constructed by different sorts of symbolic capital is useful for understanding the social context in which the biographies of adult learners are acted out. Two fields are particularly important: social capital which defines the social prestige a certain discipline has, and intellectual capital marking the scientific ranking of a discipline.

In traditional universities, for example, there is a similar distribution of disciplines and faculties within the symbolic space of the academic field (see Figure 13.1).

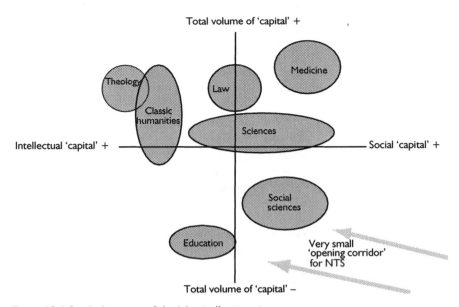

Figure 13.1 Symbolic space of the 'classical' university

Traditional faculties (like law, medicine, sciences) are divided from the 'modern disciplines' (social sciences and education), and are ranked higher within the symbolic space. Adult students are often only able to enter traditional universities through the low status disciplines such as the social sciences. In the new (UK) and reform (Germany) universities the hierarchy of knowledge with its associated symbolic power is less distinct and as a result the opportunities for entry and study are higher for non-traditional adult students (see Figure 13.2). However, it does have consequences for their biographies as a degree from a marginalised university subsequently decreases their opportunity and power in the labour market.

Contrasting biographies within the German system

Within the German context three learner biographies are common: 'patchworkers', 'upclimbers' and 'integrators'. The first two types show symptoms of being educational 'losers', while the integration type in contrast are 'winners' as illustrated by the following life stories.

Bert reflects the risk-loaded trajectory of a 'patchworker'. Coming from a broken family background he attempted several apprenticeships but did not complete any. He also began unsuccessfully a second and third school career. The introduction of a new law enabled him to enter a technical college. However, he failed to complete his studies so that during a three year period he did not obtain any certificates. His self-evaluation of his learning situation was optimistic but not a realistic one:

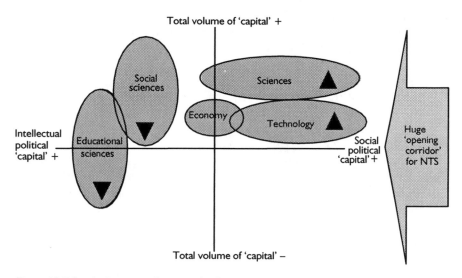

Figure 13.2 Symbolic space of new and reform universities

I hope that I will identify myself somehow with the studies, well, as an engineer or something else, so that I get a little bit of distance. I think, I hope that in a few years or perhaps sometime I'll gain some certificates as they are important.

Stephanie is a typical educational climber. She comes from a petty bourgeois family with traditional gender roles. Although she was successful at school her father did not allow her to attend a grammar school. Instead she worked as a secretary and married at an early age. After five years of marriage she divorced, bringing up her daughter as a single parent and became a working mother. In her thirties she met a university lecturer who encouraged her to begin studies in the social sciences:

Well somehow there was always a sleeping interest in me for higher connections or deeper senses, of many things. And my boyfriend has wormed this out of me somehow.

She felt a need to gain entry to the higher symbolic universe of the academic field which differs from her own lifeworld and background. The resultant educational climbing of the social ladder would be a means to sever the social links with her petty bourgeois background thus resulting in a dramatic loss of 'social capital'.

Katja's university experiences differ from those of Bert and Stephanie. She is from a working class background. Katja decided to start a second educational career studying biology but she does not perceive herself to be an upclimber.

Throughout her studies she maintains close connections with her family and friends. She tries to integrate new experiences into her former lifeworld, widening her own horizon and the horizon of her social network. She keeps her 'social capital' by changing it:

> And if I am there [her hometown] I can still visit the people there, even without telling them beforehand that I am coming. It is also not the case that we don't have anything to talk about and that we don't know what to say afterwards. They are still really good friends.

Katja's integration strategy seems to be working. At the end of her studies she achieved good results. Her future plans appear to be pragmatic and realistic. In contrast to the pessimistic study prognosis of patchworkers and the vague perspectives of educational climbers, integrators tend to be educational winners.

The German data found evidence of self-locating among the different types of non-traditional adult students within the symbolic space of universities. Whereas the patchworkers and the educational climbers (the educational losers) preferred to locate themselves within the marginalised HE institutions such as technical colleges or reform universities, the integrators entered traditional universities (see Figure 13.3). Although they exhibit a certain distance to the academic field and maintain contact with their own social environments, they do not experience barriers in entering a new social environment. Patchworkers and educational climbers choose an easier access route to university. The same trend is reflected in the choice of disciplines for study. The loser groups locate themselves in the lower status subjects, such as education and social sciences, whereas the integrators opt for high status subjects such as biology or medicine (see Figure 13.3). The winners place themselves in the high ranked spaces while the losers find themselves symbolically at the bottom.

The educational journey of German non-traditional students is risky. Integrators demonstrate what is needed to overcome the obstacles: a large amount of 'social capital'.

'Emancipators' within the UK system

The following UK biographies illustrate the emancipation type. For emancipators, studying for a degree provides a chance of breaking with a past life and starting a new biography. Despite the risks 'emancipators' are determined to succeed. While their educational biographies are mostly those of the emancipator type there is an overlap with the educational climber type. Both choose to study at an elite, 'old' university. Both are working class and illustrate the intersections between class, gender and ethnicity in constructing biographies.

Hansa is a 31-year-old Islamic Asian woman studying full-time for a law degree. She is also a single parent. She emigrated to the UK when she was a child. Hansa's parents later separated. She recalled being sexually abused by her father at the

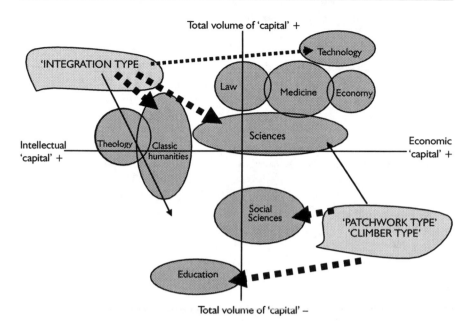

Figure 13.3 Access corridors of NTS to the disciplines

age of 13. As a child she enjoyed secondary school but cultural factors did not allow her to continue with post-compulsory studies:

> I always wanted to study. When I left school I bought a briefcase … a white coat and a stethoscope and I told my mother I'm going to be a doctor but having strict parents I wasn't allowed to study. My father said 'no'. I did get a place at college and he wouldn't allow it so I thought 'well that's it if you are not going to let me study I'm not going to sit on my backside at home – I'm going out to work'. He wouldn't let me until I promised to give him half my wages – so he let me work for Harrods. During the dinner break [at work] I used to read about medical facts … because I desperately wanted to be a doctor.

Hansa's biography here reflects the educational climber type. She had an unhappy arranged marriage in Germany as she and her daughter experienced domestic violence and received no support from her own family. She escaped to England and described this as a turning point. She refused to live with her family as she wanted her independence to start a new life. Until that point what she could or could not do had been decided for her by her father, brothers and husband. Her behaviour was about changing her identity as she was distancing herself from her family and culture by refusing to wear Asian clothes. She was stripping her identity for a new one in a similar way to Goffman's (1961) 'mortification of the self'.

After taking an Access course she hoped that a degree would lead to a profession and financial independence. A college lecturer persuaded her to apply to a particular old university because of its good reputation and following an interview she was offered a place to study law. She had also applied to two new universities, both of which offered her a place and were closer to where she lived but she turned them down. Initially she found adjusting to university life 'extremely difficult' as she felt that the Access course had not prepared her adequately:

> I don't think Access courses actually help people with university life. They are just too easy – no examinations … just assessments. They were too lenient at college. I was grateful for the leniency at the time but I'm not grateful for it now because it did not prepare me for what I was going to face at university.

She felt that university lecturers are good at introducing students to the language of law and stated that the teaching was excellent. Problems such as financial debt due to changes in the benefits and grants systems affected her studies, and at the time of interview she was heavily in debt. To survive she relied on the Access Fund like many other mature students but was determined not to let money stand in her way. She intends to qualify as a lawyer after completing her degree. In reflecting upon her life she commented:

> I've realised that history returns to repeat itself. Every time I've seen someone in the past or I've done something in the past, for some reason the past has a bearing on my future. I've used everybody from my past to build up my future.

Hansa's life experiences made her determined to be successful as an adult university student. Her goal was to emancipate herself from her past and economically support herself and her daughter by creating a new identity and life. In doing so she established new forms of social capital while largely severing her past social network and relationships in order to enrich her intellectual capital.

Diane, a 34-year-old Afro-Caribbean woman from a working class background, also decided to return to learn after ending a violent marriage. Like Hansa she is also a lone parent but has the support of her extended family, particularly her sisters. Her experiences of both primary and secondary schooling were dominated by racism from both teachers and pupils. Diane first returned to learn at the age of 25 to take an accredited course in black history at an Afro-Caribbean women's centre. This coincided with her violent marriage. She felt strengthened by the course as it looked at the role of black women:

> At that time I was in a violent relationship so it made me realise, 'this is not the situation that you're supposed to have in life so you've got to overcome things and you've got to do things'. So I made a lot of changes.

A few years later she completed a diploma in nursery nursing. The fact that her sister had returned to study for a degree encouraged her to feel that she could do the same, despite being dyslexic. A tutor supported her application to a local elite university:

> I thought 'oh my God, this is big' but when I talked to my tutor she was like 'there's no reason why you shouldn't go there, why don't you get on the course – do it'. And I thought 'all right'.

She chose to study part-time for financial reasons. She explained that she found the university environment comfortable as there were other black students and she has found lecturers helpful and supportive. Like many women she is juggling several roles (Merrill 1999), but stated that:

> I've got no choice. I think it's got a lot to do with commitment because I've decided to go to university. I thought right it needs commitment and it means hard work sometimes.

Both Hansa and Diane entered university with high expectations about academic learning and what it could do in relation to changing their identities and lives, and the aspirations of their children. They were empowered through their educational biographies. Primarily their biographies reflected the emancipator type, stimulated into returning to learn by a critical incident which acted as a turning point. However, they also reflect some aspects of the educational climber type. For example, Hansa had always had aspirations to study in higher education even at school but was prevented by structural constraints. Learning was always something she had wanted to return to as an adult; she aspired to the symbolic universe of the university. On entry to university adults have to learn to adjust to a student role and career – a process of 'situational adjustment' (Becker *et al.* 1961). Emancipators and integrators are able to do this.

Summary

Access to university as a lifelong learning adventure is not equal across Europe. The access journey in Spain is virtually impossible compared to the openness of the UK. Yet here, too, the picture is complex. Not all universities and/or not all departments want to open up their symbolic capital to non-traditional adult students. Those who do enter generally have to fit into a system which caters mostly for younger students. While institutional factors are important, the experiences and success of non-traditional adult students in the academic world also depend upon which of the five categories a learner belongs to and the type of habitus and social capital they bring with them. The past biographies of learners impact upon their university journey. Bourdieu's work on 'capital' in French universities and his concept of habitus provide useful theoretical and conceptual frameworks for making sense of the interaction between universities and non-traditional adult students at the meso/micro levels and the interplay between structure and agency and the public and the personal. As researchers we need to make explicit to policy makers and lecturers, at national and European levels, the issues non-traditional adult students face and the stories they tell in accessing the symbolic capital of universities. Universities still need to transform and redefine themselves if they are to 'have a new and a continuing role to play in terms of access and social inclusion' (Bourgeois et al. 1999: 177).

References

Alheit, P. and Dausien, B. (1999) 'Biographicity as a basic resource of lifelong learning', in P. Alheit, J. Beck, E. Kammler and H. Olesen (eds) *Lifelong Learning Inside and Outside Schools*, Vol. 2, Roskilde: Roskilde University.

Alheit, P., Bron-Wojciechowska, A., Brugger, E. and Dominicé, P. (eds) (1995) *The Biographical Approach in European Adult Education*, Vienna: Edition Volkshochschule.

Alheit, P., Szlachcic, I. and Zich, F. (2004) *Changing Mentalities in a Central European Borderline Region: A Comparative Study on Cultural Identities in East Germany, Northern Czechia and West Poland*, Görlitz: Neisse Verlag.

Beck, U. (1992) *Risk Society*, London: Sage.

Becker, H.S., Geer, B., Strauss, A. and Hughes, E. (1961) *Boys in White: Student Culture in Medical School*, Chicago: University of Chicago Press.

Bertaux, D. (ed.) (1981) *Biography and Society. The Life History Approach in the Social Sciences*, Beverly Hills: Sage.

Bourdieu, P. (1979) *La Distinction. Critique Sociale du Jugement*, Paris: Minuit.

Bourdieu, P. (1984) *Homo Academicus*, Cambridge: Polity Press.

Bourgeois, E., Guyot, J.L., Duke, C. and Merrill, B. (1999) *The Adult University*, Buckingham: Open University Press/SRHE.

Giddens, A. (1991) *Modernity and Self-Identity*, Cambridge: Polity Press.

Goffman, E. (1961) *Asylums*, Harmondsworth: Penguin.

Lea, M. and West, L. (1995) 'On biographies and institutions: changing selves, fragmentation and the struggle for meaning', in P. Alheit, A. Bron-Wojciechowska, E. Brugger and P. Dominicé (eds) *The Biographical Approach in European Adult Education*, Vienna: Edition Volkshochschule.

Mannheim, K. (1980) *Strukturen des Denkens*, Frankfurt am Main: Suhrkamp.

Merrill, B. (1999) *Gender, Change and Identity: Mature Women Students in Universities*, Aldershot: Ashgate.

Rosenthal, G. (1993) 'Reconstruction of life stories: principles of selection in generating stories for narrative biographical interviews', in R. Josselson and A. Lieblich (eds) *The Narrative Study of Lives*, Newbury Park: Sage Publications.

Scott, P. (1995) *The Meanings of Mass Higher Education*, Buckingham: Open University Press.

Thomas, W.I. and Znaniecki, F. (1958) *The Polish Peasant in Europe and America*, first published 1918–21, New York: Dover Publications.

Trow, M. (1973) *Problems in the Transition from Elite to Mass Higher Education*, Berkeley, CA: Carnegie Commission on Higher Education.

Chapter 14

Counting access

Problems and puzzles

Alasdair Forsyth and Andy Furlong

Introduction

In this chapter we intend to highlight the problems inherent with measuring changes in access to Higher Education. Specifically, we will explore some of the difficulties in describing who is, and in defining who should be, benefiting from policies aimed at broadening participation. That is, how do we know that an increase in the numbers of young people accessing Higher Education reflects a greater level of participation by groups previously excluded? In doing this, we will scrutinise the methods used for measuring levels of access and detail the problems and gaps in our knowledge that can result from these. These issues will be explored by making reference to a recent Joseph Rowntree Foundation funded research project conducted in Scotland with the aim of improving polices aimed at widening access for school-leavers from disadvantaged family backgrounds. As we will see, the problems and puzzles encountered when attempting to count access have implications for both those undertaking such quantitative research studies and those who are entrusted with the formulation of polices aimed at widening participation in Higher Education.

Background

Both the UK Government and the Scottish Executive are committed to two educational goals that while appearing complementary may in fact conflict. On the one hand, there is a commitment to increase the proportion of young people who benefit from Higher Education, on the other a desire to widen access to Higher Education as part of a social justice agenda. In one sense an increase in the numbers of young people entering Higher Education will automatically result in wider access. In a relatively short period of time Higher Education has moved from an elite to a mainstream experience and with around 50 per cent of Scottish young people now entering Higher Education, it is no longer the exclusive preserve of the privileged classes. Wider access though, does not automatically lead to patterns of entry that are more socially just and, in many senses, the benefits of an expanded system of HE have largely accrued to the middle classes among whom participation rates are approaching saturation point. In comparison to the middle classes, levels of participation among the working classes (and especially the lower working classes) are relatively poor with the gap in representation being greater now than it was in 1960 (DfES, 2003). Also, as we will argue in this chapter, levels of participation are not a good measure of inequality of access.

In order to make an adequate assessment of any movement towards more egalitarian patterns of access to Higher Education it is necessary to take account of the extent to which qualified young people are being differentially channelled towards certain courses or institutions. Here there is concern among the public that egalitarian access policies are not something that are welcomed by the elite universities which continue to draw their intakes from the small minority of young people who attend fee paying schools. We share this concern, but argue that the problem is much more deep-seated. The evidence discussed in this chapter draws attention to the sorts of statistics that must be considered by the new English Access Regulator and others who are concerned that the benefits of the current expansion of Higher Education reach those sections of our society who have largely been excluded from the benefits of past periods of expansion.

Evidence from recent research

The difficulties inherent in using quantitative measures to assess changes in levels of access to Higher Education were highlighted by a research project undertaken between 1998 and 2002 by the University of Glasgow for the Joseph Rowntree Foundation. The research project was designed to address issues surrounding the relative under-representation of young people from disadvantaged backgrounds within Higher Education. This aim was achieved by recruiting a sample of qualified but disadvantaged young people while still at school and by tracking their progress towards Higher Education.

Disadvantaged schools selection procedure

The research began by identifying schools that had below the Scottish national average level of school-leavers entering Higher Education, yet had a sufficient number of achieving pupils (ten or more) in the final school year (S6, which approximates to age 17 or school year 13 elsewhere in the UK) for a viable sample of qualified young people to be recruited. This was accomplished by making use of the school statistics published at that time (HM Inspectors of Schools, 1997 and 1998). Using this procedure, 16 schools were selected, from where a sample of suitable young people was recruited.

Each of the participating schools was located in one of four geographical areas. These areas were selected in order to represent a continuum from the inner city (seven schools), through a conurbation of large manufacturing towns (three schools) and small town former mining communities (four schools) to remote highland or island environments (two schools). As we will see, in practice this meant that each of the participating schools tended to serve localities classified as deprived by various databases. The remote geographical area was a partial exception to this, although both the schools in this sub-sample had a government designated regeneration area or SIP (Social Inclusion Partnership) located within their catchments.

Sampling disadvantaged school-leavers

A classroom survey was conducted in each school during the Spring of 1999. This involved a questionnaire being completed by all final year (S6) pupils present on the day that the researcher called (two foreign exchange students were excluded). This procedure recruited an initial sample of 514 respondents (there was only one refusal at this stage). The questionnaire was designed to measure both levels of academic achievement (including aspirations towards Higher Education) and demographics (i.e. levels of individual disadvantage).

At the time of the classroom survey, most of the respondents were aged seventeen (91.9 per cent) and a majority was female (56.8 per cent). Just under a third (30.6 per cent) of the sample were from single parent families and less than one in ten (8.9 per cent) were only children. Three-quarters of respondents (75.8 per cent) had at least one parent who was in full-time work, while more than one in eight (13.2 per cent) had at least one parent who was unemployed at the time of the survey. Almost one-third of the sample (29.6 per cent) received a bursary, given out in Scotland as an incentive to encourage more children from low-income families to remain in full-time education after the minimum school-leaving age of 16 years. This payment can be considered a good indicator of socio-economic disadvantage in itself (and as such was used as a selection criterion for subsequent face-to-face interviews). Around two-thirds (65.8 per cent) of the sample received some money from their families ('pocket money'), while around a half (51.8 per cent) were already earning money from part-time work (i.e. while still at school).

As this initial sample of young people were nearing the end of their final year at school, it was anticipated that a proportion of those recruited would progress into Higher Education in the Autumn (1999), while others, including some qualified school-leavers, would not do so. To measure how many respondents actually progressed to Higher Education, it was decided to keep track of these young people by conducting a postal follow-up survey at that time. To this end respondents were asked to provide contact details (there was only one further refusal). The aim of this postal questionnaire was to assess the success rate of disadvantaged school-leavers in accessing Higher Education.

Finally, and in addition to these surveys, face-to-face interviews were conducted with a representative sub-sample of qualified but disadvantaged young people the following Spring (2000). Some interviewees were in Higher Education, while others were not. These interviews were conducted to provide qualitative data measuring the experiences of disadvantaged but qualified school-leavers and to shed light on the reasons behind their post-school destinations. Those eligible for interview were selected from the demographic information they provided during the initial classroom survey.

Given the methodology used to recruit the above cohort it might have been expected that those who accessed Higher Education in this sample could justifiably be regarded as successes in the struggle to broaden participation within Higher Education. However, in the following sections we will outline some of the caveats to such an assertion. These include problems with interpreting school statistics, area deprivation indices, measures of individual disadvantage or personal circumstances and also the appropriateness of the targets used to measure success.

School statistics

The research project described above utilised 'official' statistics that are published annually as indicators of school performance. These statistics, commonly known as 'league tables' can be used to identify schools with high or low levels of school-leavers who progress to Higher Education. As such this information may be seen as useful to parents, teachers and young people, as well as researchers or policy makers. Whereas this may at first seem to be a good way of targeting groups who might benefit from policies aimed at broadening participation within Higher Education, there are a number of hidden factors which bring the usefulness of such statistics into question.

The research project only recruited from schools with below average rates of school-leavers who access Higher Education. These low access rates exist primarily because of low levels of achievement in such schools, which is in itself a reflection of the levels of disadvantage of the young people who attend such schools. When this is combined with the low level of retention within such schools, a further reflection of background disadvantage, rates of access to Higher Education can become particularly low. At first glance it may therefore seem obvious to target assistance at such schools and in particular at those pupils who are aspiring to achieve or remain beyond age 16. However, a closer inspection of the young people in such schools who do display these characteristics reveals a more complicated picture.

When the classroom survey was conducted, the most apparent feature of the sample was the relatively small number of pupils who remain in such disadvantaged schools until the final year (S6). In some inner-city schools with rolls of 750 to 1,000 pupils overall, fewer than 20 had remained until the sixth year. For example, one school had a roll of 850 yet only 12 pupils in S6 (as opposed to approximately 200 pupils in each of the compulsory years). In other words the underlying difficulty here is that the great bulk of young people, who attend schools located in areas of disadvantage, leave before they reach the age when they would even be eligible to sit the exams necessary to gain entry into Higher Education. The implications of this finding for policy makers being that initiatives aimed at improving the access rates from such schools would need to be targeted at an earlier age group. This of course means that increasing the level of access to Higher Education amongst the most disadvantaged young people will only come after such young people can be persuaded to remain in school in the first place.

This phenomenon exists as an expression of the greater attrition rate from education in general, in this case from secondary schools, found amongst young people from disadvantaged backgrounds. At a between schools level this means attrition is greatest in those serving areas of disadvantage, such as the schools that participated in this research project (although as will be discussed later, such attrition gradients also exist *within* such schools). In contrast to these low retention rates, schools serving more affluent areas often have a majority of pupils remaining beyond the minimum leaving age, while in independent (fee paying) schools the numbers enrolled in the final year and sitting exams for entry to university may actually exceed those in the years before the minimum leaving age. Indeed, the relative success of other schools may be in part at the expense of low achieving schools located in areas of disadvantage, as some parents may choose to send their children to these non-local schools.

Even the relatively disadvantaged schools selected for this research received some pupils from more severely deprived areas. This was true of all the inner-city schools surveyed, though in the more rural areas there were clearly fewer or no alternative (state) schools to choose from. In some cases, the respondents concerned had only transferred school during their final two years in order to sit the exams necessary for entry to university at a 'better' school. This situation was made more complicated by the effects of school mergers and closures (which is a more common occurrence with schools located in areas of disadvantage). For example, in the school where only 12 pupils had enrolled in S6 at the beginning of the year, the number of questionnaires returned was almost double that figure ($n = 23$). This happened because the neighbouring school, which had a similar intake, had recently closed and the surveyed school had gained extra pupils. Two of the other six schools located in the inner city area also 'benefited' from the mergers programme, with one gaining two, the other only one final year pupil from the even more disadvantaged catchments of the adjacent schools which had closed (where research such as this would not have been viable owing to the scarcity of young people who do not leave education at the earliest possible opportunity).

This ever shuffling school population, together with a range of school specific factors (e.g. variety of subjects being taught, quality of teaching and diversity of catchment or intake) would therefore seem to favour the use of area rather than school-based statistics when attempting to measure the numbers of disadvantaged young people accessing Higher Education. However, as we will explain in the next section, using area databases as a technique for measuring improvements in access to Higher Education can also be fraught with difficulties.

Area statistics

It was intended from the research design to recruit a sample of respondents who were predominantly resident in areas of deprivation. This was confirmed by examining the postcodes of the home addresses given by respondents who participated in the classroom survey and comparing these to databases which measure geographical deprivation. The first of these to be used was the Carstairs and Morris deprivation category system, which allocates every postcode sector in Scotland to a septile or DEPCAT (Carstairs and Morris, 1991; McLoone, 1994). According to this system, almost three-quarters (73.6 per cent) of the sample lived in deprived postcode sector (DEPCAT 5, 6 or 7) whereas none lived in the most affluent sectors (DEPCAT 1). Only nine respondents lived in the second most affluent septile (DEPCAT 2). A full breakdown across all seven DEPCATs, for all respondents, is shown in Figure 14.1.

Figure 14.1 reveals that as expected the sample was predominantly resident in areas of deprivation. However, this was only partially confirmed by using another system used to classify respondents from their postcode, the UK-wide ACORN system (CACI Ltd., 1993). This system uses exact postcodes (much smaller areas than DEPCAT sectors), each of which is allocated into one of six ACORN Categories (A to F) and 54 numbered ACORN Types. Although ACORN Types with higher numbers are usually regarded as more disadvantaged, this system takes into account many other area characteristics (e.g. ethnicity, age of population, family structure, spatial geography). The majority (58 per cent) of respondents lived in the most disadvantaged ACORN Category F, termed as 'striving' neighbourhoods (which comprises Types 39 and above). Similarly the ACORN Type in which the most respondents were resident was Type 51 (n = 55), which is described as representing the neighbourhoods suffering 'the greatest hardship' and also as the 'worst unemployment blackspots in Britain'. However, as can be seen in Figure 14.2 the sample, although recruited only in low-achieving schools, comprised young people who resided across a broad range of neighbourhoods, including some (8.9 per cent) who lived in the most affluent ACORN Category A (Types 1 to 9).

In addition to the DEPCAT and ACORN area classification systems, more than two out of five respondents (42.5 per cent) lived in neighbourhoods designated for government social inclusion partnership assisted regeneration programmes (SIPs or equivalent).

In terms of accessing Higher Education, these area disadvantage measures can be slightly misleading, especially when applied to young people such as those in this research sample. The design of the project purposively included recruiting school-leavers from a geographically remote area. Of the 81 (15.7 per cent) respondents with home addresses in this large area only one lived in a relatively deprived DEPCAT (6), only one in ACORN Type 51 and only four in a SIP area. This may be a true representation of the lack of deprivation in such remote areas, although it may also indicate inadequacies in the way in which rural disadvantage is recorded, particularly in regard of young people and especially in relation of those aspiring towards Higher Education. The most common ACORN Type of respondents from this geographical area was Type 7 (n = 15), described as 'holiday retreats' with 'high numbers of older people'. Clearly this apparent lack of disadvantage, the result of the predominance of

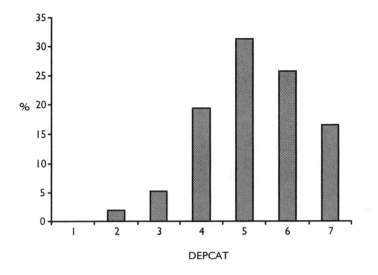

Figure 14.1 Area (DEPCAT) deprivation of the addresses of final year school-leavers attending low access schools

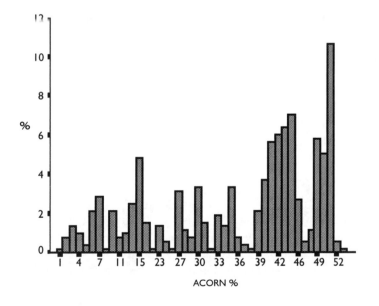

Figure 14.2 Area (ACORN) Type of the addresses of final year school-leavers attending low access schools

'affluent greys' (as ACORN terms them) in these neighbourhoods, is a phenomenon that is unlikely to be transferable to the advantage of local teenagers. In either event, any advantage indicated from these deprivation statistics is likely to be offset by the fact that all the remote area respondents who took part in the research resided too far from any institution of Higher (or even Further) Education for daily commuting to be an option and therefore for them enrolment in post-school education would necessitate a (costly) housing transition.

Even after considering the hidden nature of the disadvantage affecting the young people from the remote area, at first glance the area statistics as presented above do still indicate that the sample recruited from schools serving disadvantaged communities *does* predominantly consist of disadvantaged young people, although this was less true of the more precise ACORN measure (see Figures 14.1 and 14.2). However, a closer examination of where the young people who took part in this research actually lived revealed that using such databases can mask a great deal of hidden affluence or advantage amongst final year leavers from low-achieving schools.

This hidden advantage is a result of the way in which area statistics fail to reflect pockets of individual variance. In the same way in which pockets of disadvantage (e.g. remote area deprivation, see above) may be hidden from the statistics by predominate and surrounding affluence, this can also be true in the opposite direction where small pockets of affluence exist within poor neighbourhoods. This phenomenon was found to exist in each of the three other geographical areas studied in this research. Put simply, when respondents' home addresses were mapped, these were not uniformly distributed throughout their school's catchment area. Further to this, the home addresses of young people who were aspiring towards Higher Education were found to be particularly concentrated within these clusters. This is most easily demonstrated by mapping respondents' addresses in the self-contained small towns study area where this phenomenon could not be compounded by the effect of other schools with adjoining catchments either importing or exporting pupils. Figures 14.2 and 14.3, which map the home addresses of school-leavers recruited from two of the schools serving former mining communities, illustrate this phenomenon.

The most striking thing about Figure 14.3 ('Coaltoun') is that half (12/24) of the respondents from this community live in one small geographical area, an area of modern private built housing. In contrast only eight respondents lived in the council estates or 'schemes' that make up the majority of the community. The four remaining respondents lived along or near the two main roads through the area, where older desirable properties are located. Indeed, this geographical representation of local inequality is likely to be an underestimation of the true picture in 'Coaltoun' as these 'schemes' are likely to have both a higher population density and larger numbers of teenagers than the other two types of area. In other words, those who remain at the local school beyond the minimum leaving age until their final year, and hence those who are at least eligible to apply for university, tend to be from the 'better off' areas locally.

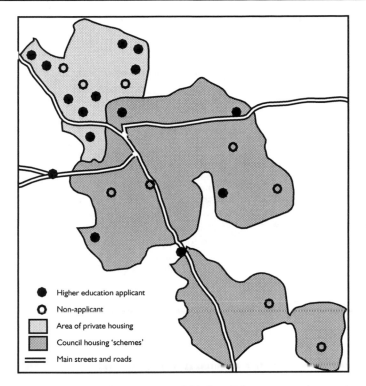

Figure 14.3 Map of addresses of Higher Education applicants in 'Coaltoun'

Almost the whole of 'Coaltoun' (population approximately 9,500) is classified as a SIP area, including the area of private housing and all the main roads (only one respondent, who lived in one of the council schemes, was not resident in the SIP area). Both of the two postcode sectors that cover this community can be categorised as deprived. Three 'Coaltoun' respondents were resident in a DEPCAT 6 sector (including the non-SIP respondent and a main road resident), while the remainder, including all the private housing residents, lived in a DEPCAT 5 sector. In other words neither the DEPCAT nor the SIP status of these school-leavers gives any indication of local variation within 'Coaltoun'.

The more detailed ACORN classification (which uses exact postcode) did present a somewhat different picture. The twelve respondents living in the area of private housing were found to reside in ACORN Types ranging between 3 and 14 (ten lived in Type 9). In contrast the ACORN Types of those residing in the 'schemes' of 'Coaltoun' ranged between 41 and 50. This would seem to imply that ACORN is a better measure for identifying disadvantaged Higher Education applicants than are either DEPCAT or SIP area status. However, even this small area measure could not explain the success of those who lived along the main

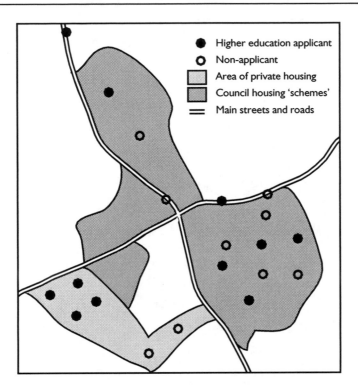

Figure 14.4 Map of addresses of Higher Education applicants in 'Minetoun'

roads, as the ACORN Types of these respondents varied from 30 to 51 and as such are more likely to be a reflection of the social mix within such postcodes between these main road addresses and the 'schemes' that they bisect.

Figure 14.4 maps the distribution of final year pupils and Higher Education applicants in the neighbouring community of 'Minetoun' (population approximately 4,000), which is located approximately 10 miles from 'Coaltoun'. At first glance the situation in 'Minetoun' would appear to be 'better', as despite having a smaller population than 'Coaltoun', a similar number of young people (*n* = 20) were recruited from the final year at the local school. Furthermore, half of these young people lived in the local council housing 'schemes' (ACORN Types 41 to 46). Although like 'Coaltoun' those final year pupils who lived in either an area of modern private built housing (ACORN Types 2 to 33) or along the main roads (ACORN Types 13 to 30) were most likely to be applying for Higher Education, half of those who lived in the local 'schemes' were also doing so.

Despite having labour market similarities with 'Coaltoun', at the time of the classroom survey 'Minetoun' was not classified as a SIP area. Of the two postcode sectors that cover this community only one could be considered deprived (DEPCAT 5, where 13 of the 20 respondents lived). The other postcode sector was DEPCAT 2 and contained the majority (7/9) of the respondents with this DEPCAT (the most affluent) in the whole research sample. At this stage, with these statistics in mind, the relative affluence of 'Minetoun' would appear to be reflected in the numbers of young people retained at the local school and applying for university. However, as we will see this does not mean that these young people in 'Minetoun' (half of whom live in 'schemes') have an advantage over those in 'Coaltoun' (most of whom live in 'better off' areas albeit within a government assisted SIP area).

The true underlying similarities between the two former mining communities are revealed in Figures 14.5 and 14.6. These take things one stage further and map the young people from 'Coaltoun' and 'Minetoun' who actually accessed Higher Education according to the postal survey conducted six months after the classroom survey. It should be noted that three respondents from each community who took part in the classroom survey did not respond to the postal survey and these six young people are removed in Figures 14.5 and 14.6. These two maps break down the remaining respondents into four categories of post-school destination: those who accessed Degree courses, Diploma courses (HND), other courses (e.g. NC, HNC) and those who were not in education at the time of the postal survey.

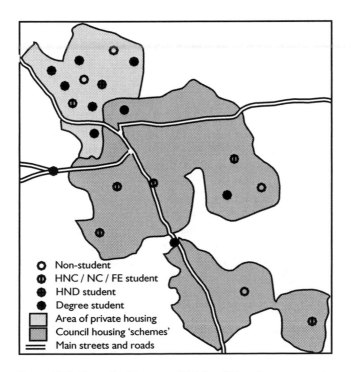

Figure 14.5 Map of addresses of Higher Education entrants in 'Coaltoun'

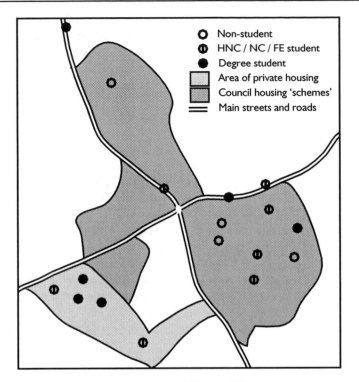

Figure 14.6 Map of addresses of Higher Education entrants in 'Minetoun'

Taking Figure 14.5 first, it can be seen that the local inequalities in 'Coaltoun' persisted, with those who enrolled in Degree courses being largely restricted to the respondents living along the main roads or in the area of newer private housing. This situation was exacerbated by the fact that the families of one Degree and one HNC student living in the 'schemes' actually moved away from 'Coaltoun' after their children became students (these respondents are both still shown in Figure 14.5). On a more positive note, most of the respondents in all parts of 'Coaltoun' were still in some form of education at this time for whatever reason (e.g. failure to find full-time employment).

When Figure 14.6 is examined, it is clear that the situation in 'Minetoun' is now much more similar to that of 'Coaltoun'. Again those who accessed Degree courses at university tended to live in the 'better off' parts of this community, either in the private housing area or along the main roads. Meanwhile those who despite living in the council 'schemes' had enrolled in post-school education tended to have entered non-Degree courses, with only one respondent from this background having successfully accessed a Degree course. The difference between Figures 14.4 and 14.6 ('Minetoun' applicants and entrants) is evidence of a continued greater attrition rate within post-school education of young people from more disadvantaged backgrounds. This pattern was found throughout the research sample at this time (Forsyth and Furlong, 2003a). Indeed data collected in subsequent years (2001–3) implied that these inequalities continue to intensify to Degree year (two years hence) and beyond (Forsyth and Furlong, 2003b), by which time the number of respondents from the 'better off' parts of 'Minetoun' enrolled in Higher Education actually increased.

The implications of Figures 14.5 and 14.6, which compare school-leavers and their destinations from 'Coaltoun' and 'Minetoun', are that they expose a number of weaknesses inherent to area-based approaches being used to measure access to Higher Education. This in turn means that any initiatives aimed at reducing educational inequalities (e.g. the so-called 'postcode premium') could prove to be counter-productive. If applied to these neighbouring former mining communities, such approaches would effectively benefit the minority in 'Coaltoun' who are already advantaged and conversely would effectively help to exclude the disadvantaged in 'Minetoun'.

The pattern unveiled by Figures 14.3 to 14.6 could be repeated throughout the whole sample of school-leavers recruited from low-achieving schools located in areas of disadvantage. That is, final year pupils at these schools, particularly those aspiring towards university, tended to live in affluent enclaves often not detected by area measures of disadvantage. As such area measures may exaggerate the success rates of statistics attempting to count access to Higher Education. Although the more small scale ACORN measure would appear to have some advantages over DEPCAT or SIP, it does seem clear from the maps shown in Figures 14.3 to 14.6 that measures of individual or family background character-istics may be a better way of quantifying improvements in widening access to less advantaged groups.

Family background statistics (social class)

The existence of a hidden more affluent minority attending schools located in areas of disadvantage was confirmed by the social class profile of the respondents. This was calculated from information provided about their parental occupation during the classroom survey. In this, if either parent was not working then respondents were asked to provide their previous occupation. The final social class profile of the sample, derived using the Registrar General's occupational classification (OPCS, 1991), is shown in Figure 14.7.

The most striking feature of Figure 14.7 is that only half (49.8 per cent) of those who provided information about their parents' occupations were classified as being in the manual social classes (IIIM to V). This surprisingly high level of non-manual respondents is in part explicable by the presence of the remote area sub-sample, who were selected on the grounds of geographical, rather than socio-economic, disadvantage and which had the highest level of non-manual social class respondents (65.8 per cent). However, even the sub-sample recruited from

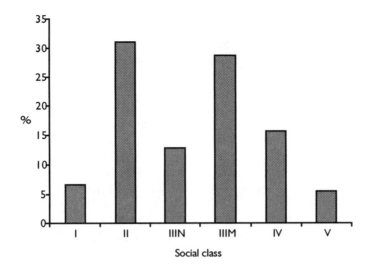

Figure 14.7 Social class of final year school-leavers from schools
located in disadvantaged areas

low-achieving schools in the deprived conurbation of large manufacturing towns
had a majority of respondents who were classified as non-manual (56.9 per cent).
If this social class profile was merely a function of the study areas in which the
research was conducted then Figure 14.7 should resemble Figure 14.1, which
clearly it does not. Unlike Figure 14.1, this class profile is not what one might
expect to find from a sample recruited in schools serving deprived communities.
Once again this is yet more evidence suggesting that the pupils who stay on until
the final year of such schools are atypical of their intake having come from the
small minority of more affluent local families resident in the community (e.g. the
local doctor's daughter in 'Coaltoun' and the Indian restaurateur's son in
'Minetoun', both main road dwellers, were in the sample).

Not shown in Figure 14.7 are the 74 (14.3 per cent) respondents who provided
no parental occupation. These individuals could give no parental occupation for
a complex variety of reasons including parents who were (or were last known to
be) unemployed, long-term sick, deceased, retired, a houseperson, a full-time
carer, a student, institutionalised or simply not present and hence their
occupational status was unknown to the respondent. When compared to those
who did provide their parental occupation, this group were found to be particularly
disadvantaged and had the smallest numbers applying to and accessing Higher
Education. Half (51.4 per cent) of these respondents were from single parent
families, which in part explains why they could not provide an occupation for
either of their parents (as in such cases often their mother is present as a housewife/
carer and they do not know what job their father does, even if they do know that
he is working). Seven out of ten (70.8 per cent) of this group were bursary pupils

at school and nearly eight out of ten (78.1 per cent) stated that neither of their parents was currently working full-time.

It was not surprising to find that these 'classless' individuals had the lowest rate of Degree level access. This is shown in Figure 14.8, in which respondents who could not be allocated to a parental social class are labelled Class 'X'. At the opposite extreme are the few Class I respondents in this research who had by far the highest rate of accessing Degree courses at this stage (and, in contrast to other groups, the HE participation rate of these individuals actually increased in subsequent years). In contrast, the Class X group had the highest level of enrolment in HNC/NC/FE courses (all of which are of one year or less in duration), which tends to indicate that these young people were aspiring to and not merely rejecters of post-school education.

Clearly this group (X) of unclassifiable respondents might be considered 'lower class'; however, this does leave it open to question where they would fit on any systems used for measuring improved access. For example, the UCAS figures for the social class of all Higher Education applicants in the UK during the year in which the respondents in this research made their applications stated that 11 per cent of Degree applicants and 20 per cent of Diploma applicants (the second highest category) were defined as 'other/unknown' social class (UCAS, 1999). It would, however, seem unlikely that all these other or unknown applicants had the same reasons for 'missing' social class information as the young people in the research sample.

With the inclusion of those with no parental occupation the 'middle class' group recruited in this research drops to 43.0 per cent of the total sample. Although at first glance this may still seem to be an excessive amount of such young people to be attending low-achieving schools, two features of this group should be remembered. First, the schools where the sample was recruited had a very low retention rate beyond the minimum leaving age. Therefore such schools need only have a dozen or so 'middle class' pupils enrolling in the first year (out of say

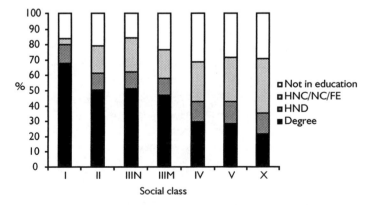

Figure 14.8 Social class and access to post-school education

a roll of 200 per year) for this to be translated into a majority of the final year pupils, because of the excessive attrition rate *within* such schools of the more disadvantaged young people. Indeed during subsequent interviews with such young people they stated that they felt attending such schools had worked to their advantage, as the teaching staff tended to earmark such pupils for special tuition. Second, these social class figures may mask the fact that many of these 'middle class' young people may themselves not be from particularly affluent families (otherwise they may have chosen to live somewhere else). The most common parental occupations in this *relatively* advantaged group were: in social class II, primary school teacher and nurse (both $n = 27$) and in social class IIIN, sales assistant ($n = 38$). Also many of these were previous occupations or those of single parents. For example, one young person interviewed was allocated to social class II because her unemployed single mother's previous occupation was auxiliary nurse. The young person concerned lived in a SIP area and in this instance her area of residence was clearly a better indicator of her relative disadvantage.

In summary then, individual family measures such as social class may have some pluses over school or area measures of disadvantage, but these too have their limitations. Like school league tables or deprivation indices, parental occupation (or income statistics) may be a better indicator of overall population changes in levels of access to Higher Education than a mechanism for identifying individuals from disadvantaged backgrounds who could benefit most from financial or other assistance.

Conclusion and implications

This chapter has highlighted the difficulties in identifying Higher Education applicants from disadvantaged backgrounds. The research described in this chapter is of interest in that despite a sampling frame which recruited only from schools with low levels of access located in areas of disadvantage and a selection procedure which identified cases from individual demographics, in practice it was actually quite difficult to find many truly disadvantaged young people who were participating fully in Higher Education. This was because when using school or area statistics, many apparently disadvantaged young people were actually representatives of pockets of local affluence. On the other hand when using individual social class or income statistics some young people appeared to be more affluent than they actually were.

The implications of these findings for researchers and policy makers should be obvious. It would seem likely that some measures implying improved access may be over-estimates in that these are merely reflecting increases in the numbers of relatively advantaged young people from low-achieving schools or deprived areas who may enrol at university. This may be good for hitting politically motivated access 'targets'; however, directing assistance to further improve access rates on such a basis would seem likely to prove counter-productive in the long run. Conversely some apparently 'middle class' young people who may actually be facing many hardships or barriers would not appear in such access statistics. In this situation there is a need to ensure that any assistance that is made available is targeted toward the right individuals. Perhaps this could better be done on a case-by-case basis as opposed to relying on blanket statistics such as school performance, area deprivation or parental social class.

Above all, the research has highlighted the need to reach out to the majority of disadvantaged young people who do not even remain in school beyond the minimum leaving age, let alone progress to Higher Education. Only when it can be demonstrated that significant numbers from this group, at least on a par with the numbers of their middle class peers, are enrolling in the longer and more prestigious university courses will we be able to report that access to Higher Education has been truly broadened.

References

CACI Ltd (1993) *ACORN User Guide*, London: CACI.

Carstairs, V. and Morris, R. (1991) *Deprivation and Health in Scotland*, Aberdeen: Aberdeen University Press.

DfES (2003) *Widening Participation in Higher Education*, London: DfES.

Forsyth, A.J.M. and Furlong, A. (2003a) 'Access to higher education and disadvantaged young people', *British Education Research Journal*, 29(2), 205–25.

Forsyth, A.J.M. and Furlong, A. (2003b) *Losing Out? Socio-economic Disadvantage and Experience in Higher Education*, Bristol: Policy Press

HM Inspectors of Schools (1997) *Leaver Destinations from Scottish Secondary Schools 1994/ 95 to 1996/97*, Edinburgh: The Scottish Office.

HM Inspectors of Schools (1998) *Examination Results in Scottish Schools 1996–98*, Edinburgh: The Scottish Office.

McLoone, P. (1994) *Carstairs Scores for Scottish Postcode Sectors from the 1991 Census*, Glasgow: Public Health Research Unit, University of Glasgow.

OPCS (Office of Population Censuses and Surveys) (1991) *The Standard Occupational Classification*, 2: 3, London: HMSO.

UCAS (University and Colleges Admissions Service) (1999) *Statistical Bulletin, Widening Participation*, Cheltenham: UCAS.

Chapter 15

E-learning, marginalised communities and social capital

A mixed method approach

Sara Ferlander[1]

Introduction

As indicated by Barraket in this volume, the rapid growth of information and communication technologies (ICTs), notably the rise of the Internet, has led to major societal changes. Castells (2001) notes the significance of the Internet by referring to it as 'the fabric of our lives' (p. 1). Digital inclusion has almost become a prerequisite for social inclusion in contemporary society (Ferlander, 2003). Studies by Wellman and Haythornwaite (2002) show that the Internet is increasingly becoming an integral part of people's everyday life. In Sweden, the country within which the study described later was located, more than two-thirds of the households (68 per cent) have access to the Internet at home (MMS, 2003). For this simple reason alone, it is thus important to investigate the impacts of the growth of ICTs.

In the literature there is disagreement between writers who see technology as a new basis for social inclusion and social capital (e.g. Lin, 2001; Wellman and Haythornwaite, 2002) and others who see it as a threat, leading to a decline in face-to-face contacts (e.g. Nie, 2001) and to new forms of social exclusion: the so-called digital divide: 'substantial differences between groups in computerization' (Fong *et al.*, 2001: 3).

Optimistic scholars consider the development of ICT to have positive effects upon social inclusion, since it enables people to participate in society regardless of temporal, spatial and other physical barriers (e.g. Timms, 1999). It is also argued that the Internet can provide a tool for a rise in social capital (e.g. Blanchard and Horan, 1998; Ferlander and Timms, 2001): 'connections among individuals – social networks and the norms of reciprocity and trustworthiness that arise from them' (Putnam, 2000: 219).

Negative voices argue that the use of computer-mediated communication will replace face-to-face contact leading to further isolation. Nie (2001) argues that the Internet keeps people indoors, staring at their computers, neglecting inter-actions in the local community. The biggest fear, however, concerning the develop-ment of ICTs is digital exclusion. Castells (2001) argues that in a 'society where most things that matter are dependent on these Internet-based networks, to be switched off is to be sentenced to marginality ...' (p. 277).

Although there has been a great diffusion of ICTs, there are still inequalities in computer use. As with most forms of exclusion, digital exclusion is organised along the same demographic lines, such as educational levels, ethnicity and age (e.g. Steyaert, 2002a and b).

In Sweden, for instance, only one fifth (20 per cent) of elderly people[2] use the Internet compared to almost every (97 per cent) young person[3] (SCB, 2003). There is also a geographical element, with people in marginalised communities being subject to what Reddick (2000) terms the *'dual* digital divide'. Fong et al. (2001) found that not only do poorer people have less access to effective computer use, but also poorer people in poorer areas lack formal training and informal mentors to provide them with computer skills.

To be included in contemporary society, citizens will increasingly need to engage in a process of learning how to use these new technologies. Learning ICT skills can be a useful tool in preventing social exclusion and increasing social capital. The focus in this chapter lies on researching the social impacts of informal ways of learning ICT. The chapter illustrates the mixed methodological approach used in the investigation of e-learning as a means of increasing social capital in a marginalised community, with a special focus on measurement of the complex concept of social capital.

Social capital: overview and definition

Social capital has recently become one of the most popular terms in the social sciences (e.g. Bourdieu, 1985; Coleman, 1988; Putnam, 1993). The concept is popular across disciplines, most prominently sociology, economics and politics. Although the explicit use of the concept is recent, recognition of the phenomenon is not. From the beginning of the discipline, sociologists (e.g. Tönnies, 1887) have discussed the ideas of social capital, even though the term itself has not been used.

Despite its historical roots and the widespread attention the term social capital has received, understanding of it is still in its infancy and there remains much confusion. The considerable contemporary debate surrounding the theoretical conceptualisation of social capital has raced ahead of the development of tools for measurement. Stone (2001) argues that in order to reach rigidity in social capital measurement, a clear understanding of the term is needed.

The idea behind social capital is that it has a positive value. Variations in social capital have, for example, been used to explain educational achievement (e.g. Coleman, 1988; Field, 2003), democracy (e.g. Putnam, 1993) and levels of crime (e.g. Sampson et al., 1997). However, there is evidence to suggest that there has been a decline in social capital in the last decades (Putnam, 1993) along with its uneven distribution (Putnam, 2002). For instance, marginalised communities tend to have low levels of bridging social capital, which is vital to escape poverty (Woolcook, 1998).

Various definitions of social capital have been presented in a rapidly increasing literature. Although the term has been defined in different ways, it is generally described as a resource accessed through social relationships. Most definitions include two aspects: the social relationship itself with its resources and the quality of those resources; and many definitions revolve around three elements: social networks, norms of reciprocity and trust. Social participation is often claimed to be a core element in social capital, but many definitions also include other elements, such as norms and trust. In this chapter, social capital is defined as *resources gained from social networks and social support, which facilitate the creation of trust and a sense of community*.[4]

Methodology: case study and research questions

The relationship between the use of ICT and social capital was investigated through a case study of two computer projects: a Local Net[5] and Internet Café, in a relatively marginalised community in Sweden. The area has a high percentage of single parent households, residents with low income and a foreign background – groups at risk of both social and digital exclusion. Specific aims of the ICT projects were to decrease the digital divide and increase social capital in the community. On the website of the Internet Café the following aims were stated (www.itcafeet.com):

> To increase knowledge about the new media and to create a place where people, old and young and from different nationalities, can meet and in that way increase communication between people in the area.

The Internet Café was making a determined effort to attract groups that might otherwise be excluded from the Information Society (and the rest of the society), such as poor people, elderly people, people with a foreign background and single parents. The prime aim was to increase interest in and knowledge about the new media among these groups, through the provision of subsidised computer access and informal learning: computer support and training. The Café also functioned as a physical (and virtual) meeting place with the aim to increase social contacts and social integration between different groups in the area. In other words, the Internet Café aimed to decrease inequalities in computer use and enhance social connections through informal ways of accessing and learning ICT.

The aim of the research was to evaluate the success of the computer projects. The first objective involved an investigation of whether the goal in increasing digital inclusion of disadvantaged groups was fulfilled. The second objective concerned the impacts of the computer projects on the residents' participation in the local community and their access to the wider society. The general research question was:

> To what extent can the use of information and communication technology (re-) create social capital and a sense of community in disadvantaged urban areas?

A mixed method approach

The research question was investigated through the case study of the computer initiatives. The case study is the method of choice when the phenomenon under study is not easily distinguishable from its context, like a project in an evaluation study. As suggested by Yin (1984), the case study uses multiple sources of evidence: a mixed method approach. In this chapter, the approach comprises research that mixes quantitative and qualitative methods within a single study. The two approaches usually tend to be highly separated. There have been a number of debates regarding the superiority of one or the other of these approaches (e.g. Datta, 1994). Objections to a mixed approach tend to be the result of a view that there are epistemological and ontological barriers to it (e.g. Smith, 1983).

However, use of the mixed method approach has been increasing since the 1980s. Bryman (2001) discusses several reasons for the use of mixed methods, such as triangulation. As described by Denzin (1978), triangulation aims to employ multiple methods to enhance the validity of the study. The variety of research methods enables each to complement and verify each other to achieve a fuller picture.

It is also argued that qualitative research facilitates quantitative research. The former research may help to provide background information, develop hypotheses and design survey questions. The inclusion of qualitative research facilitates the understanding of the survey findings. Whereas quantitative research tends to be descriptive, qualitative research tends to be explanatory. Bryman (2001) also argues that the mixed methods approach may be useful for 'solving a puzzle' (p. 454). As the outcomes of research are not always easy to anticipate, employing research methods not initially used can sometimes be helpful.

Methods of data collection

The methods of data collection included a variety of methods: documentary research, participant observation, in-depth interviews, questionnaires and focus groups.

Documentary research

The research was inspired by reading about the local community and the Local Net project in the media. Documentary research, including public records (e.g. statistics), media articles and project descriptions, was used to provide an introduction and background to the research. It also served as an important complement to other forms of methods throughout the research in terms of triangulation.

Participant observations

I became involved with the community and the Local Net project from its start. Access was gained following meetings with the project manager. A considerable amount of time was spent in the area during four years. The observations of people in the natural environment helped me become familiar with the community and the ICT projects, providing an overview of the case study. Norms, values and beliefs in the area in general could be observed, but also more explicitly in relation to the ICT projects. It allowed me to discover the everyday practices, such as how the technology was used in the IT-Café.

The insights gained through observations also helped developing questions for the surveys, interviews and focus groups. Moreover, visibility in the area was good for the creation of trust and finding participants for the research. The approach was overt, since I from the beginning stated who I was and what my research aimed to do, which is important in building trust in the researcher. This is especially important in marginalised communities, since many disadvantaged groups tend to have low levels of generalised trust. Through participation in the area, my social network expanded, facilitating access to subjects for participation in the qualitative research: the interviews and focus groups.

In-depth interviews

The first interviews were conducted with 'key people' in the project to get a general idea about the area and the project. These interviews were unstructured and open-ended, almost like conversations, using a very broad topic guide. Since the Local Net project was the first one of its kind in Sweden, the use of unstructured interviews was useful as an exploration of this new phenomenon. Like other forms of qualitative methods, the interviews were valuable as a strategy for discovery. The interviews, along with the observations, provided an important basis for the development of the survey instrument.

Later, more structured interviews were conducted to explore complex concepts, such as trust and solidarity, and investigate issues raised through the question-naire that merited a more in-depth study. The interview guide contained some general points concerning the computer projects, social capital and the local community. The discussions were dependent on the responses from the participant and allowed for a fair amount of individual adjustment. Most of the users were keen to talk and provide their opinions and often gave examples to clarify their answers. The interviews allowed personal interaction, obtaining deep and personal answers.

The interviewees, a total of seventeen users as well as non-users of ICT, themselves chose the place to meet, such as a favourite café or their homes. Much effort was put into making them feel comfortable, e.g. by the choice of my own clothes, by stressing confidentiality and by reassuring participants that there would be no knowledge based questions, but rather behavioural or attitudinal questions. This is important, especially when talking to disadvantaged groups about sensitive topics like exclusion and stigma.

Questionnaires

The questionnaire was chosen as a method to establish a description of the level of social capital in the community and a description of the computer projects, especially in order to find typical users and typical usage of computers, and also to investigate attitudes towards the projects. Moreover, the survey enabled comparisons between different groups: between different demographic groups and between users and non-users of ICT. The use of surveys also enabled some generalisations of the data, which is one of the main advantages with self-completion surveys. A large population can be surveyed, relatively cheaply (Gilbert, 1993).

A detailed survey was delivered to 392 residents: 200 (out of a 1,000) randomly selected residents not connected to the Local Net and 192 residents connected to the network. A total of 187 completed questionnaires were returned: 90 non-connected and 87 connected. In the IT-Café, 94 questionnaires were completed by its visitors. The samples were generally representative of the overall characteristics of the community population.

The main argument against postal questionnaires is that the response rate tends to be low (many do not achieve more than 50 per cent) and even when respondents do complete surveys their answers may be incomplete or unreadable (ibid.). Much effort was put into trying to maximise the response rate, since it tends to be especially low in marginalised communities, e.g. due to high mobility and low educational levels. In this particular community, many surveys had also been conducted earlier, which made the residents fed up with filling in surveys.

Two reminders were posted after the delivery of the questionnaire: one short card after three days and one letter along with a new questionnaire after a week. A considerable amount of time and effort was also put into the survey itself in terms of design and questions. The questions were based upon the initial interviews and observations, as well as upon the literature review, previous studies, surveys and scales (e.g. Srole, 1956; Ivarsson, 1997).

The questionnaire consisted of two sets of questions, corresponding to the research objectives: digital inclusion and social capital. The first set concerned questions about demographic factors, computer experience and computer usage, and perceptions of the project. The second set concerned questions about social capital: social networks, support, trust and sense of community. The measurement of social capital will be discussed later.

Focus groups

Focus group discussions were the final method used in the study. What differentiates them from other types of research is that they allow us to see how people interact in considering a topic, and how they react to disagreement. The results of the discussions give vivid and detailed perspectives and can help in identifying behaviours and attitudes which are considered socially unacceptable. Apart from this, focus groups are quicker and cheaper to conduct than individual interviews.

However, there are some disadvantages with focus groups too. Not everyone who has been invited may attend, but if some of them show up the session must be run anyway. The elderly, disabled and members from elites are especially unlikely to attend focus groups. Other problems are that focus groups can be unruly and it is hard to clearly record data (Gilbert, 1993).

As with the interviews, the focus groups aimed to clarify points raised in the surveys. They were used to explain and understand the findings from the surveys. The focus groups were useful for discussing complex and sensitive issues, such as trust online, negative uses of the Internet, stigma and community identity. They also resulted in different views about the research topic. I constantly tried to maintain a cordial and amicable atmosphere to make participants feel confident, whilst still attempting to induce contradiction around the most relevant issues.

The intention was also to investigate *online* behaviour in terms of social capital, as it had not been possible to do so in the survey. Whereas the survey mainly focused on the effects of the computer projects on social capital in the community, the focus groups also explored the creation and maintenance of social capital *online*. In that sense, the focus groups were used for 'solving a puzzle' (Bryman, 2001: 454). The initial aim was to do a longitudinal survey, comparing non-users and new users at the beginning of the project with users two years after its start. However, the Local Net did not work out as anticipated and the follow-up could not be conducted. The employment of focus groups was therefore very useful, comprising a more thorough study of computer usage.

To make sure as many as possible that had been invited would attend the participants were paid an equivalent of approximately £8 for participation in the focus groups. I also phoned the participants the day before the focus group to remind them about it. Still, some participants did not turn up to the groups as promised, which sometimes made them rather small.

In general, however, the turn-out was relatively satisfactory. Four focus groups with 12 participants were conducted. Many of the participants represented disadvantaged groups, such as single parents and people with a foreign background. In contrast to Gilbert (1993), there were also disabled and elderly participants in the groups and one focus group consisted of solely the elderly. This in itself led to comfortable participants and fruitful discussions about the important topic of ICT and elderly people.

Operationalisation of social capital

Along with the increased popularity of the concept of social capital, increasing efforts are being made to operationalise the term. This is a challenging task since social capital is a multidimensional concept, including complex elements such as trust and community. Because social capital is not a simple concept, its measurement is not a simple task.

There has been a recent increase in measurement frameworks (e.g. Onyx and Bullen, 1997; Krishna and Shrader, 1999). Social capital researchers aim to identity frameworks, which can quantify and qualify the term. Assessment tools have also been developed, using a mixed method approach, in order to measure social capital at the household, community and organisation levels (Grootaert and van Bastelaer, 2002). The complexity of the concept stresses the importance of a combination of quantitative and qualitative methods. Although the mixed approach has been used in this chapter, the discussion mainly focuses on the quantitative indicators of social capital (as it is easier to present here).

The operationalisation of social capital is dependent on its definition. The most comprehensive definitions of social capital are multidimensional. Common indicators of the concept are participation in social networks, norms of reciprocity, civic engagement and trust. Depending on the definition and the context, certain indicators may be more suitable than others. For instance, newspaper readership may be a better proxy of social capital in Italy (Putnam, 1993) than in India due to the shifting rates of literacy (World Bank, 2003).

The appropriateness of indicators is also dependent on the research level: whether the social capital is studied on a state, community or individual level. Putnam (2000) has developed 13 different measurements of social capital on a state level, which have been combined into a single measurement. Operationally what he means by social capital 'is the degree to which a given state is either high or low in the number of meetings citizens go to, the level of social trust its citizens have, the degree to which they spend time visiting one another at home ... and so on' (2001, p. 48).

Since social capital is investigated on a community level in the chapter, the concept is here defined as *resources gained from social networks and social support, which facilitate the creation of trust and a sense of community.*[6] The definition was used as a basis for the operationalisation, by looking at four elements on a community level:[7]

- Social Networks (formal-informal, strong-weak, and bridging-bonding networks)
- Social Support (five dimensions of social support)
- Trust (institutional and social trust)
- Sense of Community (solidarity and community attachment).

Structural and cognitive dimensions of social capital

Identifying key elements demonstrates that social capital is a complex concept, comprising both structural and cognitive dimensions (Krishna and Shrader, 1999). The former is concerned with people's behaviours: participation in networks and exchange of support. The latter deals with people's values and attitudes: trust and community.

In the literature there has been an extensive debate whether cognitive elements, such as trust and community, should be part of the definition or not.

For example, Woolcook (2001) considers trust as important in its own right, but sees it as an outcome rather than a source of social capital and therefore excludes it from the definition. It is argued that social capital should be defined by what it is rather than what it does.

However, many writers, including the present author, stress the dual significance of structural and cognitive aspects. Following Putnam (2001), the argument is that social capital is a complex concept: trust is a close consequence (but sometimes also a source) of social capital and therefore also an important proxy of social capital. Most writers stress the importance of acknowledging social capital as a multidimensional concept. Newton (1997) suggests that unless separate dimensions are identified, it is impossible to understand how the dimensions operate operationally, which limits our understanding of the term as a whole.

Despite this, numerous studies of social capital rely on unidimensional measures. Prominent among these studies are those using a single item measure of trust, often drawn from the *World Value Survey*,[8] a proxy of social capital as a whole (e.g. Knack and Keefer, 1997). The question 'Do you think other people generally can be trusted or that you cannot be too careful in relation to other people?' is often used in international comparisons as a proxy for social capital. Trust is a significant element of social capital, but it is also important to know how it inheres within structural components: social networks and social support.

Social networks and social support

It is generally believed that social networks and social support are crucial in the definition of social capital. Since social participation is claimed to be a core element in social capital, most questions in the survey concerned participation in social networks. A number of different forms of social networks were investigated: formal and informal, strong and weak, and bridging and bonding networks. It is important to distinguish these dimensions, since they affect social support, trust and community differently. Although the dimensions are conceptually different, in reality there are, of course, many overlaps between them.

Formal and informal networks

The first distinction was between formal and informal networks. In his early writings, Putnam (1993) concentrated on civic engagement. Membership in voluntary association is still a common indicator of social capital (e.g. Vogel *et al.*, 2003), often in international comparisons. It is generally argued that formal participation builds civic skills and provides access to information and formal support, e.g. medical services.

In accordance with the approach used by Putnam, formal involvement was measured through questions about membership in voluntary associations, voting and newspaper readership. Community involvement, contact with local politicians, local information and number of meeting-places were other indicators of participation in formal networks. In addition to Putnam's general indicators, spare-time activities, such as watching or participating in sports, going to bingo, visiting the library and attending meetings, were also measured. I think it is important to include this proxy, since it may be a more common way of civic involvement in contemporary society, also by a wider group of people, such as young people and people from a working class background.

Putnam has been criticised for his early work on formal networks when looking at social capital. The general literature on social networks (e.g. Lin, 2001) suggests that more informal networks should also be considered in analysing social capital. Newton (1997) argues that informal connections do not tend to build civic skills, but are important in sustaining social networks and providing social support.

In this research, informal social participation was also regarded as an essential component of social capital. People's social connections with family, friends and neighbours were therefore examined in terms of nature, size and frequency of contacts. More qualitative factors, such as satisfaction with the informal contacts and feelings of loneliness, were also measured in the survey. Questions about loneliness are not common within social capital research, but in combination with other questions they are simple and straightforward indications of low levels of social capital.

Social support, strong and weak ties

One of the most familiar dimensions of social capital is Granovetter's (1973) distinction between strong and weak ties. Strong ties are connections with people emotionally close to oneself, such as immediate family and close friends. Weak ties are connections with people emotionally distant to oneself, such as acquaintances. Strong ties tend to provide social support, whereas weak ties are more likely to give access to diverse information.

Strong ties were measured through questions regarding close friends, such as 'How many really close friends do you have?' and five dimensions of social support, such as questions about borrowing money, baby-sitting, talking to someone about personal problems or the need for companionship. Weaker ties were studied in terms of spare-time occupation, membership in associations and contact with local politicians, e.g. 'Do you think you have good contact with local politicians and civil servants?'

Bonding and bridging social capital

Within the recent literature on social capital, there has been a tendency to confuse the distinction between strong and weak ties with that between bonding and bridging social capital. Although the two sets of terms are similar, they are not synonymous. Bonding networks refer to people similar to oneself (e.g. similar in demographic factors or locality), whereas bridging networks concern people different to oneself. As with strong and weak ties, bonding ties tend to provide protection and bridging ties tend to create innovation.'

Bridging and bonding social capital were measured in geographical terms as well as in social terms. In terms of geographical location, the distinction was between local and non-local activities. Networks and support within the area (bonding social capital) were compared with those outside the local area (bridging social capital). Within the local area, the dimensions of bridging and bonding were also investigated in relation to solidarity and tension between residents in the area.

Trust and sense of community

The content within the structural dimensions of social capital is the cognitive dimensions, comprising values and attitudes: trust and a sense of community. According to Stone (2001), the means of measuring the cognitive dimensions are less well developed than are measures of the structural characteristics of networks.

In this research, two dimensions of trust were identified: institutional and social trust. Institutional trust is concerned with trust in the formal system (e.g. the political, tax or judicial system), whereas social trust can be characterised as trust in other people. It is important to distinguish these different forms, since they are not always related. Trust was measured using the Srole anomia-scale (Srole, 1956), which aims to measure people's sense of powerlessness and general mistrust. The scale includes five statements tapping different aspects of mistrust, including statements such as 'These days you do not really know whom to trust' and 'There is no point in writing to officials since they are rarely interested in the problems of the average man'.

A sense of community was made up of two dimensions: sense of solidarity and community attachment. Sense of solidarity was investigated through questions about social cohesion, sense of commonality and tension between groups, e.g. 'Do you believe there is tension between different groups in the community?' and 'If you think there is tension, which groups are you thinking about?' Community attachment was measured through questions about satisfaction about living in the area and local identity. Some questions from earlier studies in the area (e.g. Ivarsson, 1997) were used, e.g. 'To what extent do you feel "locally anchored" and rooted in the community where you live? (Give level of "rootedness" on a scale from 0, no roots, to 10, very strong roots)'.

Analysis and results

The analysis of the quantitative data provided descriptive statistics. Frequencies and percentages were calculated to give an overview of the results; cross tabulations were conducted to investigate differences between variables; significance was tested using t-test and chi-square as appropriate; and thematic analysis was used in the analysis of the qualitative data. Data triangulation of quantitative and qualitative results was undertaken and the qualitative data gave an interesting depth to the more descriptive quantitative data in terms of quotes and examples taken from the focus groups and interviews.

The combination of qualitative and quantitative data demonstrated that the Local Net did not achieve its goals, in terms of digital inclusion and social capital, and indeed was abandoned two years after its inauguration. In its place the Internet Café was established, which achieved many of the goals in relation to the digital divide and social contacts.

The findings show that visitors to the Internet Café, who included many disadvantaged groups, had acquired useful computer skills. The Café, with its provision of subsidised public access, informal computer support and training, made its visitors feel more included in the Information Society as well as in the wider society. The visitors also had significantly more local friends, expressed stronger social trust, perceived less tension and had a stronger sense of local identity than the non-visitors. The Internet Café was regarded as an offline as well as online meeting-place with positive impacts on social integration, and Internet use was related to networking, exchange of support and information seeking.

Conclusion

The mixed method approach proved to be very useful in the investigation of ICT and social capital in a marginalised community. In general, the mix of quantitative and qualitative methods capitalised on the advantages and compensated for the disadvantages of each approach. The combination provided alternative and complementary ways of approaching the same research question.

Qualitative methods were used both as preliminary research prior to the quantitative methods and later as a way of interpreting the quantitative results. The observations provided an important overview of the community and its projects. It also increased trust among residents and access to research subjects. The information from the observations and the initial interviews was useful for the development of an effective survey instrument, which resulted in a general description of social capital and computer use in the community. The focus groups were finally used to understand patterns identified in the questionnaire. The method was very valuable in the discussions of complex and sensitive issues, such as trust, stigma and local identity, with disadvantaged groups.

Measuring social capital was not easy. A major task was the conceptualisation of the concept, including its different dimensions. The mixed method approach facilitated the investigation and understanding of the multiple dimensions of the concept. The survey instrument provided a general description and overview of the extent of different forms of social capital, whereas the qualitative instruments enabled more in-depth studies of social networks, social support, trust and community. A clear definition, including key elements directly linked to the measurement framework, increases validity and facilitates the research of complex concepts. The development of theoretical and empirical indicators of social capital is therefore one of the most important priorities in the area.

Notes

1 This chapter is based on research conducted as part of the author's doctoral dissertation: Ferlander, S. (2003) *The Internet, Social Capital and Local Community.* Stirling: University of Stirling.
2 Between 65 and 74 years.
3 Between 16 and 24 years.
4 For a detailed discussion of the theoretical background to this definition see: Ferlander (2003).
5 A Local Net is a computer network, located in a physically based community, dealing with local issues. Subsidised home access tends to be provided to the local network, and to the Internet.
6 For a detailed discussion about the definition used see: Ferlander (2003).
7 Social capital was investigated on different research levels: micro, meso and macro, in the community. The micro level relates to an individual's participation in social networks and feelings of loneliness. The meso level concerns relations between different groups, such as different age and ethnic groups. The macro level refers to participation in the local community and in the wider society, such as voting and voluntary associations.
8 Also see Inglehart, R., Basanez, M., Diez-Medrano, J., Halman, L. and Luijkx, R. (2004) *Human Beliefs and Values* – a cross-cultural sourcebook based on the 1999–2002 values surveys, Mexico City: Siglo XXI.

References

Blanchard, A. and Horan, T. (1998) 'Virtual communities and social capital', *Social Science Computer Review*, 16(3), 293–307.

Bourdieu, P. (1985) 'The forms of capital', in J.G. Richardson (ed.) *Handbook for Theory and Research for the Sociology of Education* (pp. 241–58), New York: Greenwood.

Bryman, A. (2001) *Social Research Methods*, Oxford: Oxford University Press.

Castells, M. (2001) *The Internet Galaxy*, Oxford: Oxford University Press.

Coleman, J. (1988) 'Social capital in the creation of human capital', *American Journal of Sociology*, Issue Supplement, S95–120.

Datta, L. (1994) 'Paradigm wards: a basis for peaceful coexistence and beyond', in C.S. Reichardt and S.F. Rallis (eds) *The Qualitative-Quantitative Debate: New Perspectives* (pp. 53–70), San Francisco: Jossey-Bass.

Denzin, N. (1978) 'The logic of naturalistic inquiry', in N.K. Denzin (ed.) *Sociological Methods: A Sourcebook*, New York: McGraw-Hill.

Ferlander, S. (2003) 'The internet, social capital and local community', doctoral dissertation, University of Stirling.

Ferlander, S. and Timms, D. (2001) 'Local nets and social capital', *Telematics and Informatics*, 18, 51–65.

Field, J. (2003) *Social Capital*, London: Routledge.

Fong, E., Wellman, B., Wilkes, R. and Kew, M. (2001) *Correlates of the Digital Divide*, Ottawa: Office of Learning Technologies.

Gilbert, N. (1993) *Researching Social Life*, London: Sage.

Granovetter, M.S. (1973) 'The strength of weak ties', *American Journal of Sociology*, 78(6), 1360–80.

Grootaert, C. and van Bastelaer, T. (eds) (2002) *Understanding and Measuring Social Capital: A Multi-disciplinary Tool for Practitioners*, Washington, DC: World Bank.

Ivarsson, J.-I. (1997) *Så tycker brukarna om servicen i stadsdelen*, Utredningsrapport 1997: 3, Stockholm: USK.

Knack, S. and Keefer, P. (1997) 'Does social capital have an economic pay-off? A cross-country comparison', *Quarterly Journal of Economics*, November: 1251–88.

Krishna, A. and Shrader, E. (1999) *Social Capital Assessment Tool*, Social Capital Initiative Working Paper No. 22, The World Bank, Washington DC, online at: http://www.worldbank.org.poverty/scapital/wkrppr/wkrpppr.htm).

Lin, N. (2001) *Social Capital. A Theory of Social Structure and Action*, Cambridge: Cambridge University Press.

MMS (April 2003) *Mediamätning i Skandinavien MMS AB*, online at: http://www.mms.se).

Newton, K. (1997) 'Social capital and democracy', *American Behavioral Scientist*, 40(5), 574–85.

Nie, N.H. (2001) 'Sociability, interpersonal relations, and the Internet', *American Behavioral Scientist*, 45(3), 420–35.

Onyx, J. and Bullen, P. (1997) *Measuring Social Capital in Five Communities in NSW: An Analysis*. Centre for Community Organisations and Management Working Paper Series No. 41, University of Technology, Sydney.

Putnam, R.D. (1993) *Making Democracy Work: Civic Traditions in Modern Italy*, Princeton, NJ: Princeton University Press.

Putnam, R.D. (2000) *Bowling Alone: The Collapse and Revival of American Community*, New York: Simon & Schuster.

Putnam, R.D. (2001) 'Social capital. Measurement and consequences', *Isuma. Canadian Journal of Policy Research*, 2(1), 41–51.

Putnam, R.D. (2002) (ed.) *Democracies in Flux. The Evolution of Social Capital in Contemporary Society*, New York: Oxford University Press.

Reddick, A. (2000) *The Dual Digital Divide: The Information Highway in Canada* [Report]. The Public Interest Advocacy Center, Human Resources Development Canada, Industry Canada, online at: http://olt-bta.hrdc-drhc.gc.ca/publicat/index.html).

Sampson, R., Raudenbush, S. and Earls, F. (1997) 'Neighborhoods and violent crime: a multi-level study of collective efficacy', *Science*, 277, 918–24.

SCB (Statistiska Centralbyrån) (2003) *Äldre använder inte Internet. Pressmeddelande från SCB*, Stockholm: Statistics Sweden.

Smith, J.K. (1983) 'Quantitative versus qualitative research: an attempt to clarify the issue', *Educational Research*, 12, 6–13.

Srole, L. (1956) 'Social integration and certain corollaries: an exploratory study', *American Sociological Review*, 21(6), 709–16.

Steyaert, J. (2002a) 'Inequality and the digital divide: myths and realities', in S. Hick and J. McNutt (eds) *Advocacy, Activism and the Internet* (pp. 199–211), Chicago: Lyceum Press.

Steyaert, J. (2002b) 'Much ado about unicorns and digital divides', in J. van Beurden, P. de Graaf and T. Meinema (eds) *Bridging the Gaps* (pp. 47–58), Utrecht: NIZW-ICSW.

Stone, W. (2001) *Measuring Social Capital: Towards a Theoretically Informed Measurement for Measuring Social Capital in Family and Community Life*. Australian Internet and Family Studies Center, Research paper no. 24, Australian Institute of Family Studies,

ISBN 0 642 39486 5, online at: www.aifs.org.au/institute/pubs/RP24.pdf, National Library of Australia, Cataloguing-in-Publication Data.

Timms, E. (1999) 'Communities and welfare practice: learning through sharing', *New Technology in the Human Services*, 11(4), 11–17, online at: http://www.chst.soton.ac.uk/nths/etimms.htm, accessed on 23/10/03.

Tönnies, F. (original 1887) (1957) *Community and Society*, New York: Harper Torchbooks.

Vogel, J., Amnå, E., Munck, I. and Hull, L. (2003) *Assocational Life in Sweden. General Welfare, Social Capital, Training in Democracy*, Stockholm: Statistics Sweden, Report No. 101.

Wellman, B. and Haythornwaite, C. (2002) *The Internet in Every Day Life*, Oxford: Blackwell.

Woolcook, M. (1998) 'Social capital and economic development: towards a theoretical synthesis and policy framework', *Theory and Society*, 27, 151–208.

Woolcook, M. (2001) 'The place of social capital in understanding social and economic outcomes', *Isuma. Canadian Journal of Policy Research*, 2 (1), 11–17.

World Bank (2003) *How is Social Capital Measured?* online at: http://www.worldbank.org/poverty/scapital, accessed on 23/10/03.

World Value Survey (1990 and 1995) online at: http://www.worldvaluessurvey.org/.

Yin, R.K. (1984) *Case Study Research: Design and Methods*, London: Sage.

Chapter 16

Organisation behaviour, research and access

Chris Duke

Introduction

The first of four 'core strategic aims' of the English Higher Education Funding Council for the years 2003–8 is widening participation and fair access (HEFCE 2003). This appears to be a quite remarkable change of salience, moving access and participation from the margin to the centre of the board.

Yet, for all the importance of access and widening participation in the contemporary Higher Education policy arena, and for all the interest in and rising output of research into access, the two loose scholarly communities of widening access and organisation behaviour enjoy barely a nodding acquaintance. This chapter considers why this might be, and whether the literature and research traditions of organisation behaviour and the management of change offer any insights to those studying and working to promote wider participation. What 'research agenda' if any is now implied?

Organisation behaviour and access as fields of research, scholarship and practice

Why does there appear to be so little interest, within the field of organisational and management studies, in access?

Organisation studies 'belong' – that is to say they are perceived and usually located mainly – within the field of management and business studies. Behind that, they may be seen as a sub-set and field of application of the disciplines of sociology and psychology. Psychology inclines towards neutrality in its social identity. It commonly aspires to the status of high science. Sociology has a stronger tradition of studying and even identifying with the poor and the excluded. This is, however, less true of organisational behaviour which, like organisational and industrial psychology, has tended in the main to take more interest in – or at least to be more identified with – issues of management.

The study of access and widening participation as a movement and a policy belongs mainly within universities and a limited number of other institutional and occasionally community settings which connect with Higher Education over access. There are identities and dynamics here which go some way to explaining why so little of the work in organisation behaviour and change has illuminated and informed the practice of access, or been sought after by access practitioners.

Organisation studies and organisation behaviour groups are normally found in Business Schools and Schools of Management, the central interest of which for purposes of teaching, research and consultancy is mainly large, mainly private sector corporations. The teaching staple is the Master of Business Administration (MBA), whose clientele work mainly for such organisations. The small and medium enterprise (SME) sector has become a more recent focus of attention, partly because of its significance as in aggregate a very large employer, and also because of the intrinsic challenges which it presents for policy and management, by virtue of its character and configuration. The MBA takes diverse specialised forms and is shaped around particular market needs, with niche options. In 2002, for example, the London Institute of Education began offering a Master of Business Administration specifically in Higher Education.

Market forces are at play. The big private sector corporation is an easy and natural client for Business School organisation behaviour and change. The public sector, especially in times of privatisation and marketisation of public services, approximates or joins as a subsidiary client sector. Privatisation tendencies pose intellectual and practical challenges, health providing a prime example. Significant academic effort is drawn in. There are significant opportunities to win business through organisation and management teaching and training, research and consultancy.

As a sector Higher Education is less fertile, much less fertile again the access area within it. There may be inhibition about critically examining as a research object one's own kind of institution. The learning organisation waxes and wanes as an analytical concept, but more in the private sector than in that principal knowledge managing institution, the university. Moreover, educational institutions differ as a type from business enterprises – something we return to below. They have less funding available, or choose to make relatively little available, for research and development on themselves. Despite this large accounts are run up by contemporary (especially perhaps the 'modern') universities for management consultancy, mainly in IT and finance but also in organisation behaviour and change management, including the management of human resources. Whatever the reason, Higher Education has not attracted much of the mainly applied social science research associated with organisation behaviour and change management.

In Britain the small size and dispersed nature of the Higher Education research community is periodically regretted. There has, however, been for the past two decades a swelling volume of published work on Higher Education, exemplified by the lists of the Open University Press and a few other publishing houses. Little of this work is on management and organisational behaviour in Higher Education. Of this, still less is of interest to the mainstream of scholarship in organisation change and behaviour, occupied as it is with established subjects, clients, and sources of consultancy.

There is then only modest interest in Higher Education as a field of scholarship in the main centres of business and organisation studies. Probably the whole educational research endeavour is seen from outside as essentially about schools and schooling, and as a relatively closed community of practice. It also has low status. Seen from outside, Higher Education research is a marginal sub-set rather than an independent arena. It appears to offer little for fundamental social science insight (compare Peter Scott's observations at the beginning of Chapter 2). Within this marginal sub-set, access has been a yet more marginal field of practice. It is presumed to be impoverished conceptually and practically, of little interest beyond its own value-based and mission-led community of access workers.

If this is accepted it is not surprising that there has been little research on access which addresses the subject from the viewpoint of how organisations behave, are managed and change. Most inside are too busy doing access. Most outside lack the interest. Peter Scott's overview of research in Chapter 2 notes the value-commitment-enthused character of studies in this field. His typology distinguishes policy studies at system and institutional level, along with micro-level studies of student experience. It is (accurately) silent on organisational studies as a distinct genre.

We refer below to one study that does explicitly approach the world of access from this organisational behaviour viewpoint, and suggest what kinds of questions such an approach tends to pose. Although 'case study methodology is often criticized for its lack of rigour and generalization from a small sample' (Hazelkorn 2002: 69–82) this study also centrally addresses the generalisable relevance and utility of organisation behaviour theory to access.

Not all the fault, if fault it be, lies on one side. The world of access studies is special and distinctive. It is strongly value based, a social movement first and an educational programme and field of practice later. Marginal throughout a life which dates in Britain from the early 1970s, it was born out of early shortcomings of the post-Robbins expansion of an elite system then intended to serve all with the ability to succeed at university or college.

A raggedly clad but determined tribe, the 'Access movement' draws strength mainly within its own ranks. Solidarity around access and equity in the face of persisting elitism and exclusivity comes at the price of creating something like a church of true believers. Its discourse carries its own signs and signals, correctness of language, even self-generated and imputed opponents and enmities. Real or imagined, the embattled status of the access movement has been an anvil for forging an in-group community of the committed who are not tolerant of discourse which offends against egalitarianism and its associated style and values. The inclination is anti-establishment, towards suspecting the rich and the powerful.

Management studies, being associated with the world of corporate business, may be looked on askance. There is little empathy or common discourse between management, including organisation studies, and the access movement. The language of management and the market is deliberately intruded into Higher Education in ways that offend, which is perhaps not well advised as a way to induce change. It may be deliberately provocative, meant to disturb old assumptions and weaken protectionism. Students become clients or customers, teaching and research are core business seeking economies of scale, communities are markets with their niches, while students, research results and degrees are products, throughputs and outputs. Access, however, tends to attract and reinforce people with more communitarian values, anti-liberal in the modern economic sense but old-fashionedly liberal in terms of educational values and approach to teaching. Such people treat such language, and what is taken to lurk within it, with more or less open hostility.

This does not mean that organisation behaviour and change studies have nothing to offer to the study of access. It may explain the absence of a bumper research crop. In fact organisational studies provide tools to analyse if not to dismantle a form of managerialism inimical to access. I find the specialised literature of organisational crisis, for instance, helpful in this sense, to take a personal example (Duke 2003). Organisation studies will not, however, serve well where there is cultural dissonance exacerbated by the taint of new managerialism.

Applying organisation behaviour theory to the world of access

A comparative international study of access and Higher Education, *The Adult University* (Bourgeois *et al.* 1999), was unusual in examining explicitly how the study of organisations and organisation change contributes to the study of access and widening provision. Its third chapter, which we draw on here, looks at universities as organisations. It considers their common and distinguishing characteristics as an organisational type by reference to a literature spanning from the 1970s to the 1990s.

We are familiar with the public-private sector distinction, and its blurring as the Welfare State is dismantled or adapted to new mixed forms. Especially on the public sector side there has long been the recognition that people-oriented non-profit organisations and institutions, including educational institutions, hospitals and penitentiaries, have different functions, characteristics and defining behaviours from industrial for-profit production-line operations. This has not prevented the often indiscriminate transfer of ill-fitting management models to these institutions.

Management behaviours and organisational dynamics are not always as distinct as the missions and lines of 'business'. This may partly explain why management precepts, language and practices generalised and transferred from one type into another can offend, giving us the production-line school and the for-profit prison. Comparative study across organisational types, for example the fine work of Erving Goffman (1961) on closed institutions, can also be as highly illuminating as the transfer of metaphors, language and uninvited lessons can be offensive.

There are different, sometimes competing, typologies of organisation behaviour and change. Kazar (2001) for example distinguishes different models of change in Higher Education Institutions as evolutionary, teleological, dialectical, social cognition, and cultural, concluding that explanation is most effectively drawn from several of these models or ways of seeing. Much of his analysis is compatible with that of Bourgeois, allowing for different choices of term, such as dialectical and political.

The Bourgeois study favours a typology of *professional bureaucracy*. This includes universities, further recognising additional characteristics that differentiate them from other professional bureaucracies. Within this category, people working inside the university system are familiar with further sub-types and sub-categories, usually arranged hierarchically. All of this is especially relevant to access, in the sense that the national access mission is usually understood to mean giving equity of access into and participation in the full range of universities, not just to an implicitly inferior access sub-set.

Martin Trow (1973), looking from the far side of the United States in the 1980s, remarked of the still binary system that while the British discerned huge diversity among their universities and polytechnics, these all looked remarkably similar from California. None the less, Australia for example has various typologies of Higher Education Institutions, commonly four or five post-binary categories. Britain with its peculiar expertise in social class and classification can find as many as fifteen sub-types, looking beneath the simple 'new-old' post-binary divide. In considering access today we have to come to terms with the 'new binary divide' between Further and Higher Education Institutions. Some 12 per cent of Higher Education takes place in Further Education Colleges and that is set to grow. Access policy and practice absolutely straddles these two sectors, the relationship between which is at the heart of early twenty-first century access strategy.

Returning to the Bourgeois typology, professional bureaucracies are seen as having the following distinguishing features:

- Ambiguity and heterogeneity of goals (multiple, ambiguous, highly contested)
- Problematic technology (complex, uncertain and problematic tasks)
- Professional culture involving a demand for autonomy, and loyalty divided between discipline and institution
- Modes of labour division and co-ordination
- Professional power which is decentralised and which claims esoteric specialised expertise.

These common features of professional bureaucracies help us to understand their behaviour, and the challenges which this represents for management. Universities are also seen to have particular differentiating features:

- Fragmented professionalism resulting from

  (a) the multiplicity of academic disciplines or tribes, and
  (b) the diverse functions and goals of the institution, exacerbated by academics' individualism as autonomous professionals – hence the many jokes about cat-herding academics who unite only over car parking

- Academic governance patterns combining federated professional authority with overall bureaucratic co-ordination – hence the contemporary almost unceasing struggle between, and occasional attempt to reconcile, collegiality with efficiency, and the fact or threat of brute managerialism
- Environmental vulnerability as new pressures, new demands, and new policy initiatives, opportunities and threats pour in. This induces internal stress and pressure to diversify internally, and at system level a more strident demand for differentiation and specialisation between the missions and roles of different institutions.

A study of organisation behaviour that uses the recognition of such features and tendencies ought to help us better understand the ways that access is managed and succeeds in some institutions, and conversely, the foibles, follies and false paths through which it finds repeated frustration in others. These failures to achieve wider access may be 'institutionally determined'. They are not, however, necessarily entirely conscious and deliberate, nor even merely matters of carelessness or incompetence.

In particular, the conflicts that occur in such organisation types need to be recognised, as does the high propensity for conflict which these characteristics represent. There is conflict between multiple ambiguous goals and demands. There is conflict between social purpose and the need for institutional survival as costs rise and resources decline. There is conflict between individuals and their loose-knit tribes that pull in different directions. There is also conflict between 'classroom-and-laboratory academics' and top and senior managers trying to sustain direction and resist fragmentation.

The Adult University presents two ways of understanding a university's behaviour in respect of widening access. These are described as 'strategic' and 'structural'.

According to the first perspective, 'the organization's behaviour – in this case university policies and practices about adult access and participation – is interpreted and explained primarily by reference to the *actors' behaviours and strategies*'. The second level and kind of analysis, the structural, seeks to find the factors that explain why the actors behave as they do. What in the organisational structure and context serve as determinants of the rationale underlying the actors' behaviours in the decision process (op. cit. p.43)? This structural kind of analysis applies at both a macro (societal) and a meso (organisational) level.

Among the different strategic approaches, a political model seems to suit the characteristics of the university as an organisation better than other models, which are summarised as rational-analytic, bureaucratic, collegial and 'garbage can' (see Bourgeois *et al.* 1999 p.43). This means looking at the university in terms of interdependent competing coalitions each seeking to win by imposing their interests on the larger system of the institution as a whole. Access is typically conflictual: it raises key issues about institutional mission and priorities, relevance, quality and standards. The use of politics in decision-making 'is more likely to be observed in academic than in some other organizations, given their specific characteristics of high conflict potential; and it is more likely to be observed in decisions about access than in decisions about some other issues ...' (op. cit. p.45). When it comes to understanding why a university behaves as it does, and why access purposes seem to get lost or subverted, this approach may offer the researcher powerful insights.

Probing further as to why people behave differently, and why the story plays out in different ways between one part of a university and another, different theoretical approaches are possible within what we have called the structural approach. These are summarised as epistemic, personalist, cultural, contingency and structural-functionalist (Guyot 1998 cited in Bourgeois *et al.* 1999). They can be employed to consider, respectively, the different dimensions involved in understanding access: subject matter, the individual characteristics of faculty members, institutional sub-cultures, the relationship between institution or sub-system and its environment, and the legitimation principles which predominate in that university.

These different dimensions, and the whole structural approach, are important if the role and power of individuals are not to be over-played. Ignoring the 'strategic' approach may on the other hand make too much of context and structure. This analysis suggests the importance of balancing consideration of people and structure in organisational studies, and in the relevance and limitations of personality and leadership for making access work.

The study drawn on here presents the results of comparative empirical research on access before returning to discuss further the use of these different theoretical frameworks. What it discovers is an on-going struggle or bargaining process. Successful access depends on successful 'actor strategies in decision- and policy-making', and an organisational structure and context favourable to access. The context must be sufficiently conducive, and there must be an effective interest group configuration. Success, it is suggested in Chapter 6 of Bourgeois *et al.*, involves typically four stages: securing an appropriate decision-making structure for dealing with the issue; occupying this decision-making structure; influencing decision-making from inside; and legitimating the decision outcomes. The concepts summarised here provide us with tools for understanding, and then maybe using, 'micro-strategies' within each of these stages.

Bourgeois *et al.* conclude as follows: 'the differences that are observed in adult access policies and practices across institutions and in sub-units within institutions can, therefore, be explained to a large extent in the light of the interplay of power relationships and strategies displayed by the various interest groups in the decision-making processes that underpin these policies and practices' (op. cit. p.147). Around this there sit, so to speak, characteristics of the institution which may be more or less hospitable to access. This includes its external environment as well as internal structural factors. The study examined its empirical findings, which were both quantitative and qualitative, using cultural, contingency and structural-functionalist approaches. It concluded that this third perspective proved particularly stimulating, especially for taking into account 'the diversity of competing logics on which academic behaviours and strategies are based' (op. cit. p.154).

What does this summary review of the application and testing of theories of organisation behaviour to comparative empirical research into access in different universities and systems show? That such research has the power to define, to ask and maybe in part to answer questions about why it is that access and widening participation prove more successful as policy initiatives in some institutions, and in different parts of some institutions, than in others. It may also help us to understand what behaviours are likely to yield more or less success in what circumstances. If so the work will have predictive and operational as well as explanatory power.

It may also and on the other hand illustrate why it is that there is so little engagement with organisation theory on the part of the practice-based and value-informed world of access. It may be distasteful to have principled purposes drawn into these grubby lower levels of institutional politics and horse-trading. Ill-advisedly if understandably, such an attitude might be strengthened by the feeling that the day of access has evidently dawned, located as it now finds itself at the heart of national policy for Higher Education in Britain in 2004. It would be ironic but not surprising if this new salience meanwhile attracted more interest from organisation behaviourists outside the access field into these more attractive pastures.

The organisational perspectives characterised here as strategic and structural provide robust working tools to help us understand access better, whether for intellectual or for practical reforming purposes. The approach, tested as it was in Bourgeois' comparative study, shows that the different situations, institutions and many of the sub-systems within them are each distinctive if not unique; but also that generalisation, comparison, and transfer of analysis and experience is possible.

The whole approach may appear to have the untidy, irrational messiness, the disorderly randomness that we think of as post-modern. On the other hand it does help to enlighten and inform as to how, where and why in the administrative nitty-gritty and the living belly of the university 'organic machine' good intentions, clear leadership and well determined policies so often go astray, attenuate, or disappear without trace. It also helps to uncover why no doubt highly desirable egalitarian policies for access at the top fail to result in fairer access and greater equity on the ground.

Other dimensions of organisation behaviour and access

This chapter has concentrated on what have been called strategic and structural approaches to studying access in organisations. These approaches were brought to bear on empirical research into institutional behaviour and access in the 1990s. That work gathered different kinds of information about access at macro, meso and micro levels in diverse ways from different actors, including conventional 'non-access' students. It set up hypotheses and used organisation theory in testing these from the assembled data sets.

These approaches by no means exhaust the possibilities for studying access through the lenses of organisation behaviour. Since then the world of access has moved on and the policy environment has changed in important ways. We might now attempt a comprehensive summary and checklist of different theories, typologies and specialised research agendas through which organisational studies could widen and deepen our understanding of access dynamics. It will be more useful instead to stand back, remind ourselves why this kind of approach is valid, and ask where such kind of inquiry might lead.

The chapter started by referring to a new strategy on the part of the Higher Education Funding Council for England. That directly alters the environment for the practice of access within English UK Higher Education and indirectly beyond, for example through HEFCE's links with the institutional management work of the OECD, where it is a significant partner. The new strategy in turn attempts to respond to the new policies of the Labour Government (for the UK and not only England). At the time of writing the policy remained contested. Universities and other interest groups separately and collectively were seeking to modify it to their respective advantage.

This reminds us that the study of organisation behaviour extends beyond internal management and dynamics to the behaviour of organisations in their environments. The idea of open systems is not new (see Duke 2002, Chapter 3, on the relevance of earlier studies to the contemporary scene). Organisations interact in a rapidly changing or turbulent environment in which the interplay of forces and the making of alliances can alter the prospects of success or failure. The environment is not a given to which the university can respond only passively. (See also Burton Clark 1998, and Marginson and Considine 2000, for the way external and internal pressures change the mission and identity of the university.)

Part of the art of leadership lies in managing this uncertain environment, and in balancing and optimising time and effort between the internal and the external, to achieve and amplify beneficial synergies between what is happening and might be fostered in each setting. Networks and strategic alliances as means of management and innovation have become the focus of keen attention on the part of scholars and planners in recent years. This is as much about organisation behaviour and the management of change as is the internal. The discussion of Bourgeois et al. 1999, which drew on the work of Bordieu (1988), also embraced the wider environment, structure and culture of the society, but the emphasis tends towards internal dynamics.

In the main, the wider political and policy arena is studied in terms of public policies and the philosophy behind these, and in terms of educational and related social and economic aspirations, purposes and intentions. Examples are the UK White Paper (DfES 2003) and the HEFCE strategic plan (HEFCE 2003), even though these refer also to enhancing system and institutional capability. At the other end of a spectrum, away from the policy community of the chattering classes, are mostly individualised, usually biographical though sometimes survey-statistical studies of individual learners, their aspirations, motivations and life stories. These even more than policy studies incline to take the institution and its behaviour as a given, other than in acknowledging institutional barriers as part of the life-space within which the aspiring learner must operate.

A random but characteristic example is an interesting study of pathways of early school leavers into university education in England and New Zealand (Davey and Jamieson 2003). This looks at 300 individuals who 'bucked the trend' by accessing Higher Education in later life, numerically but mainly by case study interview and sketches. The story is told in terms of their individual motivations and social contexts. School features in the learners' stories, but the behaviour of the university as institution of destination is unquestioned and not problematised.

A full and practical understanding of access and widening participation requires the study of Higher Education institutions as well as of the broad policy arena and the situation and motivation of individuals. If this middle level of research is neglected policies are likely to be frustrated at the point of implementation. They will fail to connect with the prospective excluded learners to whom they are oriented. Individual heroism and visionary policies alike may come to nought in this middle ground.

The implication is that there remains a valid and important organisational behaviour research agenda for today's mass Higher Education era, if only for thoroughly utilitarian reasons. If this is conceded, what are the obstacles to its execution, and what kinds of questions might it fruitfully address?

Studying institutions' behaviour must attune to the changing world they inhabit, and consider how they may respond in order to survive. This world has been characterised by way of the 'three Ms' – massification, marketisation and managerialism (Tapper and Palfreyman 2000). Different institutions, depending how they perceive themselves and on the quality of their leadership, management and administration, adopt different approaches to managing change and positioning themselves in terms of 'brand' and market. Internal dynamics kick in as the leadership tries to carry the plurality of 'tribes' in its chosen direction, or to coerce this diversity into behaving like a coherent and disciplined organisation. Bourgeois' organisational analysis reminds us how complicated this can be.

In the contemporary lively UK environment, Barnett makes a neat distinction between universities and Higher Education (Barnett 2003). The autonomy of individual universities and their academic staff, and the demands upon the system to meet multiple social and economic policy objectives, pose difficult choices – for example niche diversification versus contesting position in a monolithic status hierarchy. Does one redefine one's institution as remarkably good at teaching, generally or in a particular curriculum or labour market area, apropos regional engagement and partnership, or as an access institution for particular kinds of communities?

Alternatively, is the institutional mission to be driven by claiming a place among the top dozen research institutions in the nation, where thirty others have their sights on the same few places and national funding policies aim to reduce the dozen still further? Leadership may be strong and purposeful, or weak and inadequate, in going with or against the crowd. Access, being conventionally low status and down-market, may be shunned out of weakness, since going the route of the majority feels safer, or it may be embraced as central to mission, as several new or modern UK universities are attempting in response to the 2003 White Paper (compare Duke 2002, 2003).

Either way, organisational dynamics and behaviour will be important, perhaps decisive, in determining what succeeds and fails. Passion for access and courage in choosing the less fashionable along with, or instead of, more up-market lines of business, are essential institutional strengths for the access mission. Naïveté as to what works and how institutions behave beyond the Chancellery is not a help.

We still tend to behave somewhat as if the institution were something fixed and standing apart, for all the changes pressing in from the world outside. Academic autonomy is flexibly interpreted to protect this. As a result access students are frequently square pegs to be shaved and hammered into round holes. The new paradigm of lifelong learning and universal participation has yet to displace the old. Work-based learning and e-learning are two examples of what is likely to help precipitate the paradigm change which the 2003 UK White Paper – perhaps narrowly? – failed to see. Looking further afield, if New Zealand's Maori and Pacific Island peoples constantly fail in large numbers at university, the time must come when the curriculum instead, in its larger sense, comes under scrutiny for failing the quest for enhanced performance and reduced 'failure'.

Universal lifelong learning is now a widely accepted policy proposition for the emergent 'knowledge society' – the learning society of last decade. The debate is about where the resources come from and who pays, and about what mix of economic-oriented skills and wider curriculum society requires of its Higher Education. Translating each strand of this perception of the system into effective practice takes us back to the middle level of the institution and its behaviour, where individual aspiration is fulfilled or frustrated.

The research agenda for organisation behaviour in relation to access is in many ways still the old one, but made more complex by the greater complexity of environmental change and internal-external dynamics and networks. The higher standing which access enjoys in the policy arena may make it more interesting for organisational scholars, while its new importance in policy may remove it from the ghetto of the passionate. An organisation behaviour research agenda that assists the more effective implementation of access intentions would then be more widely welcomed. This does not mean becoming the creature of managerialism, nor ceasing to ask larger questions as to where to and what for.

Sources and references

Barnett, R. (2003) 'Recovering the university', *Higher Education Digest*, Spring(45), 2–4.

Bourdieu, P. (1988) *Homo Academicus*, Cambridge: Polity Press.

Bourgeois, E., Duke, C., Guyot, J.-L. and Merrill, B. (1999) *The Adult University*, Buckingham: Open University Press.

Burton Clark, R. (1998) *Creating Entrepreneurial Universities*, Oxford: Pergamon.

Davey, J. and Jamieson, A. (2003) 'Against the odds: pathways of early school leavers into university education: evidence from England and New Zealand', *International Journal of Lifelong Education*, 23(3), 266–80.

Department for Education and Skills (DfES) (2003) *The Future of Higher Education*, London: The Stationery Office.

Duke, C. (2002) *The Learning University*, Buckingham: Open University Press.

Duke, C. (2003) 'Crisis-making and crisis-managing', in D. Warner and D. Palfreyman (eds) *Managing Crisis*, Buckingham: Open University Press.

Goffman, E. (1961) *Asylums*, Harmondsworth: Penguin.

Hazelkorn, E. (2002) 'Challenges of growing research at new and emerging higher education institutions', in G. Williams (ed.) *The Enterprising University. Reform, Excellence and Equity*, Buckingham: Open University Press.

Higher Education Funding Council for England (2003) *HEFCE Strategic Plan 2003–08. Consultation*, Bristol: HEFCE.

Kazar, J. (2001) 'Organisational change in the 21st century', *ASHE, Higher Education Report*, 28, 4.

Marginson, S. and Considine, M. (2000) *The Enterprise University: Power, Governance and Reinvention in Australia*, Cambridge: Cambridge University Press.

Tapper, T. and Palfreyman, D. (2000) *Oxford and the Decline of the Collegiate Tradition*, London: Woburn Press.

Trow, M. (1973) *Problems in the Transition from Elite to Mass Higher Education*, Berkeley, CA: Carnegie Commission on Higher Education.

Chapter 17

The case study approach to research in adult literacy, numeracy and ESOL

Rob Mark

Introduction

As the opening chapter of this volume observes, widening participation to higher education has become a dominant theme in the field of post-compulsory education; however it is but one thrust in the political imperative to improve social justice. In this chapter the focus is a related theme of literacy, and within this field of the case study approach.

Much has been written about the case study and its relevance for practice in adult education. Within the literature on qualitative research, there are as many definitions of case studies as there are writers about them. This chapter seeks to examine what is understood by the term *case study*. As with most methods or techniques in research, they have many different applications and the different types of case studies and their usages are examined. In the latter part of the chapter, the advantages and limitations of case studies are examined and their relevance to adult literacy, numeracy and ESOL (English for Speakers of Other Languages) practice.

What is a case study?

The case study is the study of a unique event or action shaped by those who are the participants in the situation. Case studies may be a study of a setting, subject, or event and may involve combinations of techniques rather than a single technique. Case studies are developed in natural settings over time and can focus on individuals, programmes or organisations, institutions or processes.

The researcher of case studies typically examines the characteristics of the focus of the observation. Case studies are normally used to collect and present information in a way that provides additional context to a situation under scrutiny and are often effective in showing how something happens or works in a real life situation.

Murray and Lawrence define the case study as:

> a detailed analysis of singularities: a person, an event limited in time, a specific department within a larger organisation, a particular form of occupational

practice, an administrative subsystem, or a single institution within clearly defined boundaries.

(Murray and Lawrence 2000: 113)

In the case study, the investigator sets out to provide a detailed account of the features of what or who is being investigated by presenting an objective view. The researchers also should provide sufficient qualifying information about the stance taken and the methodology used so as to enable the reader to make a judgement about the adequacy of the enquiry and the particular interpretation made by the investigator.

Case studies share the meanings of a particular situation with other interested parties. The ultimate responsibility of the case study researcher is to render the events of daily life in a comprehensible way. They provide insights into how and why something works in real life.

Cohen and Manion say that the purpose of the case study is:

to probe deeply and to analyse intensively the multifarious phenomena that constitute the life cycle of the unit with a view to establishing generalisations about the wider population to which that unit belongs.

(Cohen and Manion 1995: 106)

Murray and Lawrence (2000: 114) note the purpose of case studies is to identify, reveal and explain the unique features of the case. In the instance of a person or group this might include their occupational role, duties, powers, perceptions and motivations in a particular work setting. In the case of an institution it might include the study of the management of a process (e.g. staff profiles, work schedules, timetables, office practices or the management of a teaching and learning process). In the case of a process it might include the examination of the curriculum, teaching methods, forms of assessment or methods of evaluation used.

Jarvis (1999: 87) notes that case studies can form part of the practice knowledge of any occupational group and are therefore part of its body of knowledge. He also notes that they are conducted in completely different ways.

Case studies in literacy practice

Case studies have been used extensively in the filed of adult literacy practice. They have been used for different purposes including recruitment of new groups of learners, assisting learners to understand the curriculum and for improving the practice of tutors and managers working in the field.

Case studies have proved a useful marketing tool for encouraging new groups of learners to take up provision. Many adults with literacy needs lack the confidence to come forward and seek help often because of their poor perception of themselves and their abilities. Case studies of successful learners can in such circumstances highlight examples of positive role models, thus enticing adults into provision. Learner case studies can also highlight skills needed and the context in which the skills will be used, thus helping adults to see the relevance of acquiring new skills.

Case studies have also been used to provide literacy workers with a better understanding of the support needs of learners. Tutors, managers, policy makers and administrators can all benefit from case studies that help provide a better understanding of learner needs. For example, in the *Skills for Life* National Strategy document for England and Wales (2003–7) (DfES 2003), the case study is used extensively to illustrate the kind of problems adults with literacy needs are experiencing and the ways in which these problems have been overcome. The case studies include qualitative comments of learners drawn from diverse groups and those reported include a dyslexic learner, a taxi driver, a retired telecommunications manager and a tutor. These illustrations highlight issues raised in the rest of the report and help anchor the discussion about policy in adult literacy firmly within the real world of practice.

In a similar way, case studies have been used extensively in training and development to provide an understanding of the needs of particular groups. They are also used to develop tutor skills, for example, problem solving skills. By raising awareness case studies can alert tutors to the specific problems they are likely to encounter and can provide them with the knowledge and skills to solve such problems. For example, case studies can be particularly useful in meeting the needs of specific groups, such as speakers of other languages, ex-prisoners and learners with special needs.

Case studies in adult literacy cover a wide array of issues and can be drawn from every aspect of practice. They might involve learners, tutors or others involved in identifying or supporting the learning process. Case studies can focus on the role of professionals such as social workers, health workers, and community workers or they can be focussed on the curriculum, learning support or management issues in adult literacy learning.

The advent of the World Wide Web has also led to the development of new ways of accessing case studies in the field of adult literacy. For example, *Read Write Plus* (www.dfes.gov.uk/readwriteplus) is an example of an interactive website which uses case studies to enable adults to prepare more effectively for literacy and numeracy tests.

However, although the field of adult literacy abounds with examples of case studies, what has been absent is a debate about what evidence is acceptable and what methods should be used for collecting and reporting data. There is no universally accepted yardstick for measuring the quality of the vast array of case studies and the reader is left to make judgements about the validity and generalisability of each case.

Types of case studies

Cohen and Manion (1995: 107) identify two ways of carrying out case study research. The first type is based on *participant observation* where the observer engages in the very activities s/he sets out to observe. In this situation the observer becomes immersed in the activity – for example, in adult literacy practice the researcher may become part of a group or a learning process, learning with the learners or participants. Cohen and Manion also note that the participant observation approach fits in well with solving classroom problems:

> The current vogue enjoyed by the case study conducted on participant observation lines is not difficult to account for. This kind of research is eminently suitable to many of the problems that the educational investigator faces.
>
> (Cohen and Manion 1995: 110)

The second way of carrying out case study research is referred to as *non-participant observation*. Here the researcher stands aloof from the group activities s/he is investigating, for example, by sitting aside from the adult literacy class observing what is going on.

Cohen and Manion (1995) note that the unstructured, ethnographic account of teachers' work is the most typical method of observation in the natural surroundings of the class: for example, evaluating the teaching processes within the classroom setting. Thus a key feature of case studies is observation. This may mean the active deployment of techniques such as participant observation and direct observation. It may also mean the use and application of other data-gathering techniques such as surveys, interviews, analysis of documents, anecdotal data gathering, discourse analysis and ethnographic techniques, etc. The case study does not therefore employ a single data gathering technique. It employs selected techniques which best fit the facts of the case and the purposes of the enquiry, and which help to tell the story. In adult literacy, numeracy and ESOL, this has involved distribution of questionnaires to build up information about particular learners, interviews with learners to develop profiles of particular needs, discussions with groups of learners, etc.

Kane and O'Reilly-De Brún note the multi-method nature of the case study:

> Case studies are also strategies in that they use interviews, observation, and documentary materials to provide insights into how and why something works or doesn't work in real life, over time.
>
> (Kane and O'Reilly-De Brún 2001: 116)

The practitioner researcher and the case study

Wellington (2000: 91), referring to the writings of Stenhouse (1985) and Bogdan and Biklen (1982), distinguishes three major types or categories of case studies. *The historical-organisational case study* involves studying something over time (e.g. an organisation, thereby tracing its development). *The observational case study* involves participant observation of an organisation and *the life history case study* involves extensive interviews with one person for the purposes of collecting a first person narrative. A fourth category of case studies might be said to be *the practitioner-researcher case study*. This method is becoming increasingly popular and has for some time been commonplace among adult literacy, numeracy and ESOL practitioners.

Practitioners have used case studies for a number of purposes such as recruitment of new learners and preparing staff to work with adult literacy learners. The strength of practitioner-based case studies is that they can inform and assist the practitioner-researcher on existing practices and how practice might be improved.

Practitioner research is central to our understanding of practice and the practitioner case study method can be applied to teaching or management processes. The results can also be published to inform a wider audience about research undertaken. For example, an account of the effects of implementing a new curriculum or methods of assessment for a particular target group in adult literacy could be seen to be a case study which would inform practice in a particular institution or in other learning environments through the publication of the findings.

An example of this is the *Using ICT as a Hook* project reported by Mark and Donaghey (2003). This project sets out to explore whether adult literacy learners can learn using new technology and other self-supported learning resources to improve their literacy and numeracy skills. The initiative involved twenty-five different adult literacy providers each having a project which focussed on a different aspect of *Skills for Life* (literacy, numeracy and ESOL). The projects were organised in urban and rural contexts, in the workforce, in communities and with different clientele, e.g. single parents, learners with disabilities and members of ethnic communities. Each project had its own rationale and methods of working and involved a reflection and action approach to identifying goals and improving practice through a participative client-centred approach to learning.

The *Using ICT as a Hook* projects might each be thought of as a case study seeking to develop a model of practice for a particular target group. Each project provides a case study of an approach to learning highlighting the advantages and limitations of using ICT for literacy learning with the selected group. By developing personal accounts using reflective diaries the projects demonstrated how ICT can increase and widen participation in adult literacy practice. These cases, alongside other data, provide evidence of what works or doesn't work in improving participation. The information can be used in future planning of services or is useful in identifying patterns of why something works in one situation and not in another.

Mark and Donaghey (2003: 41) conclude that self-directed learning for adults with literacy needs can have benefits and make a real contribution to developing understanding and breadth of application of literacy skills. Their report demonstrates how new and innovative opportunities can develop through a project-based approach which can later inform policy and practice within the field of literacy learning.

McNiff (1996 *et al.*: 8) argues that *practitioner research* is *action research* that can be used to help improve professional practices in many types of workplaces. Jarvis (1999) also notes that practitioner-researchers know what works, are comfortable with their own body of practical knowledge and their own skills and attitudes about their practice. Teachers are therefore in a position to reflect on their own teaching processes, to study them, and to record their own reflections, attitudes, and emotions. Jarvis refers to Carr and Kemmis who say:

> action research is simply a form of self-reflective enquiry undertaken by participants in social situations in order to improve the rationality and justice of their own practices, their understanding of these practices and the situations in which the practices are carried out.
>
> (Carr and Kemmis 1985: 162)

Action research is seen as an activity that develops self-reflective, self-critical, practitioners open to enquiry and improvement of their practice. It becomes a cyclical activity where the researcher plans, carries out and monitors what is going on, reflecting on events critically. It can produce critical accounts based on this practice which can also be viewed as case studies of practice which analyse the life cycle of the phenomena with a view to establishing generalisations about the wider context to which they belong.

Jarvis (1999: 77) notes that Cohen and Manion (1995) do not include practitioner-conducted action research in their discussion of the case study, suggesting that case studies are restricted to investigations in which the researcher is either a participant or a non-participant observer. He makes the case for considering the practitioner-researcher as researcher, arguing that practitioner research can provide case studies:

> every person's practice constitutes an individual event each time it happens. Consequently, it must be studied through individual cases.
>
> (Jarvis 1999: 75)

He continues:

> case studies are both about the process of learning about and researching the specific phenomenon of phenomena under investigation and about the product of that learning and research.
>
> (Jarvis 1999: 77)

However, while case studies arising from practitioner research are primarily conducted by practitioner-researchers in relation to their own practice, it is also true that case studies can also be conducted without references to practitioners at all; for example, when a researcher observes the practitioners engaged in practice.

So far the discussion has focussed on identifying what a case study is and the various categories of case studies which exist. I shall now turn my attention to examining the advantages and drawbacks of using case studies in adult education research.

Advantages of case studies

Proponents of the case study argue that it has a number of attractions and is a useful way of examining many of the problems that the educational investigator faces.

Cohen and Manion (1995: 123, adapted from Adelman *et al.* 1980) summarise the advantages of case studies for educational evaluators or researchers as follows:

• Case study data is 'strong in reality'. The strength is because the case studies are down-to-earth and attention holding, in harmony with the reader's own experience, and thus provide a natural basis for generalisation.
• Case studies allow generalisations about an instance.
• Case studies recognise the complexities of truths and can represent something of the discrepancies or conflicts between the viewpoints held by participants.
• Case studies as 'products', may form an archive of descriptive material which can be subsequently reinterpreted.
• Case studies can be a 'step to action' and contribute to action. Insights may be directly interpreted and put to use for staff or individual self-development, and used for feedback and evaluation purposes.
• Case studies present research or evaluation data in a more publicly accessible form than other kinds of research report. They are capable of serving multiple audiences and make the research process itself accessible.

Murray and Lawrence (2000: 113) note that the main advantage of case studies is that they can be excellent for uncovering unique patterns and features of social interaction within small groups. They add to the stock of public knowledge about the person, the institution or event under scrutiny. The credibility of such portrayals and descriptions is based on the idea that the interested reader or lay person will connect the details of the case study to what he already knows of specific and general human situations.

For the adult educator, case studies can be an illuminating and insightful way of adding to knowledge and of great value to teaching and learning. They can contribute towards the 'democratisation' of decision-making and knowledge itself, allowing readers to judge the implications of a study for themselves.

They are often accessible and engaging for the reader and can be enjoyable to do. For the adult educator who is also a reflective practitioner, they can be a good way of disseminating findings on research into practice. The notion of the practitioner as an action researcher using cases of their work to extend professional knowledge is clearly an important way in providing insights into how and why something works in real life.

Problems with case studies

Despite the many advantages of case studies, there are several problems in their use.

Practical issues

Practical problems centre around a number of issues. The researcher requires a lot of time, acceptance, carefully negotiated access and tact. They can involve visits to organisations, study of their documentation, interviews and discussions with staff and learners, etc. Not all researchers will have the highly developed communication skills required to participate and engage with colleagues or learners. Where case studies are reflecting practice, an iterative 'action–reflection–action' process may be involved, which will be very time consuming. Some case studies, on the other hand, are likely to entail far more observation than participation and these require a sophisticated level of observation skills.

Validity

Problems centre around internal and external validity of the case study. The unstructured, ethnographic account of the person or group under study is the most typical method of observation and the recording of the data or observation is frequently a source of concern, especially with inexperienced case study researchers.

Jarvis (1999: 83) refers to Guba and Lincoln (1981) who suggest that with case studies there is a danger of oversimplification, exaggeration of the facts, and interpretations of selective facts. This could render the case study as unscientific, opportunistic, and unrepresentative. Cohen and Manion also refer to this problem. They note that:

> accounts are often described as subjective, biased, impressionistic, idiosyncratic and lacking the precise quantifiable measures that are the hallmark of survey research and experimentation.
>
> (Cohen and Manion 1995: 110)

There is also the possibility that the observer will lose their perspective and could become blind to the peculiarities that they are supposed to be investigating. The observers' judgement could become affected by their involvement in the group they are observing , thus affecting validity. The subjective and idiosyncratic nature of the participant observation case study is therefore bound up with the question of external validity and the need for public verification.

The case study raises a number of questions about how we know it is genuine. There is also a question about how the observer affects the case being studied and to what extent the researcher's observations and interpretations are value laden. These questions perhaps need to be addressed through a reflective approach to writing up studies. This approach has much in common with the approach of the adult educator who engages in reflective practice.

The problem of external validity could also be said to be related to the issue of sampling. Yin (1994) advocates the use of multiple case studies, over an extended period at different sites. These multiple cases can then cumulatively be used to produce generalisations. By systematically and purposefully sampling a number of cases over a period of time, it could be argued that valid generalisations can be made.

Jarvis (1999: 83) argues that case studies can be best validated internally. He notes the processes of observing, interviewing and recording are very important and suggests that provided they are sufficiently rigorous, well planned, and undertaken in the most professional manner, we should perhaps accept their reliability. He notes that the criterion of external validity cannot be proved to be valid in itself, because every practice situation is different and unique. External validity is concerned with the extent to which findings of one study can be applied to other situations. But Jarvis also argues that the case study which arises out of the practitioner-researcher's own practice is unique, and therefore the findings cannot be applied to other practice situations:

> the nature of practice dictates that we are concerned with the specific. There may well be similarities within unique and transitory practices, as the concept of habitus implies, but this is not an essential criterion for the validity of all case studies.
>
> (Jarvis 1999: 84)

A European Union Socrates funded project involving partners in Belgium, England and Ireland (Quality in Adult Literacy 1998–2000) showed how multiple cases can be accumulated to produce generalisations which can provide validity for case studies. In this context, Mark and Donaghey (2001) demonstrated how the Evolving Quality Framework for Adult Basic Education project brought together the experience of a range of stakeholders, including tutors and learners, to produce quality statements about adult literacy which could later be shared with others to develop an agreed quality framework with external validation.

In the first year of the project, a series of statements about quality were developed through a case study approach in different locations around Europe. Each partner worked with groups of stakeholders to ascertain views about quality, later developed into a series of statements on learner experience and programme management. The guiding principles central to the process were also discussed and agreed in the same way. The statements were then brought together into a European quality framework applicable in different learning contexts. In Ireland, the National Adult Literacy Agency (2002) has since developed a user guide or manual to enable lessons learnt to be applied throughout all literacy schemes within its jurisdiction. What began as a case study approach to developing quality in particular learning contexts, has since been used to create a national strategy for quality management in adult literacy and numeracy.

Generalisation

One of the problems raised about case studies is how a piece of research might be said to be applicable to other situations. The problem of generalising from a case study is summed up by Bogdan and Biklen (1982) in Wellington (2000):

> Purposely choosing the unusual or just falling into a study leaves the question of generalisability up in the air. Where does the spectrum fit in to the spectrum of human events? The question is not answered by the selection itself, but has to be explored as part of the study. The researcher has to determine what it is he or she is studying: that is, of what is this a case?
>
> (Bogdan and Biklen in Wellington 2000: 97)

Wolcott argues that it is possible to generalise:

> each case study is unique, but not so unique that we cannot learn from it and apply its lessons more generally.
>
> (Wolcott 1995: 175)

In summary, it would seem that when examining case studies, the reader, using his or her experience, knowledge and wisdom, holds as much sway as the researcher in deciding the value, or truth of the case study. Roberts (1996: 147) points out that 'as with any research, the reader has to rely on the integrity of the researcher to select and present the evidence fairly'.

While case studies are susceptible to intuitive biases and anecdote, it is possible that if sufficient details are gathered, generalisations can be made about the case. Accumulating case studies within a subject field will then permit generalisations to be made. The ability to generalise would, however, seem to be a limitation of case study work.

Jarvis (1999: 86) notes that because practice is transitory, the case study may be the most reliable way of studying it. It can be studied as part of our knowledge of practice, but it can only record and illuminate things that have already happened. Such cases can be used for teaching purposes, but they do not provide knowledge that is to be applied in a deductive manner.

The *Evolving Quality Framework for Adult Basic Education* project (Mark and Donaghey 2001) used a triangulation technique to overcome the problem of bias and anecdote in developing a quality framework for adult literacy. Views of different groups of stakeholders were assimilated using a variety of methods – interviews, questionnaires, diaries, etc. Stakeholder groups surveyed included potentially conflicting interest groups such as learners, tutors and managers, to ensure that ideas were not simply reflecting bias from any one group or location. The agreed framework represented the views of different groups from a number of locations and was not only based on the views of any one group. The findings were subject to further scrutiny at the implementation stage when each centre was invited to seek opinions from tutors and learners and feed this back into the ongoing development process.

The need to develop research on effective practice in adult literacy has also recently been highlighted in the UK through the establishment of a National Research and Development Centre (NRDC) for adult literacy and numeracy (NRDC 2003).

One of the first projects the Centre commissioned was a project entitled *Case studies in ESOL provision and learners' needs and resources*. The project is examining practices in a wide variety of dedicated ESOL provision and is seeking to establish some of the distinctive features of this kind of provision. Five case studies have been selected to show the diversity in the types of provision and learners, and the study includes both dedicated ESOL classes and other provision such as numeracy classes, classes with a focus on literacy and work placements. The case studies being developed have been carefully selected to cover different types of provision: college based; community based; employer based; different groups of learners; asylum seekers; job seekers with professional backgrounds; heterogeneous groups in the community; and different levels of language competence from basic to advanced. A further NRDC project examines *The impact of adult literacy and numeracy levels on small businesses in rural Lincolnshire and Rutland* through a case study approach (Atkin and Merchant 2004).

These research projects demonstrate the importance of the case study as a research tool in adult literacy and an acknowledgement of a need to develop high quality case studies based on rigorous methods of data collection and analysis, which has sometimes been missing in anecdotal research. Developing a range of sound and robust case studies which can be said to be reliable and valid is perhaps one of the ongoing challenges facing researchers in adult literacy today.

Conclusion

This discourse has highlighted the benefits and drawbacks of how case studies can be used in the field of adult literacy and numeracy. Case studies can give 'in-depth' information, showing how processes work, how patterns are lived out, how the ideal is converted to the real, how change occurs, etc. The main strength of case studies is perhaps that people can relate to them, even if they cannot always generalise from them. Case study research can be rich, interesting and possess wide appeal. Despite the difficulties discussed above, the case study is surely a valuable tool. Difficulties can be overcome by an open reflective approach, allowing for different interpretations to be critically examined.

The notion of the tutor or manager as researcher is crucial to the growth of professional knowledge. As more and more adult literacy practitioners begin to realise the potential of real life descriptions in improving practice, the demand for more robust case studies in the field of literacy practice is likely to grow.

References

Adelman, C., Jenkins, D. and Kemmins, S. (1980) 'Rethinking case study: notes from the Second Cambridge Conference', in H. Simons (ed.) *Towards a Science of the Singular*, Centre for Applied Research in Education, University of East Anglia.

Atkin, C. and Merchant, P. (2004) *The Impact of Adult Literacy and Numeracy on Small Businesses in Rural Lincolnshire and Rutland*, London: NRDC, online at: http://www.nrdc.org.uk.

Bogdan, R. and Biklen, S. (1982) *Qualitative Research in Education*, Boston: Allyn and Bacon.

Carr, W. and Kemmis, S. (1985) *Becoming Critical: Education, Knowledge and Action Research*, London: Falmer Press.

Cohen, L. and Manion, L. (1995) *Research Methods in Education*, 4th edn, London: Routledge.

Department for Education and Skills (2003) *Skills for Life: The National Strategy for Improving Adult Literacy and Numeracy Skills*, Nottingham: DfES Publications.

Guba, E.G. and Lincoln, Y.S. (1981) *Effective Evaluation: Improving the Usefulness of Evaluation Results Through Responsive and Naturalistic Approaches*, San Francisco, CA: Jossey-Bass.

Jarvis, P. (1999) *The Practitioner Researcher – Developing Theory from Practice*, San Francisco, CA: Jossey-Bass.

Kane, E. and O'Reilly-De Brún, M. (2001) *Doing Your Own Research*, New York: Marion Boyars Publishers.

Mark, R. and Donaghey, M. (2001) *Towards a Quality Framework for Adult Basic Education*, Report of EU Socrates Transactional Project, Belfast: Institute of Lifelong Learning, Queen's University Belfast.

Mark, R. and Donaghey, M. (2003) *Using ICT as a Hook: Review of the Learndirect Essential Skills Project*, Belfast: University for Industry.

McNiff, J., Lomax, P. and Whitehead, J. (1996) *You and Your Action Research Project*, London: Routledge.

Murray, L. and Lawrence, B. (2000) *Practitioner-Based Enquiry Principles for Postgraduate Research*, London: Falmer Press.

National Adult Literacy Agency (2002) *Evolving Quality Framework for Adult Basic Education: User Guide*, Dublin: NALA.

National Research and Development Centre News (2003) *NRDC homepage*, online at: http://www.nrdc.org.uk. Accessed June 2003.

Read Write Plus (2003) *Read Write Plus homepage*, online at: http://www.dfes.gov.uk/readwriteplus. Accessed June 2003.

Roberts, M. (1996) 'Case study research', in M. Williams (ed.) *Understanding Geographical and Environmental Education*, London: Cassell.

Stenhouse, L. (1985) 'A note on case study and educational practice', in R.G. Burgess (ed.) *Field Methods in the Study of Education*, Lewes: Falmer Press.

Wellington, J. (2000) *Educational Research: Contemporary Issues and Practical Approaches*, London: Continuum.

Wolcott, H.F. (1995) *The Art of Fieldwork*, London: Sage Publications.

Yin, R.K. (1994) *Case Study Research: Design and Methods*, Beverley Hills, CA: Sage.

Chapter 18

Researching widening access

The future agenda

Jim Gallacher and Beth Crossan

Introduction

This book has brought together a number of contributions from across the world on the theme of researching widening access. While the introductory chapter by Osborne and Gallacher seeks to provide an overview of existing research, and the questions which arise from this research, this final chapter will attempt to identify some of the key issues which have emerged from the contributions to this book, and which researchers must face, if this field is to continue to develop as one in which high quality research will underpin the development of both policy and practice. These issues relate to both substantive issues and to methodological challenges, and it is hoped that they will together contribute towards developing an agenda and a framework for work in this field. The chapter will be divided into three main sections. The first will consider widening access as a field of research, and consider how it may develop. The second will consider issues associated with methodological and theoretical approaches, and the third will identify and discuss some of the key issues for research, which have emerged from the contributions to this book.

Developing research into widening access

In his chapter, which provides an overview of the development of research into widening access, Peter Scott has suggested that despite the strength of access as a policy agenda, as a field of research it is still only emerging and is weakly institutionalised. By comparison with many other discipline areas there is an absence of large and stable research groups. There is also an absence of what Scott describes as 'canonical texts'. It is certainly the case that throughout the UK, and indeed more widely in Europe, and many other parts of the world there are few well established research groups with access as their main focus, and even although lifelong learning is being strengthened in the UK, and in some other countries, access is often not a central element in the research undertaken by these groups. This then raises an interesting challenge for researchers who wish to develop and strengthen this field. In reflecting on these issues Scott points to a possible source of strength for access research, which builds on the earlier work which he, and others have undertaken. This refers to the increasing recognition which they suggest is being given to the production of 'Mode 2' knowledge, which is often produced through action. This is contrasted with 'Mode 1' knowledge which is produced through traditional discipline based research (Gibbons *et al.* 1994; Nowotny *et al.* 2001). This leads Scott to suggest that the sharp demarcation between established and alternative modes of research is breaking down, and there is the recognition of a broader spectrum of epistemologies and methodologies. This is of particular significance for research in the post compulsory and access fields, where much of the research has been conducted by practitioners who were committed to advocacy on behalf of those who were likely to benefit from access policies, or who had responsibility for implementation and evaluation of these policies. In addition a good deal of the larger scale research which has been undertaken in this field has often been evaluation of policies or initiatives, funded by government departments, the higher education funding bodies or similar organisations. In this respect alternative approaches to research are a well established feature of this field, and are contributing to alternative research paradigms which will further strengthen this field of research. An interesting example of this process is the Teaching and Learning Research Programme (TLRP) in the UK, which was launched by the Economic and Social Research Council (ESRC), the Higher Education Funding Council for England (HEFCE) and the Scottish Executive in 2000. It now has a total budget of £26 million, and is probably the largest education research programme ever funded in the UK. Its focus is on research which will improve teaching and learning, and there is a strong emphasis on collaboration with practitioners, and on dissemination. The latest round of this programme (Phase 3), has focused on post compulsory education and training, and the projects included within it are diverse in their topics and methods.[1]

This development, and the award of a significant number of large research grants within this prestigious programme to researchers working in the field of post compulsory or lifelong learning, can be seen both as recognition of the validity of this type of research within the wider research community, and as an important means through which research in this field will be given the opportunity to develop a much stronger institutional base. However, a contrasting picture can be seen in the one presented by Shirley Walters in her discussion of South Africa, where she comments on the point that, while the need for change in the provision of opportunities for adult learners is recognised at the level of policy, there is a lack of resources to implement it, a lack of baseline data on which to build studies, and an absence of funding for research. This reflects the position in many parts of the world, and while change may come gradually in the ways suggested in Scott's chapter, this also points to the need to attempt to strengthen the international community of researchers in this field.

Practitioners within the field of access research therefore face a number of important challenges. They must consider how they can build on the distinctive traditions, which they have established over the last twenty years or more, to strengthen their research activities in ways which will help inform policy and practice, while ensuring that they receive recognition, and the funding which goes with this, in an increasingly competitive research environment. In considering these issues it is interesting to reflect on some of the issues raised by other contributors to this book.

Researching widening access: theoretical and methodological issues

First it can be noted that while there are a substantial number of chapters which report on empirical research on substantive questions, and there are a number of chapters which explore methodological issues, the discussion of theoretical issues is limited. This again may reflect Scott's point that the tradition of 'academic' research in this field is relatively weak, and there is an absence of 'canonical' texts. Theoretical and conceptual frameworks can of course be found, and one of the most influential of these derives from the work of Bourdieu, which is increasingly influencing the work of researchers in this field (Bloomer and Hodkinson 2000), and is referred to by Merrill and Alheit in their chapter in this collection (Bourdieu 1984). Hodkinson and Bloomer also use the concept of 'learning careers' which derives from the symbolic interactionist tradition, and which has also been used by Gallacher et al. (2002) in their analysis of the processes through which adults re-engage with formal learning. The concept of social capital discussed by Ferlander and Barraket in this collection, is also being used by an increasing number of researchers as a framework for analysis (Field 2003). Theoretical perspectives of these kinds will help frame the projects funded through the TLRP, and it can be expected that this will contribute to the development and strengthening of theoretical and conceptual frameworks in this field. This might be seen as an interesting example of the synergy which Scott alludes to, in which the changing research paradigms are providing opportunities for researchers in this field to gain access to mainstream research funding, which is itself contributing to further development and strengthening of the field.

While the theoretical perspectives may at present be relatively weak a number of contributors to this book point to a potentially important way of strengthening these frameworks, in which the absence of strong discipline boundaries could be a potential source of strength. These writers refer to the value of bringing together perspectives from areas of work which are traditionally quite separate. In particular Ewart Keep and Chris Duke's chapters are interesting in this respect.

Keep's chapter is an important one in that it looks at what happens after access and graduation, what is the demand for graduates in the labour market and what are the returns, both at the level of the individual, and of society. Some of the substantive issues which Keep raises will be discussed further below. At this point what is important to note is the way in which he is bringing together what he refers to as different strands of research, and their implications for policy. In particular he comments on the ways in which an analysis of labour market research can raise important questions for educational policies which have focused on increasing participation rates in higher education. However, he notes the tendency for different research traditions to pursue 'parallel courses', and makes the following point:

> In the short to medium term probably the most useful step the research community could take would be to try to bring together the different bodies of evidence, and thrash out what they can and cannot tell us, and attempt to reconcile their widely varying conclusions about the utility of mass higher education and who stands to gain from it.

There is already a considerable level of interaction between researchers working in the fields of labour market studies and education and training policies, and strengthening these links could considerably enhance research outputs in this field.

In a similar way Chris Duke's chapter on 'Organisation behaviour, research and access' points to the value of bringing together perspectives from organisational and management studies research and access research. Duke comments on the ways in which the focus of work within organisational and access studies, and the priorities of researchers in these fields have made co-operation unlikely. Nevertheless, drawing on Bourgeois' analysis he suggests that studies of universities as organisations can be a powerful approach when exploring the reasons why access and widening participation initiatives are more successful in some institutions than others, or when pursued in particular ways (Bourgeois et al. 1999).

These two examples suggest that there are important challenges for the research community both in undertaking this kind of interdisciplinary analysis, and in presenting it to the policy and practice communities in ways which increase the likelihood that they will respond to it. Nevertheless, drawing on Scott's earlier point, researchers in the field of access, and more generally in the field of lifelong learning, may be better placed to do this than those in other fields because the disciplinary boundaries are much less clearly defined.

While contributors to this book provide relatively little explicit discussion of theoretical perspectives, which could help shape future research, methodological questions are discussed much more fully. An important theme which emerges here, and which may be seen as a reflection of the value commitments of many researchers in this field, is an emphasis on methods which enable the voices of the research subjects to be heard, and their understanding of social reality to be clearly articulated. One chapter in particular may be seen as providing a valuable analysis which links theoretical and methodological issues in suggesting fruitful lines of development. Flecha and Gómez, drawing on the work of writers such as Habermas (1984, 1987) and Beck, argue that there has been a shift towards a more communicative and dialogic society, and this analysis places human agency at the core of social action. This also leads to an argument that research should turn towards dialogue, with a de-monopolisation of expert knowledge (Beck et *al.* 1994). Because human agency is given a key role in the theorisation of societies, it is argued that the research methodology must also recognise this human agency, and give it a central place. Communicative-dialogic research is therefore an approach which is based on the direct participation of those whose reality is being studied, and a joint construction of objective reality by researcher and researched. Flecha and Gómez report on how they attempt to operationalise this approach in the work of CREA through the theoretical approaches they use, the involvement of researchers from very varied social and ethnic backgrounds, their choice of research topics, and their collaboration with organisations which are active in the fields of adult education and social action. The approaches to research which are advocated involve egalitarian relationships between researchers and researched, and a process in which they both argue and share meanings and interpretations. An approach which is in some ways similar is outlined by Merrill and Alheit in their chapter. In this case the central ideas are those of biography and narrative, and they suggest that 'biographical methods in many ways complement the traditions of adult education of placing the learner central to the process and taking into account the subjectivity of the learner'. However, the approach advocated by Merrill and Alheit is one which also recognises that learners' experiences will be structured by their own positions and experiences within the wider social structure, and by the characteristics of the educational systems within which they study. These educational systems will vary at both a national or macro level, and at an institutional or meso level.

The approaches outlined above lead to an emphasis on the importance of qualitative research, in which the experiences, understandings and interpretations of the learners, who are the subjects of research, are given clear recognition, and accorded a high level of importance. It has been suggested above that this in many respects reflects the traditions from which much access research has emerged. It can also be seen as being useful to emphasise these approaches as alternatives to the more quantitative approaches, which have dominated much educational and social science research, and which have also often been privileged by policy makers. However, qualitative research must also be complemented in appropriate cases by high quality quantitative research. Crossan and Osborne recognise this in their chapter, which while exploring the distinctive contributions of qualitative research, also recognises the need for and contribution of quantitative approaches. The value and complexity of quantitative approaches is illustrated in Forsyth and Furlong's chapter which draws on their study of participation in higher education among young people from socially disadvantaged areas (Forsyth and Furlong 2003). The quantitative analysis which they undertake illustrates, not just the continuing patterns of inequality in participation in higher education, but also the difficulties of area based analysis, and the dangers that postcode analysis can mask further patterns of inequality within fairly small geographical areas. This points to the need for critical and sophisticated approaches to the use of quantitative techniques. Forsyth and Furlong also report on their use of interview data to help interpret and explain the patterns which emerge from their quantitative research, and show the value of combined and complementary approaches. The ability to use these combinations of methodological approaches will be important if research in this field is to develop, and receive full recognition in both the research and policy communities. However, the relatively weak institutional bases, and absence of research infrastructure, which Scott has commented on, can lead to difficulties in developing research capacity of this kind. In the UK the TLRP should make some contribution to meeting these needs through the Research Capacity Building Programme which has been built into it. However, there is a need for support of this kind to be developed and sustained, and for similar programmes to be developed elsewhere in the world.

Researching widening access: an agenda for research

The chapters in this book, as well as contributing to the development of methodology for widening access research, have helped identify some of the key issues in establishing the agenda for research. Three main themes can be identified in this respect. The first of these is the complexity of the patterns of inequality in participation which exist. The second is the need to move beyond a narrow concept of access to the recognition that many of the key issues surrounding access and retention raise important issues of institutional change. The third set of issues explores the impact of access, with regard to the opportunities which it creates for participants. This can also be related to the first set of issues. All of these issues are ones which can be observed in a number of different countries, and it is necessary to explore issues of similarity and difference between countries in this respect.

Complexity of the patterns of inequality in participation

The first set of issues concerns the complexity of the patterns of inequality in participation. The move towards systems of mass higher education, which has in many countries been accompanied by an emphasis on policies designed to widen access to higher education, has led to higher participation rates across society. However, this has brought with it new forms of differentiation, an issue identified by Osborne and Gallacher in their introductory chapter and which is explored in a number of other chapters. Morgan-Klein and Murphy, drawing on research which they have undertaken in Scotland (Murphy et al. 2002), point to an increasingly differentiated higher education system in Scotland, in which there are now four main sectors ('ancient', 1960s, and post 1992 universities, and further education colleges). Students from less advantaged social classes, and from less advantaged areas are least likely to gain access to the more prestigious 'ancient' universities, and are most likely to study in the further education colleges or the post 1992 universities, the least prestigious sectors. Forsyth and Furlong provide further evidence of these complex patterns of inequality. Reporting on their detailed study of participation of young people from socially disadvantaged areas they observe first of all that area based analysis of this kind can create a misleading impression of success in widening access. They report that even in areas of social disadvantage there are pockets of greater affluence, and it is from these sub-areas that participants in higher education are most likely to come. This leads them to conclude that '... in practice it was actually quite difficult to find many truly disadvantaged young people who were participating fully in higher education'. They also go on to suggest that when young people from these areas do participate in higher education they are more likely to participate in the shorter one or two year higher national certificate or diploma (HNC or HND) courses in the further education colleges than in the longer degree courses in universities, and that there was evidence that young people entering the most prestigious courses, such as medicine, faced particular difficulties.

These patterns are now being documented and explored in the UK with respect to social class, and areas of social disadvantage. However, there is a need to explore the extent to which patterns of inequality may manifest themselves in different ways in different societies. Walters in her analysis of change in South Africa has pointed out that while the enrolment of black students increased by 61 per cent between 1993 and 1999, and now represents 71 per cent of the total headcount enrolments, significant patterns of inequality can still be observed within the South African higher education system. Thus while the participation rate of 'black African' students has increased from 9 per cent to 12 per cent, it still remains well below that of 'white' students at 47 per cent and Asian students at 39 per cent. The 'black African' students also remain clustered in areas such as humanities, with low levels of enrolments in science, engineering and technology, and business and commerce. The South African system is also highly differentiated, with institutions which were historically defined as 'white advantaged' or 'black disadvantaged'. There has also been a distinction between universities and technikons, which were more vocationally and technically oriented. This system is currently being restructured, but it will be necessary to examine the participation rates of students from the different racial and ethnic backgrounds in the emerging system. Contributions to this book have not dealt with other aspects of inequality, such as gender and disability, but there is clearly also a need to explore the complex patterns of inequality in participation in these areas.

This discussion has identified a number of important issues which researchers must explore when examining the impact of policies designed to widen access to higher and further education. First, evidence presented here indicates that, despite the expansion of tertiary systems, people from the most disadvantaged backgrounds are still very under-represented. It is important that the extent of this problem, and the factors which give rise to it are explored fully in research, so that more effective policies can be developed to address these problems. The second set of issues is the evidence of growing differentiation within systems of tertiary education, and that those from the more socially disadvantaged backgrounds are more likely to enter the least prestigious institutions and courses. This is an issue which is likely to become of increasing significance as we move towards mass systems of higher education, which contain within them a high degree of differentiation, and which may have significant consequences for the participants in terms of both experiences and outcomes.

The third set of issues concerns the success of students from socially disadvantaged backgrounds who do enter higher education programmes. While this is not explored in great depth by any of the contributors to this book, it is clearly an issue of considerable importance. Walters in her discussion of South Africa points to the wide disparities in graduation rates of black and 'white' students. Average graduation rates for 'white' students are double those of black students. In the very different context of Scottish higher education Forsyth and Furlong note that those students from disadvantaged backgrounds who do enter more prestigious courses are likely to experience continuing problems which may undermine their success, and result in early leaving. The issue of the importance of retention as well as access has increasingly been recognised in the literature (see for example Boylan's chapter in this book), and will be discussed further below.

Access and institutional change

The second set of issues for the research agenda concern the need to move beyond a narrow concept of access to the recognition that many of the key issues surrounding access and retention raise important issues of institutional change. This view is expressed with particular force by David Boud who argues in his chapter that we need to move beyond a focus on 'widening' access, which can easily lead to a focus on letting more people in, but not changing the nature of the educational experience to which they are being admitted. He suggests that:

> it assumes that the problems prompting concerns about access are addressed by admission into the front door of the academy. It does not emphasise who or what is falling out the back.

This leads Boud to suggest that the focus should change from 'widening access' to 'responsiveness', and a consideration of the types of changes required if institutions are to respond to the needs of learners. In considering the type of change required Boud emphasises flexibility, and innovative forms of provision, such as work based learning. This discussion points to the need for further research into the kinds of institutional change which will be needed if access policies are to be effective, an issue taken up by a number of contributors to this collection.

A key issue raised by several writers in different national contexts is the one of cultural differences between learners and institutions. Merrill and Alheit in their study of adult students in a number of different European countries refer to a clash of 'lifeworlds' experienced by many adult students. Thus elite German universities are described as 'exclusive institutions, where non-traditional students often experience a clash of lifeworlds, a deep conflict of personal and institutional attitudes'. They suggest that there are considerable variations between countries, and even within countries, where systems are differentiated and stratified. Some institutions have much stronger traditions of connections to the communities in which they are based, while others are more clearly embedded in elite cultures. This raises important questions for researchers, not just regarding access to these institutions, but also the experience of students, and the factors which contribute to success or failure.

Issues of a similar kind are raised by Joseph Lo Bianco in his discussion of literacy. In his chapter he argues that consideration of widening access issues must go beyond academic or financial barriers to participation, and consider social and cultural barriers. Drawing on work from both Australia and South Africa (Absalom and Golebiowsi 2002; Bock and Gough 2002) Lo Bianco argues that 'the varying literate practices of the diverse fields that comprise higher education institutions mediate admission or exclusion, determine knowledge acquisition, govern performance and signify identity and professional culture'. A central task for access researchers should therefore be to make academics aware of the language and literacy dimensions of all academic activity, and their implications for students so that they can be more adequately supported in their studies.

A similar theme emerges in Juanita Johnson-Bailey and Ron Cervero's discussion of race in the USA. They suggest that in responding to the disadvantaged position of black people in adult education programmes in the USA there is a need to recognise 'the hidden curriculum, which thwarts efforts to be inclusive and democratic'. This hidden curriculum refers to student/professor and student/student interactions, and the unwritten and unspoken rules which shape these interactions. These in turn reflect the power relationships within the wider society, and these issues must be identified and addressed if higher proportions of black students are to gain access to programmes, and be successful within them. Johnson-Bailey and Cervero also recognise that the formal curriculum of texts and classroom practices contributes to this exclusion of black students, but suggest that the hidden curriculum is more influential. There is therefore a need for research into the impact of the hidden curriculum and the power relationships which underlie it, with respect to its impact, not just on race, but on other under-represented groups.

Jo Barraket's discussion of e-learning and access in Australia also raises important issues regarding the type of institutional response which will be required to support learners from the 'equity' groups, who have been recognised by the Australian Government as being under-represented in higher education. The research undertaken by Barraket has shown that the levels of 'information literacy' (Rigmor and Luke 1995) are lower among equity groups, and that this acts as a deterrent to accessing available information communications technology (ICT) resources. There was also evidence that they lacked access to experiential knowledge through their family and social support networks. In this context the support provided by the services and staff of the university was crucial to their success. However, there was evidence of a division between 'technology services' and 'access and equity services' which meant that the appropriate support was not always available to students from these equity groups. This then raises research questions about the kinds of support which students require in these situations, and how access support is integrated with other forms of provision within the university. These questions are of relevance not just with respect to e-learning, but also with respect to a wider range of issues.

The importance of research into forms of provision which are designed to support learning among students from a variety of non-traditional backgrounds and improve retention rates is now well established, particularly within the USA. This has included approaches to teaching, learning and study, programme organisation, and institutional support. This work is summarised in the chapter by Hunter Boylan, and this may provide a useful guide for researchers in other countries who wish to consider research designed to improve retention and progression rates.

Access and after

The third set of issues relate to the longer-term impact of access to education. This raises issues regarding the opportunities which participation in various forms of learning opens up for people. This may relate to their participation in the labour market, or in other aspects of society. Studies which focus on the impact of widening access on learners' longer term prospects are still relatively limited. The main chapter which focuses on this in this book is Ewart Keep's discussion of access and the labour market. Keep reports research which indicates that the rates of return for graduates in the UK appear to be holding up well despite the expanding supply of graduates (Dearden et al. 2000). However, he also reports research which shows that returns appear to vary considerably according to gender, subject, class of degree and institution (Conlon and Chevalier 2002), and that the returns for higher education Type B qualifications (e.g. Higher National Certificates and Diplomas (HNC/D)) are considerably lower than for degrees (Dearden et al. 2000). Furthermore, given that high levels of participation are relatively new, it is still difficult to predict the likely effects of entry to the labour market of successive large cohorts of graduates. The evidence on the differential rates of return depending on the qualification, subject and institution is of particular interest, given the discussion above about differentiation and stratification within tertiary education, and the tendency for non-traditional students from disadvantaged backgrounds to be more likely to study for shorter qualifications in less prestigious institutions. So far little longitudinal research of this type has been undertaken with former access students, but it is clearly an important area for future research. Research of this type should also focus on the other wider benefits of learning.

Conclusion

This chapter has attempted to draw together some of the main issues which may be helpful in developing research in the field of widening access. It is recognised that this is an area in which research is still in a developmental phase, and that the level of institutional support is often limited. However, it has been suggested that the traditions and history of research in this field have created certain strengths, which can be built upon in developing a strong and distinctive approach, which will produce research which will be of high quality in its own right, and will be of value in informing policy and practice. It is suggested that while theoretical frameworks have to date been relatively weak there are interesting areas of development, and that these can be linked to distinctive methodological approaches. It is also suggested that an important agenda for future research can be mapped out, which will involve moving beyond narrow definitions of access to wider issues of structural differentiation, institutional change, and the impact of access on learners' later lives.

Notes

1 Details of the projects that have been commissioned in this initiative can be found at the TLRP website (http://www.esrc.ac.uk/tlrp).

References

Absalom, D. and Golebiowsi, Z. (2002) 'Tertiary literacy on the cusp', *Australian Review of Applied Linguistics*, 25(2), 5–18.

Beck, U., Giddens, A. and Lash, S. (1994) *Reflexive Modernization. Politics, Tradition and Aesthetics in the Modern Social Order*, Cambridge, MA: Polity Press.

Bloomer, M. and Hodkinson, P. (2000) 'Learning careers: continuity and change in young people's dispositions to learning', *British Educational Research Journal*, 26, 528–97.

Bock, Z. and Gough, D. (2002) 'Social literacies and students in tertiary settings: lessons from South Africa', *Australian Review of Applied Linguistics*, 25(2), 49–58.

Bourdieu, P. (1984) *Homo Academicus*, Cambridge: Polity Press.

Bourgeois, E., Duke, C., Guyot, J.-L. and Merrill, B. (1999) *The Adult University*, Buckingham: Open University Press.

Conlon, G., and Chevalier, A. (2002) *Rates of Return to Qualifications: A Summary of Recent Evidence*, London: London School of Economics, Centre for the Economics of Education.

Dearden, L., MacIntosh, S., Myck, M. and Vignoles, A. (2000) 'The Returns to Academic, Vocational and Basic Skills in Britain', *DfEE Research Report*, RR192, Nottingham: DfEE.

Field, J. (2003) *Social Capital*, London: Routledge.

Forsyth, A.J.M. and Furlong, A. (2003) 'Access to higher education and disadvantaged young people', *British Education Research Journal*, 29(2), 205–25.

Gallacher, J., Field, J., Merrill, B. and Crossan, B. (2002) 'Learning careers and the social space: exploring fragile identities, adult returners and the new further education', *International Journal of Lifelong Education*, 21(6), 493–509.

Gibbons, M., Limoges, C., Nowotny, H., Schwartzman, S., Scott, P. and Trow, M. (1994) *The New Production of Knowledge: The Dynamics of Science and Research in Contemporary Societies*, London: Sage.

Habermas, J. (1984) *The Theory of Communicative Action, Vol. 1: Reasons and the Rationalization of Society*, Boston, MA: Beacon Press.

Habermas, J. (1987) *The Theory of Communicative Action, Vol. 2: Lifeworld and System: A Critique of Functionalist Reason*, Boston, MA: Beacon Press.

Murphy, M., Morgan-Klein, B., Osborne, M. and Gallacher, J. (2002) *Widening Participation in Higher Education. Report to Scottish Executive*, Stirling: Centre for Research in Lifelong Learning/Scottish Executive.

Nowotny, H., Scott, P. and Gibbons, M. (2001) *Re-Thinking Science: Knowledge and the Public in an Age of Uncertainty*, Cambridge: Polity Press.

Rigmor, G. and Luke, R. (1995) 'The critical place of information literacy in the trend towards flexible delivery in higher education contexts', paper presented at Learning for Life Conference, Adelaide.

Index